To Dianne

To God be the glory
I thank God for fellowship
such as you. I pray you stay
strong in the Lord and daily put on
His armor that as you fight to strengthen
others your heart will remain
protected.
God bless & keep you
Love in Christ Carol

WHEN WARRIORS FALL

Carolyn Marie Hudler

Copyright © 2012 by Carolyn Marie Hudler.

All rights reserved. No part of this book may be used or reproduced by any means, graphic, electronic, or mechanical, including photocopying, recording, taping or by any information storage retrieval system without the written permission of the publisher except in the case of brief quotations embodied in critical articles and reviews.

Poetry contributions by Melanie S. Dickinson

WestBow Press books may be ordered through booksellers or by contacting:

WestBow Press
A Division of Thomas Nelson
1663 Liberty Drive
Bloomington, IN 47403
www.westbowpress.com
1-(866) 928-1240

Because of the dynamic nature of the Internet, any web addresses or links contained in this book may have changed since publication and may no longer be valid. The views expressed in this work are solely those of the author and do not necessarily reflect the views of the publisher, and the publisher hereby disclaims any responsibility for them.

Any people depicted in stock imagery provided by Thinkstock are models, and such images are being used for illustrative purposes only.

Certain stock imagery © Thinkstock.

ISBN: 978-1-4497-5485-3 (sc)
ISBN: 978-1-4497-5487-7 (hc)
ISBN: 978-1-4497-5486-0 (e)

Library of Congress Control Number: 2012910306

Printed in the United States of America

WestBow Press rev. date: 07/10/2012

For my husband, John

You are my greatest encourager. I love you.

Acknowledgements

To John: I thank God for you. The Lord has blessed me with a husband who is steadfast and strong in his love for me. You have encouraged and strengthened me to finish this work, and you have loved that I remain about our Father's business. I thank God for you.

To John II, Chris and Becky: Your love and trust in me pushed me forward. Knowing that I have not always been the best for you, I am compelled by that trust to press in, and never be shaken again.

To my daughter, Melanie: You inspire me. Your heart is bigger, and your love of people is greater than I could have ever imagined. I love who you are, and I appreciate your part in this book.

To my battle buddies, Laura Lee (Beautiful), and Lana: I am blessed by your great love for me. If love covers a multitude of sin, then truly His love has covered me. He used you as a tangible banner of His love.

To the prophetic voice that stopped me in my tracks: Hylan, thank you for your determined obedience to God.

To Sandy, Ama and Lana, thank you for reading and editing and encouraging me along the way.

To all of the Aaron's and Hurr's in my life, which are too many to name, thank you for lifting my arms when the battle raged, and I was tired. Thank you for your faithful prayers.

Above all else, To Jehovah God: All glory and honor and praise belong to you. Great is your faithfulness, Oh God my Father!

Contents

Acknowledgements vii
Introduction xiii

Part 1   Battlefield of Sexual Immorality

    Kara Magdalene—Loved and Made Clean 3

    Fallen 5
    Eyesight 14
    Destruction 19
    Truth 24
    To the Warrior Fighting Adultery 28

    Lillian—God's Oath 31

    The Box 32
    The Scourge 42
    Dying Embers 50
    The Wedding Gown 60
    To the Warrior Fighting Promiscuity 68

    Amos Marcus Desi—Troubled & Warlike 71

    Imagine 73
    Snow White's Apple 87
    Burning Flame 98
    Changing the Picture 104
    To the Warrior Fighting Pornography 112

Part 2 The Death of My People

    Roni Simone—Shout for Joy Because He Hears 117

    Dance of the Gods 119
    Hope Deferred 125
    A Very Present help..147
    Abiona's Choice 162

    Diverging Paths—A Tale of Two Mothers.........................173

    Cries behind the Veil..175
    Silence in the Dark...183
    To the Warrior Fighting Abortion 188

    Reaneva Ashanti—Struggles with People.........................191

    Not Like Her 193
    I Love Her But 199
    Just a Prayer—Excuses for Gossip 204
    To the Warrior Fighting Gossip...210

    Mariel Anya—Bitterness Covered by Grace 213

    Mariel's Hammer 215
    Bitterness Takes Sides 222
    To The Warrior Fighting Bitterness 236

Part 3 Sentinels

    Arion Cadman 243

    Playground..245
    Treasury vs. Treachery 251
    The Thought Surrendered 253
    Shiri's Song...259
    To the Sentinel Guarding the Mind...................................264

    Lyell Shiri-Kalele—Loyal Friend, Song of my Soul 267

    Heart Surgery...269
    To the Sentinel Guarding the Heart...................................274

    Gabriel Alexavier—Hero of God, Protector of the
    Home 277

    Heart and Home..279
    Soul and Spirit 286

    To the Warrior Guarding the Home..................................292
Epilogue 295
Index of Scripture...305

Introduction

A NOTE TO THE WARRIOR

We are a people, made in the image of God, established in Him and ultimately drawn to Him that we might know Him intimately and have a relationship with Him for all eternity. There is a calling in each one of us that causes him to seek first the Kingdom of God. Since the fall of Adam and Eve, corruption has chased after mankind with a tenacious determination to plug up the God space that resides within each human being. All the worldly fineries that attract the human race with a showy or stylish pomp somehow get shoved into that place intended for God until it is crammed full with the things that do not satisfy.

I am speaking to Christians who have given their lives to Christ and have entered into a relationship with Him, loving Him and serving Him; and who are very much aware that this was no easy street decision. Corruption still fights to get in and clog up that God space and keep the God-Warrior from knowing the full potential of his relationship with Jesus.

In the confines of the church there are many people moving about like zombies—dead men walking, continuing to allow corruption to eat away at their abundant life and remaining in the grave, rather than seated in the heavenlies with Christ. As born-again believers, we are new creations who have been given a path, laid out for us to walk in. We must recognize that our paths may be terraced with the decay of corruption waiting to take hold and pull us away from the truth and *The Way*. We have to always be aware that our beauty is not found through the eye gate, nor through human emotions, but through the promises that lay ahead on each stepping stone that paves the path our Lord has set out for us.

Some have set their feet too far off the path and have been caught up in the fierce battle for their souls. Some have been ambushed by corruption and taken captive by the enemy, being pulled far away from the safety of the camp and in many cases losing fellowship with the saints and fighting alone. If this is you, I hope you will reach out and ask for help. I pray that in these pages you will find strength and courage and somehow find here an unseen battle buddy who has come to help you return to a place where you can heal and again be strengthened for battle. And then in the end, STAND, once again

To those who see that your brother or sister has fallen on the battlefield of corruption, my cry is this: Don't leave them there! Never leave a fallen warrior on the battlefield! James 5:19-20 says, "My brethren, if any among you strays from the truth and one turns him back, let him know that he who turns a sinner from the error of his way will save his soul from death and will cover a multitude of sins." Each of us is our brother's keeper.

Enter here into the hearts and minds of people who, though sold out to the Lord, Jesus Christ, have found themselves overtaken by the corruptions of the world that came to them disguised as pleasure and hope and fulfillment. Some are dying on the battlefield by their own volition. Others were introduced to it in the innocence of their lives. All need to be rescued. The Church suffers from the corruption that overtakes the world, but not all fall prey. If you are strong in the battle then reach out a hand to help one who has fallen.

As certainly as I am writing this I know there will be those who refuse to take hold. If there is a way to carry them away from the enemy, then do it. If you have tried and not succeeded, then pray for them to fall into the hands of God where He can reprove and bring them back. I know some will be lost on that bloody field where the enemy destroys; yet we cannot know who that will be and we must reach out to bring back and restore God's people if it is at all possible. Only some of the lies of the enemy are brought to surface here, and merely a dusting of what goes on with the inner man and the struggles we face as children of God. It is my hope that here you will be able to see inside the mind of the sinner and the struggle he faces in the fight against sin. My prayer is that this book will open hearts and minds to the possibilities for restoration of God's fallen warriors. To the Warrior reading this book: Nothing is impossible with God

PART 1

Battlefield of Sexual Immorality

Since the fall of man the world has experienced corruption of all kinds from the fall and death of a leaf to the perversion that seeps into the hearts of those whom the enemy has found lying in a heap of rubble. Many come into this world and find themselves in a place in life where they cannot seem to find the true love that their heart desires. All come into the world with a place inside of them that needs to be filled.

All are seekers of this kind of love from birth. Some find it immediately and live their lives as one who is truly loved and made complete. Others meet with a perverted kind of love that eventually throws them into a heap of rubble where they lay, waiting and hoping to find a warm embrace—a simple act of love. Some have discovered pure love in the miraculous hand of Jesus Christ only to find that like Israel, they have chased after the harlotry of life forgetting their Savior. And the Lord calls out, as He did to his people of Jerusalem, "you will be a crown of beauty in the hands of the Lord, a royal diadem in the hand of your God."

Kara Magdalene offers us a picture of the redemptive hand of God in the life of one of His people. She represents men and women alike who, while feeling as though they were on the right track in their walk with God, fell devastatingly into sin. Sometimes we are not aware of the holes in our armor until the enemy's dart finds its way into our hearts and minds affecting the way we believe and think. And suddenly we find ourselves on a battlefield of destruction, alone and in despair, thinking there is no way out.

Yet, as with His people of old, God deals with us with a loving and forgiving heart that will come and retrieve us from this battle, but only if we turn back to Him. The enemy of our souls would have us believe that there is no way out. Beloved, never forget this one thing: "With God all things are possible." Now as you follow these souls through their journey, I pray you can find here a way out for yourself, or that your eyes will be opened to realize the devastation and helplessness of another, so you can help a brother or sister who has been wounded in battle.

Kara Magdalene

LOVED AND MADE CLEAN

You shall be a crown of beauty in the hand of the Lord, and a royal diadem in the hand of your God (Isaiah 62:3).

Naked in His Presence

In a field of gray we meet.
Cold, vacant eyes pierce my being.
Austerity Laughs mercilessly.
My smile fades into the chilling arms that embrace me.
Pounding heart, darkness—I close my eyes.

I awake with it, alone, afraid
Outstretched hands, where is my companion?
Corruption strips me of life
What creature of evil wrestles me to the grave?
Exposed in its presence; All will see who I am.

In a field of gold and green He stands
Loving eyes pierce my being
Watching, seeking, inspecting my soul
For the smallest nugget of good; I reach for Him
Quivering amid a warm smile, radiance; I see

My face flushes with His rays of joy.
Opened arms, why this sweet deliverance
Life eruption dons an eternal embrace . . .
What Power of Life frees me from entanglements?
Naked in His presence, I am Clothed anew.

Fallen

She was down! Fallen to the bottom . . . Crash!
"Oh, no!"
Fallen!
"Oh, my God, why have You forsaken me?"

Kara looked back. The way she had taken was painful. Left strewn on the path were the broken hearts of many. Destruction had come her way and had taken its toll on those who had dared to walk with her. Her husband straggled behind in faithful diligence to hang on. Her friends met with affliction. The remnant of the church she had once served lay in a heap. Shame washed over her, and Kara was not sure she wanted to go on. The light faded. Reality was edging farther away.

"Lord!" she cried in an angry voice. "Lord! Lord!" She sobbed uncontrollably. "Lord," she finally whispered.

I see the sun rising, but the day is dark. The ominous clouds have overtaken the sky and hidden my sun. There is no warmth; light is distant. Lifting her head up, Kara placed a trembling hand on her forehead. She ran her fingers along the profile of her face while wondering what she would find in her reflection. Maybe she would see cheeks that were once red with life but were now pale and lackluster. She was sure there would be no more smooth, soft, and supple skin. No, not for Kara. Hers would likely be a dry, pitted face with deep lines and scars.

Her dark, swollen eyes were weary, and each deep pocket resonated defeat. The once bubbly blonde was now dispirited and defeated. She dropped her head in pitiful anguish and immediately lifted it to unleash the agony of her utter defeat. She let go of a sigh that had hung at the edge of her mouth in disgust and despair.

Loser, she thought. *No one wants a loser.*

She was confused about life and distant from the Lord whom she loved, so she didn't recognize the familiarity of this voice that spoke to the deepest wells of her heart.

"Kara, don't quit."

"No!" she cried. "I am a loser."

"Kara, I love you. Don't give up."

Again her hands were on her face. Life was at a standstill for this once vibrant servant of God. There was a time when she would have faced herself and this ominous voice, but now she could not. She wondered if she could ever again.

"Lord, no one wants a loser."

"Kara, don't give up."

Kara wanted to hang on to that voice, but it now began to fade quickly into the nuance of a fantasy. That peaceful voice was fast losing its appeal, and she was losing hope.

Her thoughts were jumbled and incomplete.

"Feel like quitting. No hope," she muttered. "Dark morning, battle lost. Need Your light, Lord. I can't see . . ."

Kara lost consciousness.

When she regained awareness, the slender woman looked around. For a moment, she did not remember where she was or what she had been through. Her narrow fingers ran through her hair as she opened her eyes.

It all began to come back to her in droves of unpleasant memories: the battle, the blood, and the filth and stench of evil that she couldn't wash off.

She dwelled on this thought a while, remembering how it had felt when it first began to cover her. First the slime of evil entered her mind. It was only a thought, she contended. But the *thought* soon became her nemesis. She had rationalized that the things she *thought* hurt no one. And anyway, how could she prevent what came into her mind? There was no need for discussion, especially with her husband—no need for anyone to know the things that dwelt in the secrets of her heart.

"Lies!" Kara screamed.

Echoes reverberating through the empty woods brought her back to reality. She had been lost in the abyss of her awful memories. Thoughts of her sin and the memories of them invaded her, and they wouldn't let up. The evil had ever so slowly begun to cover her. She felt it coming but found she was helpless. She couldn't fight it. She tried. Prayer, fasting, confession before God, and pleas of help had all failed. She tried everything she knew, but it just kept covering her from head to toe. Oppression crept in and began to work its corruption in her. But her heart had somehow been guarded against the baneful disease that plagued her mind and body. She didn't understand it. She only guessed that because she had given her heart to God that nothing, even hell itself, could snatch her heart out of the hands of Him to whom it was given. But her heart did ache.

The once tall and steady warrior now lifted a shaky hand to reach through the tattered armor so she could touch the deep pain she had in her heart, but she was amazed at what she felt. Kara jumped to a sitting position when she noticed a smooth, soft feeling. She just knew she would see herself dressed in the tatters she had sewn for herself, but after she opened her eyes she quickly shut them as if she had seen a ghost. Squeezing her eyes so tightly that they hurt, she winced in fear. She struggled to open them again—afraid that what she saw might go away.

"Not for you!" the past yelled at her.

"You don't deserve this." The haunting jeers of Christian *brothers and sisters* poked at her conscience. "You are a loser—probably never were saved. Your heart is corrupt. Too bad you don't love God anymore."

"Sinner!" hissed another sinister voice.

"Go away!" she shouted. "God, help me, please! Make them go away!"

"Open your eyes, Kara."

"I am afraid," she replied as she quaked. "I'm . . . I'm so mixed up, so confused."

"Open your eyes, Kara. Trust Me."

Kara's eyes suddenly shot open with dramatic intensity. All of the noises ceased. Her heart raced, and the sound of its beat swelled through her chest like an echo in a lonely canyon. She could see that she was dressed in silk: pure, white, comforting silk.

She cried, "This can't be! I have fallen. I have fallen."

"So what happens when warriors fall?"

Kara gasped and turned to see where the voice had come from. No one was there, but the sound of conviction drummed in her head like a Congo chant.

"Do you have an answer for Me?"

The voice pounded in her head, echoing through every sinew of her broken spirit. She wished it would go away. That voice—it made her head hurt. Confusion muddled her thoughts.

"Kara?"

She was battered and unstable, losing her grip.

"That voice," she shouted. "That voice, that voice." She covered her ears as if she were protecting them from what was to come next.

"Kara, Where are you? Why are you hiding? Why are you deafening your ears to Me?"

Kara was on her feet now in frenzy, spinning around to see who was speaking.

Silence infused the moment. The weary warrior took another deep breath, dropped her head back, and let the tears well up. Quiet and stillness lingered. There was no war, no commander. The battle that had raged around her had hushed.

"Kara." She heard the voice call her again. This time softly, gently, and faint, a whisper of her name washed over her like a warm shower. She flattened the creases of her shimmering skirt with her bruised hands and realized that while she was dressed in new clothes, the bruises remained. She noticed cuts that would form into scars once they healed, *if* they healed.

She walked over to the river and bent over while looking into the water and longing for a drink. As she lingered while trying to make herself kneel for a drink, she tried not to look at her reflection because she thought she would see the same battered look she saw on her hands. But she couldn't help it; she had to look!

"It can't be!" she huffed.

The gaunt look she had expected was not there; instead she saw beauty.

She turned away abruptly. "I'm dreaming! I don't get it. This cannot be happening. It's just not real."

Again she looked at her reflection in the water, and again she saw smooth new skin, hair that shined with luster, and a fresh, healthy appearance. She looked at her hands, which were still bruised and cut, and then back to the reflection of her face, which was new and fresh.

"I don't get it!"

"What now, Kara? What happens when warriors fall?" He whispered His question.

"Who is there?" she asked.

No answer. Her energy was waning, but her pulse was accelerating.

Down she went again to the ground, her face buried in dirt. She started coughing and couldn't stop. And in one quick gulp of air she inhaled dirt. Now her coughing was uncontrollable and she doubled over while trying to suppress it.

"Beauty from ashes, Kara. There will be scars but not all over. From your ash heap, I will bring beauty. Follow me!"

"Please, I need water."

Her tongue felt swollen and dry. She yearned for the water, and it was in abundance right in front of her. Streams of cold water were pouring over the rocks in a refreshing waterfall, and Kara longed for a drink of it.

I am so thirsty.

For a moment, she felt a stirring in her spirit.

"As the deer pants for the water . . ."

That verse—what is the rest of that verse?

"So my soul pants for You, Oh God."

Kara used all that was left of her energy to kneel at the river's edge, but she felt stuck. She had to get to the water. She fought the apathy and ignored the intense pain. She struggled and finally fell to the ground on her hands and knees.

"I am so thirsty!" She said

She wanted a drink and cupped her hands, placing them in the river pool before her. She tried to get a drink, but the cold water stung her cut hands.

She noticed a ladle at the root of a huge oak tree beside her on the riverbank. This must have been some kind of joke or perhaps a bad dream. The ladle was flat. Taking it anyway she tried to use this inferior utensil because she was desperate for a drink. As soon as it reached her mouth only a few drops remained on the ladle. She wanted more, and kept trying to get more accepting what few drops she would get.

Dipping furiously with the flat ladle she became frustrated. Before her was pure, cool water, and she wanted it more than anything. Kara once again dipped her cut hands into the water. She needed a drink but it was too painful to take hold of it for even the tiniest sip. She hung her head and cried. Her tears fell softly and her pain was released in quiet whimpers. The wind around her seemed to howl and a chill set over her that made her shrink up even more. Then, somewhere beneath the circling winds there was a rustling in the leaves, and *His* voice returned to her again.

"Kara, what happens when warriors fall?"

At first, she ignored His question. Then, almost demanding an answer, His question came again. Kara couldn't answer Him. She had never fallen before. How could she possibly know what happens when warriors fall? She sat by the tree and reflected on her life. How in the world did she get here? It seemed several years paraded in front of her like a celebration of victories. She was a strong warrior. How *did* she fall? It was a question she knew would have to be answered, but for now she didn't want to think about it.

Her thirst brought her back to the present, and trying once again to get a drink. She wanted the water to pour over her, but she was only able to scoop up enough to wet the tip of her tongue. Finally, in frustration, she plunged her head into the bank of the river and drank what she could. Trying to ignore the weeds getting in her way, she lapped up the water and then lifted her head out again, crying out, but really more for the pain she felt inside. Then she heard Him again. His voice encircled her like a powerful wind.

"Kara, Kara, Kara, Kara," the voice echoed her name in a mind-boggling reverie. She was on her feet again and turned in circles. She was looking around and panting for breath. The sky was spinning. The trees looked as if they would fall on top of her. Finally, she stopped and threw her arms down to her sides with her fists clenched.

"Who are you?" She demanded.

"I Am the One who loves you with an everlasting love." He returned once again in tenderness and compassion.

"Come to me and I will give you rest."

It all came back to her. She knew it was He who had called her out of darkness. It was the very one who led her out of bondage and placed her into a wonderful wide-open space. The Lord, who had once freed her from the captivity of destruction, was calling her name. He who had rescued her from the entrapment of evil had now returned to untangle her once again.

Her shoulders dropped, and her head hung in shame.

"Lord, I am not fit for you to be near me. Go away!"

"Look at yourself again. You are not that person anymore. Come on Kara; let's talk about your pathetic state. Reason with me; and let me make you whiter than snow. My child, look up!"

Kara's dull blue eyes looked heavenward—for answers, for peace and for freedom. Her arms no longer clung to her side, but lifted up in receiving anticipation.

"I am Yours, Lord. I cannot help myself. I need you." Her arms dropped again from weariness. She paused a moment and attempted to collect herself before she gained the nerve to ask the important question.

"Lord, what does happen when warriors fall?"

The Lord was silent.

"Lord?"

"You will either go to the Source of Life, where you can learn, or you will return to the same well and drink the same water using the same tools that will never work."

"I don't understand."

All was still, no sound of rushing water, no voice, and no wind. It was quiet

She questioned aloud her own reflection as if hoping an answer would arise from the water.

"Using tools that don't work? Returning to the same well? I think I get it."

Exhausted, the troubled middle-aged woman sat back and again leaned against the tree. She was weary. As her eyes closed she thought again about where she had been. Thoughts reverberated in her mind. Memories filled her senses with the smell of her office, the sound of the music playing in the sanctuary and then feelings—feelings of fear and frustration. And finally, thoughts of him—she hated him, and wondered how she could let him convince her that evil was good. What she had allowed herself to believe to be good was destroying her. She felt helpless, alone and trapped.

"The woman at the well," Kara said. "I wonder if she felt trapped in her relationships. I wonder if I am trapped?"

Again, the tears came. She sobbed with grief. It was as if there had been a death. She realized it *was* a death. It was the death of her dream to serve Him with the utmost faithfulness.

"Jesus, *I am* trapped. I am afraid I have walked through a prison door and it has shut tight. I may never get out."

"Kara!" God's voice returned to her with a gut-wrenching force that made her gasp. "I have opened a door to freedom for you. It will remain open until you can see it and walk through it."

Her head hung again.

His voice returned like lightning. "Kara! No one can shut it!" His words came powerfully, echoing all around her.

"No one can shut it—no one! The enemy has blinded you so you cannot see where to go. But keep your faith. The door is still there. Find it and walk through it."

"Lord, have mercy on me," was all she could pray. "Help me find the door."

Her struggle ended as she acquiesced to His voice. The sounds of His words began to quiet her mind and she lay back on the soft moss that surrounded the tree by the water. In the lull of the wind she continued to hear his voice in the distance, calling her.

"My beloved, don't forget I am the door. You know this. All you need to do is come in. Come in! Don't be like a mule, which has no understanding. Come of your own will, come to me and be assured that you will find peace and rest. My love will not fail you. Trust me and let me surround you. Listen to the song of deliverance I have put in your heart. Move toward that song and sing praises to your God."

Kara's eyes closed and her body felt light. The world around her became dim. The light began to fade into a mist of darkness. As sleep began to overtake her, she drifted into the possibility of never waking up. Something within her wanted that, but another voice in her cried out for life.

"Lord, am I dying? Rescue me, Lord. Have mercy . . ."

Sleep did not remain long. Kara awoke with a start. She immediately examined her clothes.

Just jeans and a tee shirt—rags she thought! There was no shimmering skirt, no battlefield, no stream, and no comforting voice. She had only memories of the pain.

It was only a dream; a fantasy—or was it?

"Oh God!" she cried. "Have mercy on me. I do need You."

Covered

Each day the sun shines
Smiles, soft words, a gentle touch
Still no life, can't feel very much

Trapped, trapped in a relationship.
Don't want to be in it. Surely He knows.
All the while the night moon still glows

Lies, secrets, angry words, no touch
Prisoner here—can I ever be free?
Enemy of mine let go of me.

Each day the Son shines
Night moon glows, still covers me
"Come," Jesus says. "Come follow me."

Eyesight

Kara felt she had been in the backwash of some crazy nightmare, where she couldn't feel, move or even breathe. A chill covered her thin body, and she shivered. The cool late autumn air brushed over her causing her to embrace herself and rub her arms for extra warmth. She didn't like the thought of winter coming. It reminded her of the condition of her heart, and this autumn air made her aware of what was ahead for her. Taking a deep breath she rose from her resting-place in the woods.

"It fits," she said, "autumn and the falling of the beautiful leaf. And where does it fall? It falls to a lonely death, and we remember it no more. And the coming of winter feels like my own approaching death—icy, unyielding, calloused, harsh and lonely. My own life is sort of like that tree succumbing to the cold winter wind."

A picture of a stream flashed through her mind. Suddenly she was thirsty. Another flash—the stream, had she been there? The wind howled with a lonely, eerie voice. Kara reached for her jacket. Seeing the sun setting, she thought she should get out of the woods. She knew it would get colder, but she was compelled to finish the trail. She turned and headed upward toward the top of the wooded park.

Kara thought about the woods and wondered if there was something she could glean from being out here alone. Hopefully, it would be something that would help her find hope and teach her how she could again live for a purpose. She turned her thoughts again to God.

"I am willing to learn. Show me, God, what these woods can teach me about my life. I am desperate to know."

Kara walked onward and as she walked she felt warmth envelop her. It was something she had not felt in some time. She placed her hand over her heart and suddenly her mind flashed back to a moment by the stream, where she had placed her hand over her aching heart. She stopped walking. Was she really there or was it a dream? She was not sure. Had she been here before? She remembered other times when she was hanging on the edge of despair, that she would slip strangely into the past and revisit the frustration, the pain, the anger and bitterness of growing up. She would reflect on her pitiful coming of age story that came sooner than it should for any little girl. She did not understand why the terrible memories were not haunting her now causing her to bear their weight as if she was still living in the middle of the constant nightmares. These memories usually would torment her, but not today.

Unexpectedly she felt the familiar hope of a loving God. Kara was content to rest with this feeling. She knew that the time would come again to wrestle with life's questions, but for now she would rest here in His warmth. There were no hoops to jump through here. She realized that even if God *did* have a hoop to jump through that it would be so deep and so wide that no matter where she jumped she would still land right into His arms.

The leaves on the trail covered Kara's boots. She furrowed through them as if making her own pathway. As she walked she recognized that these leaves were once green with new life's abundance, and then they became radiant and colorful. Now they were fallen.

You were once a great provider, she thought as she looked at the tree in front of her.

Kara sat on a bench that was midway to the top of the trail and stared at all the trees. She thought of how they protected those who journeyed here from the pressing heat. Perhaps the travelers were thankful for the refuge, but many that walked this way took their shelter for granted, and they closed their eyes to the discomforts that lie beyond the shade of the trees. Some who chose the way of this path simply didn't understand the fight that weathered around them. The protection from the scorching heat was provided by the mighty trees as people travelled the way of this path to the top.

"The Way," she spoke the words quietly.

A flaming sword flashed before her eyes. The Way was her destiny. She was a warrior! Wasn't she? Kara struggled trying to remember. It was as if she were trying to remember a dream. In a disturbing instant only pieces were revealed to her mind. A shaded line separated reality and other worldliness.

She remembered that at one time she provided shade from the burning heat of Hell. Her prayers covered friends who had gone astray, and those who were just beginning their journey. Her counsel had opened the eyes of many to a new understanding of God and His choices for them. Often she stood in the gap between them and the fiery darts of the wicked enemy, but never had she taken a hit such as this.

A wave of excitement filled her. She realized that the woods did have something to teach her, and she realigned her focus on the trees she admired. Only three weeks ago the trees still boasted vibrant shades of red, yellow and orange. Passersby gaped in awe and marveled at their beauty. But Kara knew that very few understood, or even cared about, what took place both internally and externally for the trees to produce such an explosion of color. And probably not many stopped to announce their thankfulness for the provision they offered.

Then their leaves fell, and only a precious few people realized the beauty that would come out of the fall. It seemed that when the leaves fell so did the hope of new life, purpose and importance. Few saw that the trees still had a design given to them by a great designer, even after all of the leaves had hit the ground. There was not much faith in their restoration.

Kara moved in. She needed a closer look.

I am like that tree.

She knew some would see her as one who has provided shade for many people's hearts, and that they may even reflect on how she had grown to be spiritually colorful, vibrant and beautiful. And she was aware that so many would say, *Oh, what a shame! Kara has fallen.* They would not understand that she still had purpose because her heart still belonged to Jesus.

Kara smiled. "It is okay," she quirked. "Maybe someday they will understand. Maybe someday they will come to the woods and see my carving on the trees, and maybe the woods will teach them something about life."

Kara grabbed a handful of already brittle leaves and crushed them in her hands. A small acorn that she had not seen rested in the middle of a now sifted remnant of the trees. She shook her head and sighed with a breath of understanding.

"I did not know you were there," she said, talking to the acorn. "I only saw you after the sifting." She paused. "Hmmm, after the sifting,".

She was ready to go home now. She had found her eyesight, and she knew what she needed to do. Kara could see that her position in life was dark, but not hopeless. She knew she still had purpose, and that new life would shoot up again. Most of all she knew that God still loved her, and He still saw her as beautiful. She called this spot by the bench, the sieve, because it was her sifting place.

As she headed back to her car she prayed, "Lord, sorting through the debris in my life will not be pleasant for me or for those around me, but I know it is necessary. I want to be a woman of integrity. Sift out the pretense and all that is not useful to you. Amen."

Kara started to put the acorn in a small leather bag that she carried in her backpack. Instead, she dug a small hole and buried it.

"Now grow," she charged the small acorn. "Grow tall and splendid."

Bird of Death

Bird of death, I hear your call, but answer I make thee none
You cry my time is nearly up, still, to you I will not come

You marked my tomb before unsung, but the grave I twice refused
At three you think that all is won. now death, I really am amused

Bird of death with beady eyes, He will announce the time
And I will go when He is ready; my life is His, not thine

Destruction

The day began to creep through the sweet light and into the shadows of evening. Kara descended the trail knowing she wouldn't reach the campground by dark. As the final rays of sunshine split into shimmering beams among the trees they seemed to pull the dusk up from the earth and play with it until the darkness took over. She lingered a bit to enjoy the dance of those beautiful rays, and then began to hurry back down the trail.

After some time, the healthy gait that enabled Kara to do the long hikes was waning. She was losing her strength and somewhat lacking in her ability to think clearly. Though tired she kept walking. It seemed to take an eternity.

An eternity, she thought, and with that thought she felt a pain in her side. It was as if someone had pinched her. She ignored it only to find that the pinch returned with increasing intensity.

"Ouch!" she squealed and then stopped instantly. Kara looked around in all directions. Nothing was there.

"Calm down, Kara," she said to herself. "You are letting yourself get alarmed over nothing. You must have gotten into something that is irritating your skin. There are no eyes in the woods watching you. There is certainly no invisible creature attacking you."

Again the pain came, now with stabbing intensity. A large bird flew over her. She wasn't sure exactly what kind of bird it was. It was getting so dark she couldn't tell, but she knew it was a bird of prey. Kara fought to keep fear at a distance, but it chased her and penetrated her thoughts so deeply that she found herself struggling for air.

The bird flew in closer. "Eternity!" it screeched. "Eeeee-ter-ni-ty, Eeeee-ter-ni-ty!" Again and again the bird circled, and though she tried to tell herself that the call of the wild was playing tricks on her mind, the bold and fearless outdoorswoman ran through the woods trying to escape an unknown stalker. She ran faster with the downward slope of the trail, running so fast that she didn't feel the branches slapping against her arms and legs. She felt dizzy and her thoughts were suddenly nonsensical.

"No! This cannot be happening to me. I have to keep going. This isn't real. It is too dark. I can't see where I am going."

"Eeeee-ter-ni-ty, Eeeee-ter-ni-ty!"

Haunting screeches kept after her, not giving her an opportunity to let up. Kara ran even faster until she heard a loud thud. It sounded like something big had fallen. She lifted her head. It was she who had fallen. Face to the ground, she looked up.

What happened? Did I pass out?

She lifted her head.

"Fallen? No, it can't be," she cried. "I am not that person anymore."

Kara's wrist hurt. Other aches nagged at her—the pain, and the thoughts of eternity. The shaken warrior lifted her head as she spoke once again to God.

"Lord, this must be what forever is like without you—always running with fear, and always looking over your shoulder, never knowing if your predator will finally catch you. Lord, I know I have a lot to do, but I *can* do it. I know I can. If I can only get out of these woods, I can leave all my sin and filth here. No one has to ever know the thoughts and intents that filled my heart. I can start over, tuck away the painful memories and leave them hidden forever."

A limb cracked behind Kara and made her jump. She noticed a small light off in the distance. Once again shaking off the dust, she stood. Her head hurt and her eyes felt fuzzy. Kara was scared and feeling lost. She looked around to get her bearings.

That must be the campground, she thought. Then she noticed another light in a different direction. She stood examining her whereabouts. There were two paths.

"I have hiked these woods so many times," she said, scratching her head. "I have never seen this split in the trail before."

Both paths looked dependable, both seemed right, both appeared to have a light at the end. She knew she had to choose and the choosing would bring a fight, but why? The battle was behind her; at least she thought it was. Kara closed her eyes trying to remember the face of her enemy, but she couldn't see it. She could not even remember the mien of the battlefield. Did it look like this?

Her memories flashed in front of her like an intense drama, sharpening her awareness. All of her senses were overwhelmingly powerful except sight. She tried again to picture the battlefield, but she could not see it. All she saw was darkness. Every time Kara strained to picture the battle a small revealing light would make an entrance, then a cloud of sudden darkness would overtake it.

Her other senses were more clear. She could detect the delicate, sweet smell that lures one into a state of reverie. Warriors always recognize it. It is the scent of battle and of fighting for a cause—a honeyed aroma that turns rancid once the battle is upon you. It was that sweet smell of battle that engaged her. Then the cold feel of loneliness would enter. Kara had chosen to be a loner. She thought she could fight alone, but had no idea how fierce the battle would be. Nor did she know how entangling the enemy's schemes were.

And then there was the thirst. No matter how many times she drank during the formidable fight, she remained thirsty. Memories were competing for control of her mind. She had memories of lying on the ground while the enemy and his hordes pressed around her at this intimidating intersection. How the thirst became her cry for mercy as well as her wails of anger and fear. She remembered the thirst growing, but thirst for what? Was it water?

"Waaa." She choked. "Ugh! waaa, water!" She coughed. What was going on? She tried pulling herself back to reality, but the emotions were squeezing at her throat. It all seemed so real.

You are in the woods at Baxter Park. Get a grip and move on, Kara!

She tried to pull out of this strange stupor.

She cried for water again, this time leaving stillness behind in the scattering maelstrom of the woods.

"Somebody, please give me water!" She yelled. To her amazement, she was released from the grip of horror. Then she remembered the clothes, shining and soft. They *were* clean. Had it all been a dream? Why couldn't she shake this thing that seemed to cling to her? Why did she have to continue fighting? Why did she have to choose a path? Why couldn't He just pick her up and take her the right way?

"Why, Lord, why? Help me. I don't know where to go." She paused, looking at the paths.

"Oh, who cares, anyway? It probably does not matter which path I take. I am just living out some crazy fairy tale and need to get a grip."

Kara started down the path to her right. She was tired and just wanted to get back to her car. Although she felt uneasy she shrugged her shoulders and went on. she kept walking, but it was taking too long. She began to worry. Maybe she *had* taken the wrong path, but all paths lead to the light don't they? Kara gave up thinking about it. She reasoned she would get to the same place in the end. Or would she?

Life is just life," she thought. *"God will keep me no matter what I choose. But if this is true, why is there such a battle?*

She knew the battle was in her mind; it only appeared to be external. She allowed the enemy to take her to a place that she was not allowed to go. It was a place that looked new and refreshing, one in which she was deceived to believe would meet with God's approval. She knew all along though that God would not approve. God did not look upon adultery with favor. Why did she go there? Why did she believe a lie?

Kara finally saw the campground. She hastened her pace to get to the lights. The hike she had begun seemed like it was days ago. Now running she moved closer to her car. Many thoughts filled her in a grand finale of questions.

Why am I panting? Why the panic? Why is there nothing here at the end to signal a victory?

She was glad to be at the end, but cognizant that there was nothing special here. Being here in the campground was no better, and it was no worse. Her mind still swirled with myriad thoughts. Her emotions were still controlled by fear and anger, her heart still ached and she was still extremely thirsty.

"When will it end, Lord? When will I be free?"

"My loved one, when you know the truth and live it, then you will be free." He answered immediately.

Kara looked upward because she knew who spoke to her, and she knew that what He said was true.

"And you will know the truth, and the truth will set you free." She said in acquiescence. "I do know the truth. Help me live it."

Kara opened the door to her car, and as she drove quietly home, a nagging question resounded in her thoughts and she entertained the thought of returning home.

Who am I, really? As each sunset passes, I see myself disappear into the horizon. True self, who are you? As each sunset passes, I see myself disappear into the horizon. True self, Where are you? Who are you? God knows. He knows who I am, and he has hidden my identity in a secret place—in the soul of His Son.

Sanctuary

Wait for me in your sanctuary.
Wait for me I am coming back.
It's hard to see, Lord; my soul does lack.
I yearn for home, your sanctuary.

There I was formed—in your sanctuary
Here I am purged; refined as gold
I am on my way to my home of old.
I am turning back to your sanctuary

Hurry to My Sanctuary
Lord, sin covers me with decay
My frame has begun to peel away
Still I am running to you, to your sanctuary

Truth

He waited for Kara outside her apartment. No one knew she lived here but him. Feeling like an outcast in the community, she stayed to herself and remained hidden most of the time. Setty was the last person she had wanted to see after the long grueling battle she had just faced. She wished it were her husband, her kids or some of the dear friends she had set aside in this pitiful plight she had undertaken. She pulled into the long driveway that led to her secluded place in a hidden corner of the town. It was small and suitable, but it was not home. She missed home and wanted to be there with the man she had fallen in love with years ago.

She had many nights wished her husband would come for her and instead she came home to find . . . *this*—a pitiful remnant of a battle once lost. Like an old confederate soldier he had lingered in the midst of emotional and spiritual war not realizing the fight for freedom was already won.

His face reflected the lines of one who could not come to grips with defeat. Perhaps, Kara thought, it was because he was not able to stand in the end. Tricked by the enemy's lures, he recoiled under the weight of battle and ran leaving his troops on the battlefield. He ran away from them, and he ran away from God. He tried convincing her to run with him. She nearly did, but the words of a familiar song made her stop. She realized that Jesus was her sanctuary and she ran as fast as she could back to Him.

Kara remembered from her seminary class that a sanctuary was a consecrated, inviolable asylum. How fitting it was for her right now because she really needed this place of comfort. How she longed for this sanctuary—how she longed for her Father's house. She wanted to be enclosed in the place where He alone could reach her. She desired to rest in that place where she could be set aside and not touched. She wanted it, but she seemed to have forgotten how to find it. As soon as she turned in her driveway she knew it was not here, and she dreaded what was yet ahead for her.

As he waited for her to reach the garage, he leaned against his Mercedes with all the arrogance one could possibly contain in a single existence. Kara pushed the remote to open the garage door and watched him walk across the driveway. Arrogance seemed to naturally follow him.

"Can I come in?" He asked.

"I suppose so. But you cannot stay. I want to be alone. So whatever you have to say, make it quick."

He continued talking as they walked through the door.

"I have to tell you that there is no way back for you, Maggie Mae," he spoke bluntly and followed his words with a momentary silence. She knew he was searching for a reaction to calling her Maggie, but she said nothing and waited. His little pause didn't hold. The lengthy construction of his sentences mingled with memories of the sundry events of Kara's day made his usual reverberation of self-exaltation sound like an annoying mosquito buzzing around her ear. As usual his conversation was enunciated with a surplus of words that he so cleverly used to skirt the truth. She did not realize this about him at first. After she became tangled up with him, she saw it. He was always verbose and always using that player's vernacularism to cover up his true nature.

Setty was a tall man, who tried to portray a country boy, but his true self always came out. She thought that it was his urban upbringing that motivated his swaggering, and mostly irritating demeanor. She watched in disgust as he entered in and went straight for the fridge.

"Where's the wine, Maggie dear?"

"I told you," she said squeezing the words through her teeth, "when I got rid of you, I got rid of that stuff too. And my name is *not* Maggie. Maggie is some stupid alter-ego that you dreamed up."

His lanky frame made him appear to walk with even more haughtiness than he may have normally displayed.

"You used to let me call you Maggie, what happened?"

"I think you should go," she said. "Go on, get out of here."

"Look, Maggie," he said. "Just give me ten minutes, and then if you still want me to go I will."

"Fine, you have ten minutes, but my name is Kara—Maggie is dead!"

"Just think for a minute." he Said. "Think about it. Who in the world will have you now? There is no other place for you to go, *Kara*, and you know it."

"Haven't you got anything new to say," she snapped. "I think we have discussed this before, and my view is still the same."

Setty interrupted her.

"You know the bottom line is that you have sinned. There is no turning back," he said angrily. "You have no other choice, but to keep going without looking back—no more church, no more nosey people, no more head ache."

Those song lyrics dominated her thoughts now.

Hurry to My sanctuary. Lord, sin covers me with decay. My frame has begun to peel away. Still I am running to you, Lord, to your sanctuary.

Kara spun on her heels and walked hastily over to the couch. Sitting down she let out the tears she had desperately tried to hold back. Setty came over and sat next to her. He put his arm around her shoulders, and she sobbed even more. Kara began to feel herself giving in.

Help Lord, she silently prayed.

I cannot hold on to you any longer. You will have to hold onto me. I give up.

Setty moved in closer, but Kara disrupted his plans.

"Your ten minutes is up," Kara said, putting her hand up in front of his face.

"Now please leave."

"You can't do this to me now that . . ."

"I can't do this to *you*!" she shouted. "Get out, Setty."

Kara looked away.

"I never knew it before, but I just recently learned that your given name is really Seteh. It's strange how I never knew that about you till now. Oh and by the way it just so happens that your given name is also the name of the Egyptian god of chaos. Did you know that, Mr. Trouble," she said cynically. "The name fits," she sneered. "You are an imposter from the beginning trying to hide who you really are."

Suddenly, Setty stood up. When Kara's eyes followed him she couldn't believe what she was seeing. It was like she was back on that battlefield again. Everything seemed surreal.

What is happening? she thought. Her mind was reeling, trying to sort the dilemma. Setty seemed taller. He looked like a giant. Fear began to fill her. Never had she been so afraid. Surely it was just a lack of sleep. His face was distorted. It bulged and protruded at his cheeks, all the while distorting the shape of his mouth. He pointed his finger in her face like it was a weapon aimed to kill.

"You are a child of Hell!" He said. His voice was rough and piercing. Kara feared what would happen to her.

God help me! she cried in her heart.

"Did you hear me," he bellowed. "You are a child of Hell, and nothing can change that now, *Maggie*!"

Kara heard the Lord speak the words to that song to here.

"Hurry, Kara," He said. "Hurry to My sanctuary."

Kara breathed a sigh of relief.

"Thank you Lord," she said.

She felt strength arise within her that she did not know she had. Surely God was with her because all of a sudden she was standing over Setty and looking down on him. Now she was pointing her finger in his face.

"No, *Setty*," she spat, staring into his distant eyes.

"I am a child of God, saved by grace. Now, get out of my house, you god of chaos and never return."

To her relief, he left and all was quiet.

Now what? Kara thought. She glanced at the picture on her wall. It was a picture of her family. Looking at it moved her to action. Kara was in her car in no time and almost speeding to get to her family. She pulled into the driveway of the place she once called home. There was little activity around the house. The kids were gone now. Only her husband would be there. Would he receive her? With tears rolling down her cheeks, Kara entered the house and sat down next to her husband.

"Everything I want or need is here. Please forgive me. I want to come home."

Silence lingered for a while. Kara knew there was much to do, but it was not up to her to do it like she had thought. Her sin could not remain hidden. It would be brought to the surface and purged. Knowing this, she still proceeded. As her husband embraced her she turned her thoughts heavenward.

"I am in your hands, Lord. Have mercy on me.

To the Warrior Fighting Adultery

Adultery is a sin, yet not a sin that a man or woman, who is a true follower Christ would intentionally walk into. It is one that slowly and surreptitiously comes upon the person who is hungry for something. The longings that we have are instinctive and powerful.

A longing to be loved, accepted, or recognized can instigate a wrong relationship on the grounds of seemingly good intentions. The pinnacle of an adulterous relationship is reached by an ever-ascending climb from the innocuous base of the innocent relationship. The enemy hates the man and woman of God, and seeks to thwart the beautiful person and ministry that God is growing.

Generally for the person who is undoubtedly sold out to Christ, this morsel looks like spirituality. Godly people long to be spiritual people. They recognize that there is more to this world than what they can see. Therefore, the enemy makes the sin look like it was meant to be in God's eyes. Suddenly the Christian is at war with the emotions often fighting against reason. The mind becomes a gruesome battlefield where all the darts of the enemy are let loose and the unaware can succumb to the barrage.

Many Christian people have fallen in this kind of battle. It is not because they were not prayed up, nor is it necessarily because they failed to read Scripture or be at church every time the doors are opened. Many have fallen when in the midst of a mighty walk with God. They were reading daily, memorizing Scripture, praying, doing ministry and chasing hard after God. So what happened? They failed to see or they failed to admit who they really are. They allowed a small discrepancy to continue until the enemy was able to get a hold of it and make it larger. In other words the hole in the dam could no longer be sustained.

Adultery can be forged from the festering fires of open wounds from the past. Often times we think we have fixed everything. Like Kara, we choose to leave the pain of sin, whether committed by us or against us, hidden. We hide it beneath a false burial, but like the seed hidden beneath dead leaves, a sprout will soon appear. Until we have learned to deal with those sins, laying them bare before God, no amount of raking will cover them. No effort on our part will prevent the seedling from shooting up again. Like Kara, we have to admit who we are before God and before our spouse. Then, we can look for the healing to come.

When moral failure occurs it is devastating to the one who loves God. Human nature says we should deny there is sin. The enemy will try to convince us that it is too late, especially when dealing with sexual sin. He will tell one who has committed adultery that there is no going back. Beloved, there is always a way back. Just stretch out your hand, and let God take hold of you.

The next temptation is to disguise the sin. Satan will try to convince you that no one needs to know, and all you have to do is confess to God. This ignores the Scripture that tells us to confess our sins to one another. God's wisdom provided a door of escape in that we confess our sins to one another. Confession is the beginning of healing. Remember the woman at the well? Christ needed to confront her because her sin continued to bring her to the same old watering hole, using the same old tools, and reaping the same old junk. She tucked her sin under the religiosity of the Samaritan people and hid from the truth.

We can sweep dirt under the rug and try to hide it, but the dirt is still there. Cleansing won't take place until the rug is flipped back and the dirt is uncovered. Jesus came along in this woman's life and exposed her sin, not to harm, but to heal her. Our Lord's ultimate goal for her was healing and restoration.

So what happens when warriors fall? Just look at history and examine the battles. All of the same things that happen on the historic battlefields happen in the battlefields of our spiritual life. Some warriors get up and walk away and spend the rest of their lives trying to forget. Some lay wounded and find it impossible to get up. Some are fortunate enough to have another come along and carry them out of the war-zone. Some walk away, but never recover from their wounds. Some suffer terrible loss that will never be regained. Some die.

Then, there are some, like Kara, who because of a great God and dedicated battle buddies, find a way home. These are able to trust themselves once again to the Great Physician, who heals their wounds, and brings forgiveness and restoration.

The Bible says that in the last days there will be hard times. As the Day of our Lord draws nearer the enemy will fight harder. This means the Christian will be under fire more. This does not mean that there is no way back for the repentant sinner. There is always a way back. Adultery is not the unpardonable sin. It is a sin that can wreck a human spirit and leave hurtful scars, but there is always a way back. This is the message to give to God's people.

The response of the church is always love and compassion. It is always prayer and petition, and it is always true concern. Never are we called to waylay our brother or sister in Christ with judgmental words offered in the name of prayer. If they are entrapped by sexual sin, they need no entanglements of this sort. If you know that your brother or sister is caught in the web of adultery, untangle them, but do it carefully.

Remember that when Jesus uncovered the Samaritan woman's sin he was careful with her heart. He showed her love and compassion. He did not tell her what a wretched person she was. He only pointed to the truth and exposed the pain that led her to a lifestyle of sin. He offered a door to life. He fed her starving emotions and nurtured her broken spirit. Shouldn't we do the same?

Lillian

GOD'S OATH

*You shall no more be termed Forsaken, and your land shall no more be termed Desolate, but you shall be called My Delight Is in Her, and your land Married; for the L*ORD *delights in you, and your land shall be married (Isaiah 62:4).*

The Box

An old man came to visit me
And gave me a tiny box
Of sickness, death and disease

Vaguely wrapped it was
In a fashioned manner
A simple spark was now inflamed

To open it was not my desire
A tiny, crescendo now fatal fire

Bright glow, burning slow
Billows of smoke, I feel I may choke

Curiously I had to see
Though I sensed a nagging calamity
I only wanted to watch

An old man gave me a tiny box
I wish to give it back to him
His sickness, death and disease

The Box

Yenene paced the length of the walkway just outside the exit doors of the Fisher Square Auditorium. He counted the minutes before the teens would make their way out. Agitated and restless, his pace quickened with the rate of the second hand on the clock. He was so keen on the time that he swore he felt the pulsating rhythm of the seconds ticking away on his wrist, as his watch beat away at minutes.

"Just one, Lilith, if I can catch just one sleeping teen, it will have an effect on many. You just watch your uncle tonight. Watch me! I *will* catch one sleeping."

The old enchanter had been hanging around places like this for years, always on the prowl for the sleeping mind. He had been at it at least a couple of generations. He was getting old, but his age did not show. People said he had magically kept himself young. His youthful appearance was important, which is why his work was best done at night. The night made him look better.

Lilith, his niece, was only a teen. Her face was pale and pain etched across her brow. Her eyes spoke hauntingly of anguish in life. She was used to only one thing—him. Everything was about her uncle, his work, his desires, and even his daily routine was depraved. She sometimes feared she was becoming too accustomed to his evil ways, and too often she rationalized that this was her life. She wasn't entirely desensitized to his wickedness, but at times like this, she simply let her thoughts and actions become glazed over and ignored his evil. Lost in thought, Lilith was not aware that her uncle had stood next to her until she felt his breath on her neck and smelled the noxious odor of his breath. Her skinny legs buckled at the thought of him being near her and she moved to step aside.

Yenene did not let her get far. He grabbed a small piece of her thin black hair from the nape of her neck, and she winced as he pulled it to stop her.

"Going somewhere, Lilith dear?"

"Uncle, that hurts. Let go! It really hurts," she said tightening her shoulders to ease the pain.

"Look over there," he said, wiping his nose with his sleeve.

"These kids are always so drunk with foolishness when they come out of these *salvation e*vents, that they don't really pay attention to the people of the night and how they look. Don't worry, Lilith dear. They won't notice the ashen look about your face, nor see the dullness of your hair. They will be so high on their emotions that their eyes will be closed. Most will walk on by us, but I know I can catch just one sleeper. I know I will. You just watch."

He let go of her and patted her head.

"I know you will work hard for me tonight, won't you?"

Lilith wanted to be free from him. She wanted no part in the evil he had in his heart, but he *was* all she had. And his ways were all she knew. Still, she wanted to run. Something greater told her that his box was no good. Words from her past leaped into her heart as she saw him pull out the box out and rub his hand over it.

"The thief comes only to steal, kill and destroy."

She heard those words as if her grandmother had spoken them at that very moment, and indeed wished her grandmother could stand right in front of her and finish the verse. Lilith knew that it ended with words of hope, but she could not remember them. All she knew was the thief that stood before her. He had robbed her of her own family when he took her from them ten years ago. He stole her hope of happiness, her youthful beauty and her virginity.

She was so young when he had fooled her with his box of poison. That box, once opened unleashed the demons that destroyed her innocence and left her with pain and regret. She hated Yenene. At times, she even hated herself, because it seemed she was becoming just like him. She would have preferred to be good and wise like her grandmother. She wanted to be close to God. Being here at this event made her want it even more.

While her uncle was not looking Lilith drew closer to the door and slipped inside the building. The spiritual swell of the building was imposing, and she wanted to linger. She felt she was at the edge of the surge, waiting for just the right moment. It was like waiting for the perfect wave to surf. The auditorium was full. Over five hundred teens sat quietly, but still hung on the edge of their seats. The speaker was in front of the podium, on his knees, whispering some sort of prayer. As Lilith watched he began to rise, and with each movement upward his voice raised in equal crescendo.

"It's not too late to change," he began calmly. Raising his hand he looked over at the keyboard player. The music began.

"It is never too late," he reiterated with more excitement. "Don't believe the lies of the Devil. Your soul will not die if you turn to the Savior."

"It is almost supernatural," said Lilith holding her hand over her heart.

Except for the voice of the speaker, silence still covered the auditorium.

"Turn to Him," he whispered. "You say you are no longer a virgin? Give Him your wounds, your scars and your sin. Be born again in spirit and in truth. Let Him renew your mind and your body. Let Him fill you and make you new."

Yenene grabbed Lilith from behind.

"What are you doing?" he demanded. "Why are you listening to this garbage?"

He spun her around, digging a long fingernail deep into her skin.

"You are of the night, and night people don't enjoy the luxuries of foolhardy thinking. So get your mind off of this and on what you are supposed to be doing. There is none of this kind of hope for you. You are just trash, girl. That is all you will ever be—just trash."

He pushed her away leaving that nail curved at her shoulder, scratching as it clung to her withdrawing body. Lilith ran out the door. She tried to hold back the tears, but could not. She thought she would just keep running, but the clamor of the emerging crowd made her stop. It was as if some hypnotic trance had overcome her. She was so conditioned by this scenario that she simply reacted. Deep down, she knew it was the magic of the box. It somehow made her think differently. She could hear the voice of deception echoing through the night air.

"He will make you feel special." the voice suggested. "How can you not want this? Remember, you will be a princess for a night."

Lilith knew she would be left empty in the end, but this was her world. She reasoned it would always be this way. Even though there were times that she was keenly aware of the disgrace of this work with her uncle, she always came back to a distorted way of thinking. Her only certainty was *now*. Her only truth was the *flesh*. So, she determined to make the best of this night.

Yenene followed her outside, and standing beside her he interrupted her thought.

"This is what life and *God* intended for you, Lilith. So, just go with it. Are you ready?"

No one would have guessed that just ten minutes earlier she had loathed herself, her uncle and their way of life. She acquiesced to her uncle's lies and did what he wanted.

"Ready," she sighed.

As she lingered, she watched the teens come alive. Feeling a sense of loss for the life she wanted, she imagined what it might be like participating in this event. But, her uncle's voice quickly crashed through her reflection.

"I own you, mind, body and soul. Your spirit doesn't belong to God anymore. It belongs to me." He laughed loudly and pressed her.

"You belong to the dark side, and the only way you can get any light at all is to steal it from one of those sleeping boys."

They both turned to face the large glass doors to watch the crowd that came from the auditorium. Teenagers flooded the lobby, gathering around tables where speakers were signing books, and where music CD's could be purchased. They were excited, some were laughing, some jumping up and down, some still crying from the intense pull at their emotions.

Yenene looked for the one who was trying to be the center of attention. He knew there were some that attended these events because they were crazy about the person that asked them along. Intent only on winning the heart of another, they were possibly not affected at all by the pleas and promises of virginity. It did not matter if they were preacher's kids or street kids, he could spot them easily.

Kambo was the delight of all the girls. His dark skin and curly hair accented his round boyish face that was a mix of African and English features. The youthful blush that lingered on his cheeks made him even more attractive to the girls. He was handsome, and he knew that all the girls thought so.

A senior in high school, Kambo had two months remaining until he left for summer missions and then he would be off to University to enter a Pre-Med program. Everyone in town knew him as Pastor Joseph's kid from the Community Church. He was a confident and zealous presence among his peers. He moved in and out of the other teens who were engrossed in the effects of the conference. His busyness kept him from noticing Jamee as she sneaked up behind him and grabbed the loop of his designer jeans.

"Guess who," she said covering his eyes. "No don't guess. I couldn't take it if you said another girl's name. She removed her hands from his eyes and jumped in front of him, still giddy and excited about the evening.

"'Bought us a souvenir."

She held out her hand and opened it up revealing a pair of the dog tags that were being promoted during the concert. One was for her and one for him.

"Because we are made in the image of God, we should commit ourselves, body and all, to Him," he said repeating the catch phrase of the evening. He put the chain around his neck and revealing the side that said, *Image of God.*

"Thanks Jamee!"

"Hey Kam, are you going straight home?"

"No, I got a hotel room. Would you like see it?"

"Kambo!"

"Alright, yeah, I'm walking home."

"My dad is picking me up," she said. "He should be here soon."

Lilith saw something in this blithe, handsome teenager. His movements were animated and his smile intoxicating. She liked him.

Yenene pimped over toward her. His shoulders leaned forward as his stocky body leaned into his walk, revealing his self-engrossment.

"I bet you have spotted a sleeper, haven't you?"

Lilith looked at Yenene with disgust.

"Oh yeah, I see him," said Yenene. "It's Mr. bright-eyes over there? Light even shines through his dark curls and spills into his playful eyes."

Again Lilith looked at her uncle as she listened to his fake light-heartedness, and stared at him as he spit on the ground.

"That's right. My speech was too fanciful. I am just reminding you. Don't let yourself go there. You hear?"

Lilith closed her eyes wishing he would go away. She watched her uncle as he waited until the time was right. She knew it would not be long.

Jamee poked Kam in the side.

"Come outside with me while I wait for my dad."

When they walked out the door, Yenene approached them with his box.

"A gift for you, son, maybe someday you will give it to your young lady friend."

Kam stared at him and then at the box. The old man held out a beautiful box made of teak wood and inlayed with gold trim. It was small and intricately designed. He put it in Kam's hands.

"Here, look at it."

The box was made well. It was smooth and easy to the touch. Kam tried to open it, but couldn't.

"It's locked!" Jamee said shivering.

"Look, Jamee, it's really pretty. What could be the harm in a box?"

"I don't know, but I don't trust it."

"How much, Kam asked?"

Yenene stared at Kam with a look that made Jamee turn away.

"Free. I just make them and give them away."

"Thanks man, I will take it."

Lilith was standing right there quietly waiting to see what would happen. She knew that once he took the box it was all over for him. She would wait until the right moment before she moved in. She knew what to do next, and she was ready. There was a tap at her soul that felt like a pinprick. She knew that when all was said and done that she would hate herself and her esteem would plummet, but she was unable to stop. Yenene was right. This was her life and she had to move with it.

Jamee's dad honked as he pulled up to the curb. "Hey Kambo," he called out as he opened the passenger door in front. "Come on, Jamee, let's get on home."

After Jamee left, Kam tried to open the box, but could not figure out how. This was Lilith's cue to move in.

"Here, let me show you how. He gave me one too, and I can help you get it opened. It really isn't that hard after the first time. You just get used to it."

Kam was puzzled by her approach, but he had been sleeping too long and did not understand what she was really saying. He watched and waited as she opened the box. Suddenly, it seemed something had taken hold of him. The box no longer captivated him. His attention was now on Lilith. He gazed at her and something inside of him went crazy. This was not a feeling of social intimacy. It was a salacious, carnal feeling. He had felt this before, but never with such intensity. The skinny young girl with jet-black, stringy hair suddenly seemed like a ravenous beauty to him. He had forgotten the box. She was all he wanted. A small voice arose within him beckoning him to cry out for help, but he ignored it. Desire had overtaken him.

The next morning Kam woke in a strange place. The box lay on the table next to the bed, and his dog tags were inside of it. Lilith slept soundly next to him.

He cried out as he sat up on the edge of the bed.

"Oh my God, What have I done? I can't believe I bought into this lie."

He tried to think back on last night's events. How did he get here in the first place? What made him so dull in his thinking?

"That box!" He said. "It looked so attractive."

"Noooo!" he yelled, as he looked down at the naked body of this girl. Lilith woke when he screamed but did not even turn around. She didn't want to see him, nor did she want him to see her.

It always ends this way, she thought.

"No, I didn't do this," he shouted! "I don't even know your name."

Without turning around Lilith whispered, "my name is . . ."

"No!" he interrupted. "I don't want to know your name."

Kambo stumbled around the room until he found his clothes and hurriedly put them on losing his balance as he pulled up his jeans. He had no idea where he was or how he got here. He didn't remember drinking. Did she slip him something? What exactly was in that box? What would he tell his parents? What would he tell Jamee? Should he lie, tell the truth? Why didn't he pay attention? Oh God! Why didn't he listen to Jamee?

Half dressed he opened the door of the bedroom and turned back to look at Lilith. She was facing him now and regretted that he could see her.

"I don't know who you are, but I am sorry I ever saw you," he said.

As he ran out the door he could hear Yenene laughing, and he ran harder and faster.

Kambo Harris, you have lost out, pal. You are finished!

How could he tell his family or his girlfriend where he had been? He decided he would have to come up with a lie. He would have to cover it and go on—pretend it did not happen and start all over. He walked into the house and everyone was in the living room. His mom had been crying, and his dad looked angry. Jamee and her parents were there.

"Kam, where have you been?" His dad asked.

Kam opened his mouth to answer and with every lie that he told to cover up his sin he felt more deeply nauseous.

Jamee watched him closely.

"Kam, where are your tags?"

He looked down and realized they were gone. His thoughts went to the box sitting beside the bed.

"That stupid Box!"

"What? Do you mean the box the old man had? Did he take your tags? Kam! What is going on? Talk to us!"

Jamee was in tears. "What has happened to you? What does this mean?"

Kambo remained lost in thought. That box! The thought of it made his stomach tighten in knots. His mind was playing tricks on him now. The box, the dog tags, and the girl—like menacing demons they all sashayed before his eyes. He envisioned the words on the tags like an icon swirling in front of him. That powerful imprint on the back of the tags moved in front of his eyes.

Image of God, he thought. *That's not me now.* He covered his eyes as if to keep from seeing it. His heart sank. It was as though the message stamped on the tags *was* God.

And now, Kam thought, *God has departed from me. My heart is hidden from Him, locked away in a stupid box. I may never be able to reach Him again."*

A silent whisper deep within him said that was not true, but Kam shoved it deeper and listened instead to the voice from the box. He felt sick and ran to the bathroom. When he looked in the mirror he saw it. The flush in his cheeks was gone. Darkness had moved in.

Eclipse of Life

Loneliness, my only friend
Death, my sorrow's delight
Seclusion, my only escape—
Life, my illusion at night

I close my eyes to a friendly world,
And awaken to clamor and strife.
Longing for freedom, dying a slave—
To myself, to the world, to sin

Trying to escape, I keep running away
From time, from fate, from shame
I quicken my step and hurry my pace—
Eclipse of Life, in shadows I stay

The Scourge

The Shower pulsated as it beat down on Kam's back. It was as hot as he could make it. He just wanted to be clean again. Still trying to unveil the cloud that had covered his mind while uncovering his weaknesses, he could not accept what he had done. He had never seen that girl before, but now he would never forget her. The picture of her plagued his thoughts. Even when he tried desperately to forget her, the events of their evening together seemed to be nailed to his memory. He did not want to think of what they had done, and he chastised himself for entertaining the thoughts. He wondered if he would ever see her again. He had to get some answers. Who was she? Where did she come from? Why did she have to seduce *him*?

"Oh, God!" he said as he pounded the shower wall. "Why me? You know this is not what I wanted. I wish I could go back in time."

"Kam," his mom called out. "Are you okay in there?"

"Yeah, mom, I'm okay, just tired."

"Well, your dad and I want to talk when you come out. We will wait in the living room for you. Are you sure you are okay?"

"Mom!" he growled. "I am all right. I will be down in a minute!"

He knew they were going to question him again. What would he say? How would he respond? The truth was not an option, and he couldn't keep telling them that he was out walking all night. They just were not going to buy it.

Kam ran down the stairs and hurried to the coat closet before his parents had a chance to know what was happening. He didn't waste any time trying to leave. He threw his coat over his shoulder, but his haste was to no avail. His baseball bat fell into the opening between the hinges on the door and caused it to swing back open when Kam had tried to shut it. In one mighty thrust the door came flying back and met him square in the face, knocking him to the floor. The clamor immediately drew attention to what he was doing, and he was suddenly in the midst a family melee.

Still dizzy from the confrontation with the closet door, Kam just knelt there. His head hurt, his heart ached and his soul lacked the strength to even want to get up. At that moment, He nearly told them the truth, but when he began to open his mouth the voice from the box called out hauntingly to him.

"They would not understand," said the voice of an old man. "You are on your own now, boy. You made a grown up decision, and you must live with it. They can't change your path. They can't help you now. It *is* too late."

Kam was nearly in a panic. Could they see through him? Did they know? Maybe *she* had told them? Maybe he should just get it out, but how could he?

"Call the doctor, Joe," Kam's mother ordered her husband. I think he must be hurt pretty bad."

Beads of sweat emerged on Kam's forehead.

"NO!" He yelled. "I am fine. I mean, I will be fine. Just leave me alone for a minute. Go away and quit crowding me! I will be fine," he said.

"You are making too much of this, Kam," said the voice from the box. "It was just one night—one time. Tuck it away and forget about it. Get on with it and quit acting like it is the end of the world."

Kam's mother put a hand on his shoulder. He spun around and confronted her with hostility and attacked the love and compassion she wanted to show to him. Not realizing that his response to her had come from somewhere in the darkness, Kam spat out his words as he removed her hand from his shoulder.

"You are making too much of this. It was only one night—one time. It would be nice if we could just get on with it and quit acting like this is the end of the world."

His mother was taken aback by what he said, but what she saw in his eyes impacted her more. Her son had encountered darkness. She knew it, and she was helpless to intercept it. Some ugly thing had taken him but she did not know exactly what it was. Not exactly sure what she was fighting, she felt weakened. She knew there was trouble, and no amount of effort could make her relax. Evil had provoked him into a skirmish and had won.

"Maybe, he is right, Marie," Joseph said as he drew near to his wife. "Maybe we are driving him mad with our overreacting. He is a senior, and generally very responsible. Let's back off and let things rest."

Marie drew back from her husband. Tearfully she agreed. She knew that pushing him would do no good.

"I will back off from him, but I plan to draw nearer to God. Something has happened to my son and I can't help him unless I know what I am fighting, but I can still pray for him."

From her bedroom window, Lilith watched the sun set. Grateful that she could stay home tonight, she took refuge in her room, where she found quiet, peace and rest from the wearisome voice of her uncle. Her thoughts turned often to Kam. She wondered if she would ever see him again. She guessed not. Turning quickly from the window Lilith stood in front of the mirror. Her reflection, revealed a sixteen-year-old girl who looked like a thirty-year-old prostitute.

Why do you even look, Lil? You know you will hate what you see. If you are so unhappy with your life, change it!

The same thoughts kept returning. They were like an old fashioned spanking that followed the bad little girl around, continually whipping her, chastising and belittling her. They always came to torment her. These thoughts haunted her with ghosts of a better life. She pulled at a strand of her dark, stringy hair and tucked it behind her ear. But looking into the mirror made her yank it quickly back in place so she wouldn't have to look too long at the darkness enfolding her eyes. She pulled her hair almost in front of her eyes completely.

"UGLY!" She screamed. "Why would anyone ever care for such a miserable wretch?" Lilith grabbed her brush from the rickety stand beside the mirror and brushed vigorously slamming the bristles against her head with each stroke, and yanking at the knots until it made her cry.

"Papa, why did you let him take me, why?"

Her heart was racing and she cried harder. "Why?" She threw the brush down and ran out of her bedroom. Her uncle was about to come in and they ran into each other. She upset the tray he had in his hand, sending her dinner scattering on the floor.

"Stupid girl, what is your problem? I will be glad when you are through with these hormonal years so that we can settle into a comfortable life without all this emotional preoccupation that you seem to have. Well, come on help me pick this up. It is, after all, your dinner."

Lilith looked at him and suddenly those immortal Biblical words that were delivered to her by her grandmother came rushing into her mind vying for her soul.

The thief comes only to steal, kill and destroy. I have come that they may have life and have it abundantly.[1]

Strength arose in spite of her frailty, and she surprised even herself when she pushed her uncle out of her way. Caught unaware, he fell to the floor, stupefied by her strength and her tenacity.

Lilith's breathing was already labored and her balance out of sorts. She awkwardly backed up to the back door. Then as soon as she was out she ran until she could hardly breathe. She did not know where she was going, but she was determined she would not go back there. Never again would she set foot near her uncle. Never again would she lure some unsuspecting soul to take hold of her uncle's lecherous box, and never again would she sell her own soul for want of a sick kind of love.

Holding her side and trying to keep in the pain, Lilith stopped and sat on the bench in the park. A moment of quiet became her enemy as she began to think about the ache in her side, and the even larger pain in her heart. Just as the tears began to escape she noticed nearby movement.

"Great!" Lilith spoke under her breath as she saw someone approaching. She did not want anyone to see her like this.

It would not help, she thought.

All anyone would do is to ask if I was alright, and then go away and forget all about me. I am dirt—a tiny smudge on the clean lives of all these business people, family people and church people who pass by me every day. No one sees me. They look right through me. Maybe I am not only ugly, but also faceless.

She didn't want a stranger see that she was crying. She didn't want to deal with any knights in shining armor. She tried to stop crying, but without reserve her head sunk into her hands and she cried harder, shaking and sobbing irrepressibly. Her eyes were like grainy mounds and left no doubt to her emotional state. She was sure that whoever had been coming her way was standing over her wondering if they should talk to her or call the police, but when she looked up there was no one.

"I knew it," she said aloud. "No one cares! I am nobody, a scourge on society." She stood and pulled up on her low rider jeans, and tugged her tee shirt to cover her bare belly. She felt naked. It felt like many eyes were watching and waiting to take her. Faces of the many men who had invaded her, not just the teens, older men too—and her uncle. Disgust turned in her stomach and made her sick.

Suddenly she knew something was wrong. Footsteps were pounding behind her. It startled her and her heart began to race at the sound. Heavy breaths were upon her and she turned to see who or what was coming. Pain, like she had never encountered assailed the back of her legs. Again it came and took her to her knees. A loud pop resounded as her knees hit the pavement and twisted underneath her body. She didn't have a moment to think. She was only cognizant of one thing. The pain kept coming harder with each strike. Everything was growing dim.

"Filth, that's what you are—stinking filth. You want to be a scourge. I will give it gladly."

Harder her assailant struck. In an echo she could hear him yelling, but she could not make out what he was saying. The only thing her mind was registering was hot intense pain.

"But, I have come that you might have life and have it abundantly."

Those words! Who was saying them? She knew she was hearing someone.

She heard the voice again. The pain was still there. The evil surrounding it filled her consciousness. Pain, evil, hurt and shame all pointed to the thief.

"Who has come?" Lilith asked in broken words.

"Stupid girl, your stupidity will kill you. It is me, your dear uncle."

"No, who has come," she asked.

Yenene stopped beating her and grabbed her throat.

"Now will you come back and obey me? If you don't I will leave you here for dead. No one will help you girl—no one!"

"No!" she said deliriously. "He has come."

"There is no one here, but you and me."

Lilith opened her eyes and stared at her attacker. Breathing in raspy pants she grabbed his arm and squeezed.

"It's Jesus! Jesus has come to give me life."

"You are sounding like your grandmother." He wrestled her grip from his hand and kicked her with each subsequent question.

"And where is she, huh?" His heel thrashed the side of her face pounding her nose to the pavement.

"Is she alive?" The heel of his boot was now pressing against her skin holding her face to the ground. His weight continued pushing against her and rubbing her cheek into the grit of the pavement. It felt like needles were flung from an arrow and landed just below her eye. A kick to her back made her scream.

"Can she help you, support you or care for you? Well, I have come to give you death." Yenene kicked her in the ribs reciting a single word with each kick.

"You—are—a—scourge."

Lilith was no longer feeling anything. She could barely hear this madman, and soon the words of death and scourge that repeatedly fell from his mouth gave way to another voice. Lilith saw herself sitting in the front pew of the church with her grandmother next to her. They sat so close that Lilith could feel the warmth from her body and smell the fragrance of her perfume. The preacher was saying something about being a soldier of God.

"Hold on, Lil," he said, hold on. A soldier is fighting for you. Freedom is coming because someone is on her knees fighting for your life."

Lilith could feel the resistance of her body against her uncle's attacks, but she could no longer see or hear him. She saw only that old southern preacher pointing his finger at her and calling her name.

"How did you get here?" She asked.

It made no sense. He had not been around since she was a little girl.

Everything felt surreal. He couldn't be here, yet she could hear him plainly talking to her and calling her by name.

"Hang on, Lil, hang on. Sometimes there is only one thing that stands in between your old way of life and freedom. It is the soldier of God, the soldier fighting for you on the battlefield using the weapon of God, which is mighty for tearing down strongholds. Hang on, girl. You are a blessing because God made you so. Hang on"

An abrupt hush hung over her now, and the beaten teenager lay in silence for what seemed like hours. She didn't mind. It was a relief that her assailant was gone.

Lilith tried to examine her situation. Through swollen and bloody eyes she could see the shadow of a woman kneeling over her. She was untangling locks of blood-clotted hair trying to gently clear her eyes. The numbing shock had begun to leave and Lilith was beginning to feel the intense beating her body had taken. She winced in pain, and when the strange woman bent down and gently touched her bruised face the memory of her grandmother seemed close enough to touch.

"You are a blessing, child. Always remember that."

Kara sat on the ground next to the teenager's limp aching body, and Lilith could feel the warmth.

"Grandma, is that you? It has to be you. The preacher said you were praying. Can it be you, Grandma?"

Lilith suddenly pushed away from Kara and turned her head unknowingly rubbing her cheek into the rocky pavement.

"But you are dead!" She whimpered. "Grandma, can you pray from heaven? Is it you? Are you the one?"

"Hush, child," Kara said. "Shhh."

Kara held her and rocked back and forth praying for this girl, humming a soft melody to lull her to rest. As she rocked, she heard the girl saying something. Kara leaned closer to listen.

"Oh Lord!" Kara whispered. "She's singing the song."

Kara now began singing the old familiar tune and held her closer.

> Look up little girl; you are not alone; see He is by your side.
> While you slept, He left His throne; and crossed the deep and wide.
>
> He touched your world; He loves you. See, He touched your mind.
> And as you live He will see you through, and never leave you behind
>
> He touched your heart, now let Him in. Remember Him my dear.
> Awake little girl you are gonna win. See now your Lord draw near.

Lilith's chest heaved to breathe out more of the words. One eye was now swollen shut and her body was shaking from shock. Her lips were quivering, but it did not stop the words from coming though. Kara saw her strength and wept even more and prayed harder.

"Lord!" She cried, "Another fallen warrior. How long, Jesus? How long has she been fighting for her freedom?"

A chill ran through Kara. Suddenly she knew that more than just chance had brought her here. It was no accident.

"Father, thank you for your timing," she prayed. "Could it be that you will indeed use me again? Am I up to the call? Am I ready for the battle? Oh, help me, Jesus, to choose you and your weapons of warfare. Help me to . . ."

Lilith groaned and Kara gently caressed the young girl's swollen face.

"Help is here sweet girl, don't worry. Your help is here. You just hang on. Someone is praying for you. So just hang on."

Kara kept singing.

The gentleness of the song, the sound of crickets and frogs reining in the evening lulled Lilith into semi-consciousness. She was fading. An airplane flew overhead and seemed to Lilith to move slowly. Even nightfall descended like a cascade of cotton balls—slow, quiet, and deliberate. Lil's head dropped into Kara's lap.

Kara wept as she prayed because it had been two years since she had fallen and she felt God would never use her again. She wept because he had called her to the side of this young girl. What would have happened if she had not come along and interrupted the cruelty of that man. Would he have killed her? Suddenly she ached all over.

"Lord, spare her," she prayed. "Save her from her enemies. See her through her trial of hurt and sorrow. Bring her from the darkness and into your glorious light. The sirens broke through the moment of prayer, and Kara gave way to the paramedics as they hurried to Lilith.

Dying Embers

Kambo looked at the young girl he had just spent the night with. The morning light pirouetted over her in a heavenly performance.

"Who are you?" he queried in a whisper. "Oh, Lord! Who am *I*?"

Even the rapturous rays of sunshine could not change the reality of this dank, musty room. This was as far from heaven as one could get. Kam knew there were no angels dancing here. How did he end up here—a hotel room relationship with prostitutes that ended with doubt and despair? He had fallen, and all was lost. That ill-fated night was months ago. It was one night, but it had changed his life forever. He wanted to blame the girl with the box, but every time the anger arose within him he scoffed at the irony of it. He didn't even know her name.

No Kam boy, it is your own fault. You chose your hell, and made your bed in the midst of it. No going back. You just have to lie down and take it.

He stroked the hair of the sleeping girl. The battle raged within him as he lowered his hand to her breasts and entertained thoughts of staying a while longer. His emotions moved from anxiety to despondency, until in anguish he cried to be freed. Regret flooded him because sin had found him again, and he hurried to pack so he could leave before she awoke. He couldn't bear to have her look at him.

"I can't stay here any longer. Forgive me, Mandy," he said as he backed away from her.

"Mandy," Kam said, repeating her name. "At least I know your name."

Shaking his head and quietly backing up, Kam hoped she would not awaken.

"Forgive me," he whispered. "I pray you will find all the love and happiness you are seeking." He blew her a kiss and left.

The streets of the city were nothing like home. Noise surrounded him and troubled his mind even further. He had strayed far from home, and he missed his family.

No going back now. Those words jabbed at his spirit. He longed for home and the soft breeze blowing in the back of the house where he liked to sit in the twilight of the evening. He missed the peace and the solitude of home, and he missed Jamee. Most of all, missed the presence of the Lord, and he prayed for God to draw near. Everything around him beckoned him home. A billboard advertised a tranquil retreat called, "Just Like Coming Home." Then, Kam passed a church and his heart jumped as he read the sermon title on the marquee, "The Prodigal Comes Home."

Was God putting all of this in front of him? He knew the desire to return to his family and to God was already there. These signs just stirred the smoldering fire that lived inside of him already.

That voice from the box came back to haunt him. *What are you thinking? You can never go back. They are going to know your sin. You won't be able to keep it from them. It's too late—no turning back now. They won't forgive you, and neither will God.*

"Shut Up!" Kam yelled, holding his ears. "I *am* going home."

Kambo sat on the edge of the highway with a sign in his hand that advertised his destination. He was tired and lonely. Nothing was going right. Cars passed by, and no one even looked his way. Night was falling and the mosquitoes were thick. They began to swarm around his head. Buzzing and biting at his ear. Then suddenly a chill came over him. He felt he was getting sick.

"Lord, please get me out of here," he prayed. "I know I don't deserve it, but I ask you to hear my prayer and help me."

After sitting on the roadside for so long, this once vibrant and resilient young man buckled to the weight of his weariness and rolled over into a heap on the side of the road. He covered himself with his denim jacket and fell into a deep sleep.

Dreams filled unconsciousness. Thoughts of family dinners became a theatrical display in his sleeping mind. He could smell the lilacs that grew just outside the kitchen window. The hammock was nearby and it was that time of day he loved so much, where the sun and the moon seemed to pass one another—one on its way to slumber, the other just beginning its shift. His dreams took him to a springtime evening at home in the back yard. The cool air swept over him. It was at first, a calm, light wind that moved beneath the setting sun. Then the clouds thickened, turning the pink and purple sky to deepening shades of gray. The soft, gentle breeze began to whisk up the loose dirt from the flowerbed and toss it over the hammock. It became more powerful, and as a storm approached, he heard his mother calling.

"Kambo, come back in," she beckoned. "It is too dangerous out there. Come on, now, before it's too late!" Her voice suddenly became desperate. "I am waiting for you, so hurry in."

The wind was now furious, and the temperature was rapidly dropping. Kam was cold and shivering. Refusing to move, he kept swinging, back and forth in his hammock.

What are you waiting for, he asked himself as he watched the storm overtake him. He seemed to be an outsider looking in as he exhorted himself to go in out of the storm.

Vividly he saw his mother in the doorway waving at him. "Come in, Kam. Don't stay out in the storm. That is why you have a home. Come home. Come home, son, come home."

He woke with a start and knelt down and prayed to the Lord.

"God forgive me; I want You and I want home. I want to return to a life of purity, starting with a purity of heart. Please take me there."

He waited silently for a response.

Be careful, Kam. Kam had to be sure he had heard from God, so he waited for more. A verse from Proverbs rang through his mind with clarity.

Let not your heart turn aside to her ways; do not stray into her paths, for many a victim has she laid low, and all her slain are a mighty throng. Her house is the way to Sheol; going down to the chambers of death.[2]

Kam's thoughts turned to the night of the concert, when he had taken the box that changed his course. He could remember the dramatized rendition of that specific verse. There was the beautifully clad dancer swirling around a throng of young men who appeared to be pillars of strength. One by one as she danced around them they fell to the stage floor in a beaten slump.

He repeated out loud the words from the speaker.

"Do not let your heart turn to her ways. Do you hear the warning? She will take you down."

Kam shook his head. There were too many memories of that night, and he was drowning in those memories. He needed to turn his thoughts back to prayer.

"Lord," he said. "I know I was wrong. Is this all you have to say to me? Will you only remind me of my wrong? Is there no other word that you have for me, possibly a word of hope and encouragement?"

But that inner voice reiterated the same words of admonition.

Do not let your heart turn. Don't stray from me and follow her paths. Kam, There is a way that seems right, but it will lead you to death.

"Lord, I promise I will follow you," Kam said. "I will turn back to purity as I turn to head home." Kam stood up and began walking home.

As he walked Kambo reflected on the past months. They had been like Hell for him—like years spent in combat. He kept thinking that his battle was against that box. It seemed crazy, but he believed that for the larger part of these past months, it was the box that had controlled him. He hated the choices he had made. He was always in strange places around people he didn't know well, and many ways he was non-existent. There was no one to go home to each day, and now he didn't even have a house to live in. There were no friends to help out, and he was far away from his family.

So, this is what it is like to be unwanted. He had never felt this way before. He was always the popular one. It had never crossed his mind what it felt like to those whom he considered smaller because they did not have the good things he had. No wonder the battle he faced now was so harsh. Life had always been all about him, and he never really thought of anyone else beyond what they could do to fulfill his needs.

He had moved so far away from what was familiar. He was low man now. Kam was on his way home, but home was still many miles away. He realized the fight to get home would be fierce, and that arriving home would not ease the conflict, nor remove the scars that he would endure.

Night had fallen and the Colorado air was colder now. He pulled his jacket closer and walked on, hoping to get a ride. Highway 96 was lonely. He fought fear as it began to arise in him. He wished he could go back and everything would be all right. He longed to be at the café with Jamee enjoying her company, but he knew she would not want him now. That would not stop him though. He had to go home and try to start over. He knew this was not the life he wanted to live. He did not belong in the arms of prostitutes. Why he allowed himself to end up in such a place he did not know. But he was glad to get away.

This is my time. I am coming home. No more playing this game of chance with my destiny. I am on my way out, and I am not changing my mind.

A small red mustang passed him at high speed. Then suddenly stopped ahead and began to back up. Kam was hoping it would be someone to give him a ride. It was getting colder and he was tired. He ran to the passenger door, and looked inside. A young woman inside was smiling. She was beautiful, and he was taken immediately by her presence. He said nothing, but only stared in the window at her.

She tossed her hair back, laughing at his obvious fascination. He was unaffected by her laugh, and just stood there more bewildered by the moment.

"Hey party boy! Need a ride?"

Kam hesitated. This could be risky. He felt the kindling of lust crackling within him and was amazed at how quickly he could forget his vow. It was an intense moment for him. His reasoning skills began to kick in, and he was making up all the excuses he could think of to find no harm in riding with her. Finally he decided he was too tired to not take her up on the offer, and since there was no one else to give him a lift, then he was compelled. Suddenly, and seemingly out of nowhere, another car stopped and offered assistance, but Kam sent this older man on his way. He could not resist the company of the driver of this red mustang. He reasoned that she was not much older than he was. Surely she would not cause him to break his promise to himself and to God. How could she possibly prevent him? He was set on regaining his life.

And, if something happens, I will begin my journey to regain my life when I get home. For a moment Kam's heart was quickened. *Where did that thought come from, Kam? Run! Run for your life! Run now, while you can. Your journey back home begins here and now.*

Kam stood there a moment, rationalizing.

"Come on Sugar," she said in a syrupy sweet voice. "Get in."

He looked inside the car gawking at this beautiful girl. From head to toe he discovered every inch of her body. The evening breeze blew gently through the dark strands of hair that fell in thick waves to her waist. Her waistline was tiny and sloped intricately to a pale playboy bunny that displayed the one place not tanned of her beautifully bronzed skin. Her skirt was low on her hips and rode high on her thighs, revealing long legs that glistened with oils. She was an amazing beauty, and he was taken with her.

"Well, do you need a ride or not?"

Kam's legs trembled as he moved closer. Urgency arose within him screaming of danger. He could feel the heat rising. Once more the voice that arose within him was almost yelling, telling him to run.

Don't get in! There is a way that seems right, but it will lead to you to death.

"Well, Sweetie?"

Again this young enchantress took his thoughts captive. How could he walk away? What possible harm could a ride do? Kam thought no more of the warnings, and got into the car.

"I can handle this," he said. Then, realizing he had spoken out loud his face flushed with heat. Turning in his seat he faced the window so she could not see his embarrassment. He did not want her to have even the slightest idea that he was so absorbed by her beauty.

The young woman chuckled.

"Can handle what?" she asked teasingly.

"What is your name?" Kam responded, changing the subject.

"My name is Leila. What's yours?"

"Kambo, but my friends call me Kam."

"Where are you going, Kambo?"

"I am going to Fisher; how far can you take me?"

"All the way." she said, glancing longingly at him. Enunciating every word, she reiterated her answer.

"I am prepared to take you all—the—way. I can take you as far as you want to go."

It made him uncomfortable the way she said it. He cowered a bit from this sensual advancement, and found himself relishing it at the same time.

"Are you going to Fisher?" he asked.

"I wasn't till now, but I don't have anything else to do. So I will take you."

"But it's over three hundred miles."

She reached over and lightly touched his temple with her fingertips.

"No problem. I have plenty of time."

Kam panicked. He was no longer sure of what he wanted. He thought it was home and purity and God, but now his mind was whirling. Reason was leaving him as he began imagining ways to respond to her. He tried to remain calm and not reveal his uneasiness. Every time he looked at her he was taken completely by her unusual beauty. There was something very unsettling and almost amoral about her, but he tried not to think about that. How could someone so beautiful possibly possess the potential for evil?

That sweet voice interrupted his thinking and pulled him back to the moment.

"I have to get some gas, love," she said as she edged up to the pump. "Be a doll and pump the gas for me while I run to the girl's room?"

Kam quickly responded and got out to pump gas. While she was gone he thought about his promise to himself and to God.

It's not too late. Run! The voice again was filling his emotions making his hand tremble as he held on to the gas pump. *What can possibly go wrong,* he thought.

"We are in the car, traveling in daylight, and I have no money for a hotel," he mumbled to himself. "I think I am safe enough."

"Not as long as I am here," Leila said as she put her arms around him from behind and squeezed her body closer to his."

Kam jumped and pulled the gas nozzle out of the car, letting gas run all over the ground before he realized what he was doing.

"Leila," he said, "You can't."

But she held on even more, laying her head into the back of his neck.

"Can't what, Kam? I can't think that you are the best looking thing I have seen in a while? Can't wish I was close to you?"

"Leila, stop. Don't do this. I made a promise. Please, I just need a ride. That's all."

"Okay, handsome, but if you ride with me, I will put you to the test."

Kam was relieved for having passed this test. He was now feeling dauntless. He thought he could now overcome anything. *Victory,* he thought, as he got into the car and again put himself in the way of temptation.

"I *can* handle this."

Leila chuckled. "I heard that before. So does this mean you are still riding with me, party boy?"

Again embarrassed that he had spoken his thoughts out loud, Kam started to turn away, but then a sense of arrogance welled within him and he looked directly at her.

"Yes, we are still on," he said, "all—the—way."

Then his heart sank within him.

What made you say it that way, he thought. Even as he thought it he knew the answer. He was sure he could handle himself. If a situation arose he would run, but for now he was too cozy with the presence of this beautiful girl, and he was not about to change that.

Silence fell between them as they covered miles of lonely, isolated roads. The daylight hours were being overtaken by the cool, mysterious breezes of a Colorado night. They were getting close to home, and Kam felt the nearness of his family, and the hope of a new beginning filled his thoughts. Most of the way home he ignored the desire he had felt for Leila. Instead, he sensed a more urgent need within him. He needed home and was on his way. A sign just ahead gave him assurance that he would make it. The name of the city illuminated on a green and white sign that told him he had only fifty miles to go.

"Yes," his voice bolstered, "almost home."

"Yeah, and I need to stop for a minute, Leila said. I noticed there is a park at the next exit. Do you mind? I am getting really tired."

"No, I don't mind. I need a break too."

Leila stopped at a place near a stream.

"This looks good. We can take a short break here, and have a snack and get something to drink.

Leila jumped out of the mustang. "Kam," she said. "Grab the cooler in the back. There are drinks and some food in it. I will grab the blanket."

Kam hesitated but did not retreat. He grabbed the cooler and followed her to the side of the stream, where she spread out the blanket for them to sit on. He had not come this far to fail, and was determined to keep his distance. Still, he felt uneasy, unsure of himself. And once again he reiterated those words, only this time he added a little more.

"I can handle this, God," he said.

There is a way, Kam that leads to death!

Kam was shocked at the voice that reverberated in his mind. Was it really God? How is it that he could get so close to home and be in danger? Nothing had happened yet.

"Run!" The voice was now audible

"Come on! Run!"

Kam looked behind him and saw a father chasing his son.

"Run," he heard him say again as he chased his little boy toward the car.

Kam fell back on the blanket, relieved that it was just the voice of another person. Or was it?

"You sure are an uneasy person. Relax and take in the cool air. We are almost there and . . ."

"Leila?" Kam turned to see why she had quit talking. Her lip was quivering and when he looked at her she burst into tears.

"Leila, what is it? Did I do something?"

"No. It's just that I am so lonely. Truth is I have nothing to go back to, actually no place to go to, and I . . . Oh never mind."

"I'm sorry, Leila. Come here."

He wrapped his arm around her and she buried her head into his shoulder and cried harder. The more she cried the closer he held her, and she embraced him back clinging tightly to him. She was not crying now, but he was not willing to let go of her. She smelled good, and she was holding on to him and moving in closer, breathing heavily on his neck and into his ear. In a sudden and hasty moment lust overtook him. He no longer resisted her, and once again the strong and vibrant warrior fell on the battlefield of promiscuity. Another battle completely and forever lost. He ignored the awful feeling in his gut and drifted off to sleep.

As he slept he dreamed of holding her next to him and feeling the sensual release, but when he turned to look into her beautiful face she was repulsive. Her soft, exquisite face was replaced by a hellish distortion. She grabbed him and pulled him close to her. Strangely, he felt a fresh sensual stirring as she was breathing slow and longing breaths into his ear. Forgetting the awful face he had seen only minutes before he succumbed. But again the nightmarish face returned in front of him, and it was closer than ever. Her whispers were hard to discern. Then, without warning she was pinching him, and her whispers became loud and clear.

"Death to you," she said. "Death to you!"

He broke away and looked at her again and saw the face of a hideous monster that was disfigured and covered with boils and open sores. Everything about her embodied evil, and she had a hold on him that he could barely escape.

"Death!" she whispered as she breathed hot long breaths toward him. He tried to free himself from her grip, but he couldn't. He saw in her eyes, his reflection melting away. His tanned complexion turned ashen before him. His eyes began to hollow out, his hair turned white and his face became a skeleton. The sight of it made him scream, and it woke him. He was relieved that it was only a dream.

Leila was up and moving fast.

"What's your hurry?" Kam asked

"I have to get out of here, now!"

"Alright, I will help you."

"No, Kam, I am not taking you any further."

Kam was puzzled at her sudden change of heart. He followed her, carrying things to her car and helping her pack. Maybe she was just kidding.

"This is it, Playboy." Leila said, smiling at him. It was not that winsome smile that she had when he first got into her car. What was going on?

"You don't have far to go now," she said. "You can make it."

He was not believing that she was just going to leave him, especially now.

"How can you just up and take off now, especially after . . ."

"Look, Kambo, face it. You have been had. I hate pretty-faced guys like you who think that they can just do what they want and get away with it. Before I die I will find as many as I can who are just like you and screw their lives up.

"Before you die?"

Leila stared at him with a hatred he had not seen before.

"I have AIDS," she said coldly. "Because of guys like you, I am going to die a slow and painful death. Call this *The Revenge of Leila*."

Kam was stunned. He couldn't believe what he was hearing.

"Payback time, my dear Kambo, she said. Closing the door of her car, Leila spun her tires and raced off leaving Kam alone in his hopelessness.

The Wedding Gown

"Come on Lil, we have been over this before." Kara said standing at the closet door. "We need to decide what you will wear. Tonight is important. You need to do this for yourself. You know if you don't you will regret it."

"But what if *he* is there? I haven't seen Yenene now in over a year, and I am afraid he will be there and take me back."

Kara chose her words carefully. "Lil, he signed over guardianship. He cannot make you do anything, and I will be there with you."

"You don't know him, Kara. He has ways that are compelling."

"Lil, don't do this to yourself. What is your name?"

The young girl responded slowly at first.

"Lillian Holt."

Kara nodded. "Go on."

"Lillian means God's oath, and I am no longer Lilith. I am God's promise, and he has made me new. I am not that person anymore."

"Don't forget it Lil, you are God's promise. Yenene cannot hurt you. Now, decide, will you? What are you wearing tonight?"

Kara watched as Lil smiled. Lil's demure smile always softened Kara's heart. She had not once regretted taking her in. She sat on the bed remembering the months of counseling and the constant reassuring that her life was worth living. There were many letters and inquiries sent to discover her roots and find pictures of her grandmother. That was the final connection Lil had needed. After six months of searching, finally a letter had come. It was from her grandmother's preacher asking her to come and visit him.

He remembered Lil and all that had happened. As the two of them listened to him talk, Lil's story began to unfold in an epic Kara had not imagined of this young girl. They met with the preacher in an old country church that sat in a quiet town in Alabama. The old preacher looked the same as Lil had remembered. With a trembling hand the old man took Lil's hand as the first words came out of his mouth.

"Your mother gave you the name Lillian because you were a promise of God to her. That's what your name means—God's oath. I was her pastor when she was just a small child, and I can tell you her life was never easy. Nevertheless, she was always relying on God to bring her joy. After she married your dad and found out she was pregnant with you she worried because she wanted you to be free of the hardships that she endured. She prayed for you from the time you were conceived, and she told me that one day while she was praying for you that God had assured her that her prayers were answered. She named you Lillian so that she would always remember that God promised you would be free."

The old preacher went to the pulpit and retrieved a Bible. When Lil saw it tears filled her eyes. It was her grandmother's. She could tell right away by the turned up leather on the corners and the inscription, *Psalm 103:17*. She recited the verse from memory.

"But the steadfast love of the LORD *is from everlasting to everlasting on those who fear Him, and his righteousness to children's children."*[3]

"Your grandmother took great care of you after your mom died. Lil, do you remember the day you accepted Jesus as your Savior?"

Lil slowly shook her head.

"No Sir," she said politely. "Well, I remember all that happened, but I can't tell you what day it was or how old I was."

The preacher opened the Bible, and handed it to Lil to read the note her grandmother had written: *Today my sweet Lil accepted Jesus as her Savior.*

"You were just five years old," the preacher continued. "But within a couple of months I could tell you were already a mighty soldier enlisted in God's army. You were quite the prayer warrior for one so young. Then in just a little over a year your grandmother passed away. It was a Sunday, and she had left her Bible in church that day. After the funeral I went to give it to you. I thought you would want it. But you were nowhere to be found. I was told your uncle took you away and no one knew where. I held on to this Bible and prayed the Lord would help me to one day find you so I could give it to you."

Lil's voice interrupted Kara's daydreaming.

"Kara, Kara? Hello! Where are you?"

"Sorry Lil, I was thinking of our visit with that old southern preacher. What were you saying?"

"I was asking if I could I try on the dress you wore when you were remarried to Tom? If it will fit, I would like to wear it."

"You want to wear *my* dress?"

Lil stirred on the edge of the bed, wondering if this was going to appear too trite, and that Kara might laugh.

"It is the dress you wore when you recommitted yourself to your marriage. It represents a promise of purity and a symbol of newness. Isn't that what I am doing tonight? I am going to the conference to help others, but also to make a renewed commitment for my life. I am facing the evils and telling them I will no longer be a part of them, and at the same time I am stepping over a personal line to freedom. Am I right?"

"Yes, you are right. Does the dress mean that much to you?"

"It does. After all, it *is* your wedding dress. It will represent my commitment to Christ—to be His bride. It is because of you that I am here today, trusting God and looking at things like I do. I would really love to wear your dress."

Tears were rolling down Kara's face, though she tried to hold back the emotions.

"Don't start that," Lil said. "Besides I really just want to wear it because you have good taste in clothes," she said, trying to lighten the moment. Let's get ready."

The ride to the auditorium was quiet. Both women knew this was not going to be easy, but Kara knew that Lil was strong and she would be fine. And Lil knew that Kara was there as her support. Not much was spoken between them until Kara whispered a prayer for strength. Lil looked around at the crowded auditorium, and as she stepped up to the microphone the hum of voices began to decline. She didn't falter, but spoke immediately and clearly with a voice that commanded attention.

"My name is Lillian." It means God's oath. My mother gave it to me because she believed God's promises to her, and she felt that I was a promise. Mama died shortly after I was born. Papa was already depressed from her being sick for so long. He couldn't handle her death, and didn't know what to do with me. So Papa sent me to live with my grandmother, who was a loving and godly woman. She took care of me and loved me and introduced me to Jesus. By her leading and teaching I accepted Jesus as my Savior when I was five. She told me that I was now a child of God, but that I was also one of His warriors. So we began to pray together because she said that's what warriors do.

My world was beautiful, and I had begun to forget the pain of my mother's death and my father's abandonment. Then, my grandma died too. Papa wasn't involved in my life much, and he didn't want the burden of a child so he gave me away to my uncle, Yenene. I didn't understand at the time, but now I know that Yenene was an evil man, and the world he thrust me into was evil. He gave himself the name Yenene when he began to practice the occult. He always told me he was a wizard and that is what his name means—the wizard who poisons one who is sleeping. Yenene changed my name too. He called me Lilith, which means storm goddess, spirit of the night."

Lil paused and caught her breath. Her heart was pounding. What would they think? Some of them are her age. Would they recognize her as the one who stood outside this door with her uncle? She wavered, but saw Kara off to the side cheering her on.

"I'm a warrior that fell," she continued. "At age seven my uncle made me his prostitute, and since then my battlefield has been one of promiscuity. You might say it was not my fault, and that I didn't ask for it. Well, let me tell you that even when a warrior of Christ makes a decision to sin, it is not always something he or she would have asked for. Sin has a way of overtaking us. Whether it broke through into our lives by the attack of another or came through a door that we opened ourselves, is irrelevant. The thing to remember is that if we allow it, sin can overshadow all of the blessings and good things in life.

The auditorium was quiet as the teens were on the edge of their seats listening intently to Lil's testimony.

"I am here tonight," she said sounding somewhat like that southern preacher, "to publicly announce that I have reclaimed my true identity as Lillian. I am God's promise. I want to give testimony to you and bear witness before God that I am not that person, Lilith, any more. Christ has reclaimed my life, my heart and my virginity. I want to give assurance to those of you who have found themselves fallen on the battlefield of promiscuity. There is still hope for you and your life can be made new in Christ."

She paused a moment and remembered to pray to the Lord as her grandmother had taught her. She bowed her head and whispered silently, "Lord how do I proceed?"

Without hesitation she then lifted one arm into the air and prayed the Scripture that her Grandmother had quoted so many times.

"The thief comes only to steal and kill and destroy. I came that they may have life and have it abundantly."[4]

With passion in her voice, she addressed her audience with more fervor than she had the entire evening.

"The Yenenes are waiting just outside these doors with a box of clever lures. Don't even go near them. The box will be wrapped beautifully, but inside you will find death."

Kara was keenly aware of someone standing in the crowd looking unsettled. A young man began walking toward Lil, and before Kara could react he was on the stage. One of the ushers had tried to remove him, but he pleaded to have a voice. Lil looked at the haggard young man. He looked tired and worn, but she recognized him right away. It was him. He must hate her for taking his simple life away from him. She wanted to run, but the words from that familiar encouraged her.

Look up little girl, you're not alone. He is by your side. As you live, He'll see you through, and never leave you alone.

Lil spoke into the microphone to the usher who was struggling to get Kam to go back to his seat.

"Please, let him come forward."

Kam approached the microphone. He desperately searched for the right words. He knew he had to warn them. He believed he had strayed too far from God to ask Him for protection now, but maybe he could help others. He began to recite some of the lyrics to the song he wrote, and the worship team added blends of music as background.

> The doorpost where my heart once hung remains a memory
> The refuge I seek in my homeland above is reaching out to me
> But for now I am stuck in between
>
> And as I search to know why I ache inside, no words can give it meaning
> That longing, searching, far off feeling, that makes me ache inside

How bittersweet this time I linger till you call to take
  me away
From my tenure here on earth I come to be with you
  always
Until then I wait, and . . .

As I search to know why I ache inside, seems no words
  can give it meaning
That longing, searching, far off feeling, that makes me
  ache inside

Kam had finished but the worship team kept playing softly. He realized that he was just standing there listening to the music with his eyes closed and in front of all these teenagers. When he opened his eyes he could see why the praise team kept playing. Teens were crying, hanging on to one another, and flocking to the front where there was room to get on their knees. He had no idea the song would have that affect. Some of the students were still in their seats looking at him. He turned to look at Lil and then back at the crowd that was still in their seats.

"I can testify to what Lillian is saying. Almost two years ago I left this conference, and accepted the trappings of lust. I was shackled by selfishness. I cared only about myself, and I did not pay attention. God tried several times to bring me back, but I believed the lies of the enemy, and kept playing my sexual games. Now, I have found out that I have made contact with someone who has AIDS."

More teens got up and ran to the front to pray. Kam started to walk off the stage, but he stopped and went back to the microphone. He looked over again at Lillian. She thought that surely he would point her out as the cause for his dilemma. Her heart raced and she turned to run, but Kara was right there behind her.

"I am here, Lil," she said, "It will be okay."

Lil turned back toward Kam, and as he came up to the microphone she reached for Kara's hand. Her legs felt weak. She had not expected this.

"Lillian," Kam said with a humbled and tender voice.

"Please forgive me."

At that moment there was not a single person sitting, except one. Every student in that place had gone to the front to pray, but there was someone standing in the back. Her arms were folded across her chest tightly, and she was fighting back the tears of anger.

Kam looked straight at her as she turned to leave. When she walked into the light he noticed it was Jamee, and he ran after her.

"Jamee wait," he called out. "Please talk to me," he called again, running after her. Jamee stopped suddenly and turned to face Kam.

"I hate you Kambo Harris. What do you want from me now? You have ruined everything. I cannot believe you did this to me. I never want to see you again!"

"Jamee, I'm sorry; please forgive me?"

She took a deep breath.

"I can't," she said, and then turned and ran away.

Kambo sat on the wall of the flowerbed outside and watched helplessly as she ran.

Lil saw him and went out to find Kambo, but hesitated when she saw him. She turned to look back at Kara who nodded for her to go on.

"Kambo, can I join you? I want to give you something."

Lil held out her hand toward his face and Kam saw the tags that he had forgotten even existed. When he saw them he lost control and cried. Those tags were a sign of his redemption. God had indeed returned. He looked up at Lillian. She really did look different—somehow more at peace.

Kam stared at the tags in her hand, and finally took them, quietly cupping them in his hand.

Lillian turned to walk away

"Thanks," he said.

Lillian stopped, and without turning around she asked, "Will you forgive *me*?"

Silence dominated for a moment, and then He answered.

"Yes."

"Can we be friend?" she asked.

"I might have AIDS."

"That's okay, she said, facing him.

"I have recommitted my life to Christ and reclaimed my promise. I only want friendship, nothing more. Besides, you might not have AIDS. The odds are in your favor.

"I do need a friend." He said.

They sat quietly for a moment. Then Lil took his hand and bowed her head. Taking the cue, Kambo did the same.

"Lord," she prayed. "We are like sheep, and we tend to go astray. Even though we turn from Your love, You always receive us back. Thank You. Amen."

Kam opened his eyes to see if she had really stopped praying.

"That was a short prayer," he said.

"It was enough for now. Maybe the next time it will be longer."

"Agreed," Kambo said. "I look forward to the next time."

To the Warrior Fighting Promiscuity

The fight against promiscuity is a tough battle. In our culture there is really not much left to the imagination concerning human sexuality. By the time of marriage many couples have already experienced sex with one another and often times they have had multiple sexual partners. The head of morality seems to have turned away as if to embrace this as an acceptable way of life. Most people in our modern culture concede the idea of sex outside of marriage as normal.

The tragedy of this social dilemma is that it promotes all kinds of perverted behavior. Lillian represents one of the tragedies of a culture that is loosely bound to an absolute moral standard. Far too many have allowed perversion to dominate their lives and minds. There are some that are given over to reprobate thinking, and are not satisfied with the norms of human sexuality. Thus, they begin to crave the corrupt and distorted forms of sexual behavior. They prey on the innocent, and bring corruption into these innocent's lives. Sadly, the innocent one becomes vulnerable to replicate the depraved soul who once inflicted an unfair and unwholesome view of life upon their minds and bodies.

Lillian depicts the innocent whose only desire was to be loved, and one who would go to any end to gain even a moment of any kind of affection—no matter how distorted. Unless someone can set this person on a path toward the true lover of her soul and point her heart in His direction, she will keep the pattern of destruction alive in her life only to pass it along to the next generation.

Kambo embodies the self-centered Christian who thinks he cannot fall. He uses his charm to maintain his good standing. He claims good values and morals. He sets boundaries, and makes his vows to wait for marriage, but, his greatest problem is himself. In his immaturity he thinks he can achieve all of these lofty goals on his own. He believes he is strong, and does not rely on God. As a result he tends to walk too closely to the edge, until one day he finds he has fallen. He discovers that all of his charm and wit cannot pick him up, and his pride keeps him from facing others and confessing his sin. It takes a while for the

Kambos of Christianity to be restored, and sometimes their restoration comes too late, or not at all.

Yenene is everyone's temptation. He is the trickster that has a box with your name on it, and will decorate it in a fashion that is meant to lure you to take it and open it. He is the enemy of your heart—the strongman who seeks to destroy you. He lies in wait like the lion that looks for someone to devour. He pays attention to the weaker Christian, waiting to catch him off guard. He looks for the one who is sleeping. Even a small inoculation of his poison can take over the Christian mind like a raging cancer. Yenene is the destroyer. He cares for no one. He hates God and all that the cross represents. He hates you.

The Bible says: "He lurks in ambush like a lion in his thicket; he lurks that he may seize the poor; he seizes the poor when he draws him into his net."[5]

This enemy crouches at your door every day waiting to pull you down. The good news is that the Lord Jesus Christ waits for you too. He doesn't crouch as one who must hide, but He stands at your door as the King who longs to bring you to His Kingdom.

"Behold, I stand at the door and knock. If anyone hears my voice and opens the door, I will come in to him and eat with him, and he with me. The one who conquers, I will grant him to sit with me on my throne, as I also conquered and sat down with my Father on his throne."[6]

If you open the door to the adversary, you will meet with destruction. If you open to the Lord Jesus Christ you will find help in your time of need. Who is knocking at your door? If you have never let Jesus in, do it now. He will give you strength to overcome. He will protect your innocence, your life, your heart and your mind. While you dine with Him the Yenenes cannot affect you. If you dine with Jesus and the enemy knocks, let Jesus answer the door. Resist the enemy and he will run away. Jesus can open and close the right door when it comes to your thought life. Let Him do that for you.

Finally, I want to offer a word for those who have fallen. Don't give up. Let God restore you. He can and he is willing. Listen to the Lord. Your adversary will tell you it is too late. I would encourage you lift up your eyes to the Lord. With Him it is never too late. Read Psalm 103 and let your heart begin there. Let God renew you.

Prayer

Lord, I want to let you into my life, and I choose right now to open that door. I know that the life I have lived and the things I have done are not right. I admit that I am a sinner, and I need you in my life to help me overcome. I ask you to forgive me for the wrong I have done, and come into my heart. Please bring people into my life that will teach me about you. Come into my heart and life and be the Lord of my life. I ask for forgiveness of my sins and want to have a relationship with you. Lead me to do Your will.

Amos Marcus Desi

TROUBLED & WARLIKE

Come now and let us reason together says the Lord, though your sins are as scarlet, they will be as white as snow; Though they are red like crimson, they will become wool. If you are willing and obedient, you shall eat the good of the land; but if you refuse and rebel, you shall be eaten by the sword; for the mouth of the Lord has spoken. (Isaiah 1:18-20)

Pictures

Pictures fall before unguarded eyes
To embed an image into the soul

Iconic laces tied unscrupulously
Around the heart gone astray

Fetters threaded through muted places
Weave tightly into knots

Then bind the spiritual muscle
And weaken the soldier's will

Imagine

Amos Marcus Desi, prominent community member and respected leader found himself in a place he never dreamed he would be. His journey had landed him in a depressed area of town. He didn't like being alone, but he reasoned that this place was no more dangerous than any other large city he had encountered. His ministry journeys led him to perform at various concerts, and had taken him to some pretty depressed areas. Being in a place like this was not so foreign. His dismay was more about *how* he wanted to end up, than where he landed. All he wanted to do was run away, but he couldn't escape this time. Constant tormenting thoughts and feelings assailed all of his good intentions and thwarted the most promising goals to change.

The small framed man held his hand up to his forehead to block the setting sun that was in front of the street sign he needed to see. He wanted to make sure he was headed in the right direction. His face revealed a determined resolve that echoed the desire of his heart, and he decided that he was going to go to the church he had passed earlier. Negative thoughts slipped back and forth in his mind, returning each time with more power.

If I could just kneel down to pray, He thought. *Maybe someone would be there to talk to me maybe even help me. Lord, I desperately need the help.*

He started to turn the corner in the direction of the church, but decided to walk around the block once to clear his thoughts, and circle back after that. That's when he saw it. In front of him an old wooden sign swung with the movement of the breeze that whirled through the city. The sign was cut like a snowflake around the edges and its wood was weathered and chipped in places. It hung low on one side and creaked eerily when it swayed. Amos covered his ears to block the disturbing noise. Suddenly his heart raced. It was happening again. He tried to resist. but was helpless against the monster that lived in the dark caverns of his mind.

Cars whirled by, children played and couples passed in animated chatter, but he did not notice them. An empty silence surrounded him. In that moment he heard nothing but the creaking sound of the sign as it acquiesced to the wind and moved back and forth. The only thing that stood out on the sullied clapboard was black bold letters that incinerated the senses of this desperate young man. His eyes fixed on the sign he read, *Fantasy Tavern*. If that were not enough, when the sign swayed with the windy current of the early evening breeze it was lifted just enough to reveal the neon sign that advertised with large block letters, **ADULT ENTERTAINMENT CENTER**

The war began. His mind seemed to be on fire with passionate thoughts of beautiful women. Pictures from the past flooded his brain and he soon found himself following the emotional scent of lust. His brain reacted to the mental pictures of yesterday, and suddenly he was fighting the need to find and see more pornography.

"Oh, how can this be so bad?" He asked himself. "Who am I hurting? Can I help it if I am made this way? Why does it feel so wrong? Who says it is wrong any way?"

Question after unanswered question reeled through his mind. Rampant, ravaging untamed thoughts took hold of his being and carried him away. His mind was plundered like by the enemy who had seized the spoils of war. He knew he was losing again, and he was powerless against this enemy. How would he escape?

A man's voice interrupted his thoughts.

"It's closed."

"What?" Amos turned abruptly to find a man standing next to him. How long had he been there?

"I said it is closed!"

Startled, the young musician gaped at the large black man beside him. He towered over Amos's five foot nine inch body by at least six inches. He was older, maybe mid-sixties, but his build was solid. His shaven head revealed the layers of skin on the back of his neck. His thick brows stood out on his face, but that did not detract from the gentle look in his eyes.

"It's been closed a long time now," he said nodding toward the adult bookstore. "That's when Fantasy Tavern became such a hit. People who were used to the triple X started coming here to waste away hours chasing dreams that would never come true. But, then, by and by, it closed too."

Amos stood there feeling uncovered—like someone who had just been busted in a sex scandal. This man could not know his thoughts, but it appeared he did. He was not sure what to make of this conversation, and was afraid that if he spoke it would give him away. This sin of his was a secret that no one knew. How could a stranger know? The heat rose in his face, and his high cheekbones were now accented with the shade of embarrassment. This stranger's eyes pierced right through Amos' soul.

"You gonna be alright, friend," he said. His voice was not judging, though it was penetrating. Amos turned his head away from this intimidating man and started to walk away, but the old man was not going to let him go yet.

"Take care, friend. Spring time nights in KC can be chilly."

In exasperation Amos stopped and looked back at him.

"Who are you?"

"You can just say that I am just a friend."

The whole scene was overwhelming—the phantom building, the creaking sound of the sign yielding in haunted symphony with the wind and this mysterious man who appeared in the midst of his troubles.

"How long ago did the tavern close?"

"About a year ago. Funny thing was that it closed exactly one year after the bookstore closed. It was to the date."

"So what happened?" Amos asked as he stuck his hands in his pockets.

The old man moved in a little closer. "What do you mean?"

"I mean why did it close?"

Chance's eyes danced as he laughed. "Prayer, my friend! I prayed for it to close and God answered my prayer. It's as simple as that."

He laughed some more and held out his hand. "Chance is my name. What's yours?"

"My name is Amos. I am a ways from home. I live in Elkhart, Indiana."

"Well, Amos from Elkhart, Indiana, would you like some coffee and conversation? I'm only a couple blocks away. We have to walk since I don't own a car."

Amos looked up at the sign and then back to this strangely engaging man. What he really wanted was to pursue this heated ambition that had formed in his mind. He was more interested in satisfying the need that was aroused. Even though he fought to break away from the habitual opiate of pornography, he could not do it. At times like this he felt helpless, and wondered if he would ever be freed from the shame and scandal of his own mind. He would on any given day make his vow to be renewed in mind, but then all of a sudden something would trigger the pictures that were stored within. Once the lion was awakened he had to respond. He could no longer help himself because the lecherous power was too great.

In a flash, those carnal cravings sunk into his mind, and he was detached from all else. Amos was familiar with this song. Its melody was rather discordant, but the tune lured him like a sailor's nymph. He was so beguiled by the images that the sign had placed in his brain that he forgot where he was and who was with him. Breathing as if he were struggling for air, his chin dropped into his chest and he heaved a final deep sigh.

"How can I be released from this adversity?"

"Hey man, my coffee ain't that bad," Chance said laughing. He knew this young man was far away, fighting an unseen enemy, and he wanted to bring him back to the present without much ado.

"Sorry, I was somewhere else," Amos said. "Coffee does sound good, but honestly the conversation sounds better."

Chance talked freely as they walked. He spoke with hands that cut through the air. His head was always shaking back and forth, and his eyes lit up with every peak of his conversation.

"Oh yeah!" his voiced pealed with excitement. "This here section of town was actually known as KC's hall of iniquity. It was alive with all sorts of hell's invitation. Mercy me! There were drugs, prostitutes, porn—you name it. If it fell under the heading of lust, it was here."

Amos stopped walking.

"And now it's dead around here. Shouldn't you have just left it alone? It seems it would be better than this—tattered signs hanging by a thread and buildings falling apart. It looks like a ghost town. Is this good? Who are you to stop the progress of people's lives and maybe even their livelihood?"

Chance laughed quietly. "I really didn't do anything. I just talked to God about what was troubling me. He's the one that moved the mountain, or in this case the establishment."

Amos looked back once more at the old tattered sign.

"So did they relocate or die out?"

"I don't know."

"But, what good is that dead place now?"

Chance paused in front of the church that Amos had planned to visit.

"This is my place."

The lighting in the parking lot illuminated the bald man's face as he looked soberly at Amos. His brow furrowed again to form one line.

"Where'd you say you were from?"

"Elkhart, Indiana."

"Ain't that a small town with cows and corn?"

"What has corn and cows got to do with my question?" Amos asked defensively.

"Plant much corn, yourself?"

"I've done a bit, so what?"

Chance's uncompromising expression was deeply intrusive. His eyes pierced through Amos, digging right to the quick of his soul. Silence was broken when Chance finally spoke again.

"It dies, my friend! The corn dies. Seeds are produced and a healthy and useful stalk of corn grows out of an old dead seed. Do you get it?"

"Where do you come from?" Amos asked.

The older man chuckled. "My name is Chance and I come from this here church. I keep records. I maintain the records of the most important place in the city. I log when the doors of this here church are opened and when they are closed. I keep account of those that come willingly and . . ."

He chuckled again in his deep bristly tone. "I record those who come kicking and screaming. I keep records my friend, for the Lord. But let's not go there now. I will tell you more about *my* calling later. I'd be better off to hear about your calling."

Chance led the puzzled young man around to the back of the church to a small apartment. When he opened the door for Amos to enter, a rush of soft, warm air came out of the door. It offered a pleasant and strangely magnetic touch of energy.

"Come on in," Chance offered. "I will make some coffee."

Amos looked around the modestly decorated apartment. The walls were bare except for one. On it a picture hung majestically above an opened Bible. It was a painting of Jesus unlike he had ever seen. The face of the Lord seemed to embody all races and represent many emotions. At one angle there was peacefulness and at another there was joy. Imagery poked out of every facet of the painting. He saw battles being fought in harvest fields. There were brush strokes that resembled powerful angels emanating from the Savior's eyes, and just before his outstretched arms was the tired body of a battle-weary soldier.

Near the Bible was another table with an old-fashioned church kneeler.

Church, he thought. *How long has it been?*

He ran his hand over the table and the kneeler, then back again to the painting, and then to the Bible, which was opened to the book of Matthew.

"Come to me, all who labor and are heavy laden, and I will give you rest. Take my yoke upon you, and learn from me, for I am gentle and lowly in heart, and you will find rest for your souls." [7]

At reading this, he asked. "Learn how to struggle through the legalism of religion? I will *never* set foot in a church again. What am I doing here anyway—having coffee with some crazy man who thinks God hears *and answers* his prayers? Why do I even care about this picture? It's just a picture."

Though his anger blistered at the sight of this painting, he was drawn once again to its mysterious ambiance. A mystical shroud hovered over the painting like a sacred waterfall of untapped secrets. Amos's hand was shaking uncontrollably. He protested the sense of awe, and fought against the pervading trepidation that was arising within him. A foreboding was rumbling in his stomach and moving upward until his heart began to pound. What was this unseen power? Was it the mantle that hung like a mist inside this apartment?

Amos shook his head, running his fingers through his the fine strands of hair that had receded from his forehead. He walked away from the picture, lifted one arm up and shook his fist in the air. He beckoned reason to intervene. It was just a picture. He just needed to walk away from it and refocus. But he could not help but turn his gaze back upon it.

He was again staring at the picture, looking for the obscurities that made it a distinctive work of art. That's all it was—just art. The many pictures that were concealed within this one painting fascinated him. Several faces of Jesus came passionately alive. They were all stirring. They were actively moving him to a place he did not want to go. It was that familiar place of self-examination. Those faces were all so different and yet so familiar. One was pensive, another was laughing, and another revealed a true man of sorrow. Amos could relate to that one. There was an old church in the background, and women knelt beside it praying. Soldiers gambled on the porch of the church which was just in front of an open door that accentuated a veil torn in two. There was so much to see. The longer he looked the more he noticed.

The painting was beautiful, yet disturbing, empowering, yet crippling. Behind the church was a graveyard which had some open graves. Amos remembered the passage that spoke of the death of Jesus and how the dead had come out of the grave. The thought of it always seemed too much like a nightmare theatre to him. He shivered as he imagined those graves opening up. As he reached out to touch the painting, the entire room was illuminated by lightening. Amos was startled by a larger-than-life image in the shadow of that flash.

"Lord! You scared me," Amos said shaking his head as Chance made his way closer. He was relieved, knowing it was only this old man who had appeared in the midst of his tense moment. Chance put the coffee down on the table.

"It happens all the time. The picture is powerful, ain't it?"

"Yeah, where did it come from?"

"A good friend of mine gave it to me, painted it himself. He is an artist, a creator of beauty. He is the kind of person you would call an alien in this world."

"Humph," Amos replied. "I guess next I am supposed to ask what you mean by *alien*. But I already know. Guess you could say I have been there and bought the tee shirt. I feel like an alien. Guess you could say I am an outcast in my world."

Amos pulled a chair out from the table. His shaking hands reached for a cigarette in his top right pocket. Chance's gaze zeroed in on his new visitor with one of those intense looks.

"I don't need to explain what I meant if you don't want me to. But, I will say why those things you are pulling out of your pocket ain't good for you. They ain't good for me either. So, you know what to do."

Chance did not quit staring at him until he put the cigarettes back in his pocket.

"I could talk about how those cigarettes will kill you, my friend, but I think you have more to worry about than what can kill the body. Am I right?"

Amos wondered who he had hooked up with. As much as this quirky older man troubled him, Amos found a need to be around him. Chance was eccentric and yet pleasantly simple. He had a certain serenity that Amos secretly wanted. His meager existence revealed a man whose pleasure and happiness in life came from more than what a material world could offer. He knew it was his relationship with Christ, and wished he had the same thing.

"I'm ready to listen." Amos said. "Let's talk about your artist friend. What do you mean that he was an alien in the world?"

"My friend's name is Simon," Chance answered. "He got his name because his mother swore that he could hear her deepest thoughts even before he was born. She was just a girl, and not married when she got pregnant. Simon's dad left town and was never seen again. His momma had to work hard to prepare a home for them, and she often missed out on the good fellowship the church she called home. That was this church. It's in the records."

Chance rubbed his chin and watched closely to see if Amos was listening.

"Simon is a different kind of man. Yes sir, he was different even before he was born. His momma said that every time she felt overwhelmed by her circumstance, she would swear that her life wasn't worth living, and that she should just give up and die. Just as soon as she said those words he would kick. It happened so many times that she said that boy heard her, and was trying to tell her that *he* was worth living for."

Amos was attentive, and Chance didn't miss an opportunity.

"Simon's name means *he who hears*, and I'm telling you that man hears from God like no other person I know. He makes it clear that this world ain't his home and that he is just a passing through. That's what I mean by alien. Look, he's there in the picture."

Chance pointed a leathery, weathered finger at the place where Amos would find Simon in the picture, but all Amos saw was a man, whose face was unrecognizable because he was looking upward. The face was overlaid on the outstretched arms on the cross next to the bowed head of Christ. Baffled by this man's self portrait in the painting Amos looked to Chance for more information.

"I don't get it. Why is Christ's head bowed and Simon's looking up"

Chance tenderly placed his large hand on Amos's shoulder.
"Makes Matthew 11:28 and 29 come to life, doesn't it?"
"What do you mean?"
"Like I said, my friend, Simon, he hears. He heard the message of Matthew clearly. You see, Jesus said to come to him if you have burdens, and He will give you rest. Simon found that peace because he discovered that Jesus paid the price for his restlessness. Jesus put all that transgression on Himself. That's why his head is bowed. He also heard in that verse that to take the yoke of Christ was to take rest for his soul. So he is in the picture, yoked to the one that enabled him to look up. Do you know what a yoke is?"

Amos remained silent and waited for the old man to tell him.

"A yoke is a wooden frame that joins animals at the head so they will work together. You can see that Simon's face is next to the Savior's face. He painted it that way to remind him to keep himself joined, in his mind, to Jesus, so he can work together with Him."

"I get it." Amos said. "Say no more. I get it."

The room was quiet; there was no more rushing wind, no whirling thoughts that resounded in Amos's head, no panic rising to a bleating octave in his heart. There was momentary silence in Amos' mind. Chance saw it. Peace was passing over Amos. It was definitely a moment to record in the church records, and likely a moment where some of this young man's demons would flee, if he would let it happen. The peace was there, knocking at the door, but struggle remained in his eyes.

"Choose peace, Amos," Chance whispered. "Choose peace."

Amos read the inscription across the bottom of the painting. *There beside that crown of thorns, I place my head, my mind; yoked with Him; united as one; Together, fixed in one accord.*

He then pulled a picture out of his wallet and handed it to Chance.

"Her name is Jamee. She's my wife."

Chance smiled, but not the full smile.

"She's a beautiful lady"

"Yes, she is, but she's been hurt so much in her life. I found that I couldn't help her. I couldn't ease her pain. I couldn't make her forget even for a minute. We've been married for three years and I knew within the first three months that she really did not want me. She was in love with someone else, who had hurt her."

Amos hesitated, "He ended up being HIV positive, if that tells you anything. After Jamee and I got married she got really depressed and withdrawn, and I guess I got really lonely. Before I could stop it, I became involved in a virtual dating agency on line. Jamee came into the room one day when I was deeply involved in the site—if you know what I mean. In her mind, it was just like I was cheating on her. I told her she was stupid for even thinking like that, but she was right. I didn't realize how hooked I was, until I got caught. I hurt her even worse than she had been hurt before. I still couldn't stop the pictures in my head, and I couldn't make the desires go away."

"Where is your wife now?"

"Back home with her parents. She's thinking of filing for divorce."

"And you?"

"What do you mean?"

"Why aren't you at home fighting for her?"

"I guess it's just easier to run. And the truth is I don't want to quit what I'm doing."

Chance was quiet. He looked at Amos, and noticed he was getting sleepy.

"Can I ask you something?"

"Go ahead," Amos answered without opening his eyes.

"You ever give your life to the Lord and ask Him to deliver you from this addiction?"

"Well, I was a leader in our church, isn't that close enough?"

"No," Chance said. "You have to ask Him to forgive you. Would you do that now? I will pray with you if you want?"

Amos put his feet up on the couch.

"Not now. I'm tired, Chance. I am so tired"

As he began to drift off to sleep he noticed the air was getting colder around him and he stiffened his body to try to stay warm. Then he felt the heaviness of a quilt being laid over him.

"Thanks Chance," he said, and then fell into a deep sleep.

"Hey mister, Are you needing some help? How can I help you?"

Amos heard the voice as he was waking up, but it was unfamiliar. He felt the hand shaking him and looked up. He lay there for a moment trying to think about what happened before he went to sleep and then realized he didn't know this person. Amos jumped up, startled.

"I must have fallen asleep. Who are you? Where is Chance?"

"Who is Chance? I'm the preacher here. My name is Simon, and I am sorry to say, I don't know anyone named Chance. Are you okay? You need a place to stay for a night or two?"

Amos looked at the man standing over him. He was kind and seemed to be genuinely concerned, but he wasn't Chance. Amos panicked.

"You've got to know him. He's the keeper of the records for your church. He lives here in this apartment. He invited me over for coffee."

Amos looked around.

"The picture, it's gone! Wait where am I? Did someone move me? What is going on here? I know I am not going crazy. Who are you?"

"Again, I am Simon, the pastor of this church. There is no apartment here, and no one named Chance who keeps records. You are in the sanctuary of the Apostle's Church."

"Wait, your name is Simon? Are you an artist?"

"Well, I have to be a bit creative to run a church in this area of town, but I'm not an artist in the truest sense of the word. I just come to church, make sure the doors are open and tell everyone about how much Jesus loves them."

Amos jumped to his feet.

"This is some kind of trick. What time is it?

The preacher was deliberate, and in some ways a bit slow in his movements. He was probably near Amos's age, but his mannerisms made him seem older. Something about him was piercing. Amos noticed his calloused hands. They were not like he would expect from a pastor. Back home all of the pastoral staff were the clean-shaven type with soft hands. But this guy even had dirt under his fingernails. He was not the typical pastor.

"It's 4:00 a.m.," the preacher said. "I had unlocked the door earlier, and was coming back to see who was here."

"What do you mean?" Amos asked.

"Well, as I prayed this morning, the Lord blessed me and told me to go unlock the doors because I would soon have a visitor."

"God talks to you?"

"Not audibly, but I do try to listen and hear what He says to me each day. It's more of an impression in my heart and conscience, only I don't believe it's my conscience, but that of the Holy Spirit directing my day for the glory of the Lord."

Amos looked up at the cross on the wall.

"Simon, one who hears," he whispered. "You hear from God?"

"Yes, I believe so."

"But you don't know Chance?"

"Afraid not, my friend. So tell me, what's your name; and why are you here?"

"Do you mean, here in this church or here in Kansas City? Amos asked.

Simon sat quietly for a moment before answering.

"You choose," he said. "I'm listening either way."

"I don't know if I can explain why I am here in this church. Well, I could tell you what happened to bring me here. It's pretty clear in my head, but it seems too much like a dream and makes no sense. So I will tell you why I am here in Kansas City."

The pastor nodded. "I'm listening."

Shifting in his seat uncomfortably he said, "My name is Amos. I am, well, I *was*, the music director at my church in Indiana. And long story short? I needed to get away so I could figure out the *next* piece of my life. My wife left me and went back to her parents; she is probably visiting the lawyer today. I told Chance all about this already."

Amos realized when he mentioned Chance again that this *Chance* person was probably a dream. But he had to pursue some possibilities.

"Hey, Pastor Simon, I have to ask something. Was there an Adult Entertainment Center and a place called Fantasy Tavern not far from the church that closed up?"

Simon took his hand off of his chin, and sat up looking straight at Amos.

"I have been praying for that Tavern to close, but it hasn't yet."

"Oh man," Amos said standing up quickly and pacing as he continued to speak.

"This is too strange. You mean to tell me it is still there? But I saw the sign. It was barely hanging there. It looked closed down to me."

"Yeah, I think they just leave the sign hanging so people can see the neon sign behind it. That Adult Entertainment place is closed. In fact, in another two weeks it will be one year ago that it closed. And the tavern popped up right after it. But it isn't really a tavern so much as it is another porn place. The sign hangs there and exposes the neon advertisement for the real reason they exist. But you don't need to be going there!" Simon stood up next to him.

"You aren't thinking of going there are you?"

Amos said nothing. He didn't know what to say. This was just too strange. How could all this be happening? It seemed he was in the middle of a dream or something.

"Amos, are you alright?" Simon asked trying to help. Then he realized what was happening with this curious traveler.

"Oh," he said. "You, not being the music director at your church any more, is because of an addiction, right?"

Amos nodded.

"To porn," Simon asked.

He looked up at Simon and saw the tears welling up in his eyes.

"Yes, to porn," he said. I'm really not trying to get away to think. I'm running away from having to look at all those people who now know. I can't go to church anymore and look at them. The sorry part is that I don't want to give it up. I keep finding ways to justify it even though it is already costing me a lot of grief."

Simon's heart went out to this man. He wanted to help him, but knew that what he really needed to do was to go back home and find restoration, and to reconcile as much as he could with those whom he had hurt. But for now, he thought, maybe a break would help him to collect his thoughts and find some time with God.

"I think eventually you do have to go back and face everyone," he said, placing a hand on Amos's shoulder. Give it some time though. For now why don't you stay a couple of days, and at least get your thoughts together. I have an extra room at my place. There is no one there but me. You will have peace and quiet and maybe some time to think. If nothing else you'll have a decent meal. I'm a pretty good cook."

"Well, if you are sure it will be alright," Amos said. "It sounds good to me."

"It's good," Simon reassured him. Still, a nagging feeling lingered in the pastor's mind that it was not going to be an easy journey.

Snow White's Apple

Amos wasn't sure what this was going to be like and though there was no hesitation about staying with this stranger for the next few days, there was a sense of uncertainty. The drive was short. He thought it was close enough that they could have walked, but this was after all, Kansas City's high crime district. It was probably not a good thing to walk this time in the morning.

"This is it?" Amos asked.

"Yep, I know it isn't much, but it's mine and it's paid for. I like that it's close to the church. I could walk if I needed to."

The house is small, he thought looking at it from the outside. It needed some work. Some of the guttering was hanging and the siding needed repair. The place really needed a good handy man.

"Maybe I can do some work around here for you to earn my keep. I'd feel better about that anyway."

Simon laughed. "Looks that bad huh?"

"Well," he said, trying not to hurt Simon's feelings. "Let's just say it could use an upgrade, and I am the person who can give it what it needs."

"Yeah, I'm not very good at that stuff. I do better at soul repair."

"So are you out to fix me?" Amos said.

"No, I don't actually do the repair, Jesus does. I just point people toward him."

Simon opened the door.

"After you," he said.

Amos entered into what appeared to be the living room. It was small and cozy, considering its lack of household accessories. Other than the two weathered looking sconces that accented a framed certificate of ordination, the walls were scarcely decorated. There was one decoration that caught his eye. On the wall near the couch, a large oak frame surrounded a drafted pencil sketch of Jesus on a plain white canvas. Inside that outline was another picture that was obscured by the light coming in through the window. He edged closer for a better look.

"That's really weird," Amos said as heart raced, and his mind flashed back to his dream or whatever it was with Chance. The picture was blank except for this outline, but what caused his heart to race was the sketch of the person whose head was lifted upward.

"What's weird?" Simon asked as he walked near the picture.

Amos just shook it off. "Oh, nothing really, it's just that the picture reminded me of a dream I had. The picture I saw was more vibrant, though. It was like one of those pieces you see in a gallery that is finished in pastels with more details and color."

"Well," Simon added. "I drew that sketch."

"I thought you said you weren't an artist," Amos interrupted.

"I'm not. Well, I can do some things, but it is so much of a labor for me that I don't pursue it. It doesn't come naturally. I did this as a reminder to me that God will supply all my needs. As you can see, I am not getting any younger."

Amos watched Simon lean against the wall as he ran his fingers through his hair.

"I want to someday be married," Simon continued, "but have not met that right one yet."

Simon's thoughts trailed off.

"I had originally sketched that picture for my mother. I hung it here to remind me that when the Lord is ready for me to marry, He will bring me someone who will be the right one to complete my life. So I have in the picture me looking up to God as I rest on the outstretched arms of the Lord. I am waiting in Him, and one day the right person will come along and finish this piece of art with the story of *our* lives."

"What if that person can't draw?" Amos asked.

"She'll be a very talented artist, who will make this picture and my life a beautiful piece. I am confident of that."

"How can you be so sure, man? Do you think you have a direct line to God or something? I mean you can't possibly know something like that."

Simon apprehended the moment and answered with a question.

"Do you have a direct line to God, my friend?"

"Well, I was the music leader in my church," As soon as he said these words that sense of déjà vu struck and took him back to his encounter with Chance.

He heard that old man's voice just a clear as if he were standing right there.

"Jesus said, to come to him if you have burdens and He will give you rest."

Simon interrupted Amos's thoughts of Chance as he continued to tell this wayward minister of music about the truth of the Gospel. But this stubborn young man refused to hear it.

"Amos, he said drawing in closer, being a leader in the church doesn't give you a relationship with Jesus any more than standing in the U.S. makes you a citizen. You have to be born in this country or grafted in by a desire to embrace its tenets in order to experience the freedom of citizenship. Likewise, in order to have that *direct line* to God you have to be born again into His family—grafted in by confessing the sins that hinder your freedom, and asking Him to forgive you and change you. Have you ever done that?"

"Well, no, I guess not."

"Would you like to now? I can pray with you."

"Not now, Simon. I just need to go for a walk and clear my head. Do you mind if I get away for a while?"

"No, you go on and do what you need to do. Just be careful out there."

Amos left and walked toward Fantasy Tavern. He stopped at a bench just a block away, and sat there trying to convince himself to go back to Simon's apartment to pray with him to be freed from this craziness. As he sat near the building a young woman, seductively dressed, came up next to him. Her short skirt hiked further up her thighs as she sat next to him, and she sat so close he felt he couldn't breathe.

That's pretty bold, he thought. She didn't know him or what he was capable of doing, but she was offering complete exposure, and he knew it.

She said nothing at all. She handed him a business card, and walked away. The card said it all. It read: Selene's Dream, Your dream too—Fantasy Tavern.

He stood up and watched her walk away, and then looked at the card. He knew he should throw it away, but he stuck it in his pocket before he began to walk back to the pastor's house. He didn't hesitate to show Simon the card when asked how his walk went.

"I tried to throw it away, but I can't." he said, looking at Simon.

"Then give it to me. I can throw it away," Simon said holding out his hand.

"Can't do that either," Amos replied, putting the card back in his pocket. Just pray for Jamee that God will help her. I am not going to change."

"Amos," Simon said hesitatingly. "I called your wife. She's coming here next week."

"What? How'd did you get the number? How'd you talk her into coming? Man, you shouldn't have done that. It won't change anything."

Simon held a cell phone in his hand. "You left this behind. I thought you two needed to fight this out together, and that maybe this would be a safe place to do that. You'd be surprised how willing she was. Now, can I have that business card?"

"No, I will get rid of it."

"Man, don't. It's like Snow White's apple, and it will keep you under its spell. Give it up now, before it's too late.

Amos shoved it further into his pocket, and sat down on the couch.

"When can we get started on those repairs," he said changing the subject.

Simon started to object, but Amos stopped him.

"Please, enough about my issues."

Simon decided to let it drop for now. There would be other opportunities.

Sitting next to the business man on the bus, Jamee noticed as he opened his brief case that a Bible sat inside of it. She wondered if this person was a true person of God. She didn't have a lot of faith in people. She had been hurt so many times, and felt she couldn't afford to trust anyone—well, not guys anyway. She remembered last week when Pastor Simon called, and asked her to come to Kansas City. She was hesitant to believe that he really wanted to help.

When the phone rang she held the divorce papers in her hand, and was feeling the turmoil of this decision. She reflected on all the horrible feelings she was harboring against Amos. She knew it really wasn't his fault entirely. She should not have married him when things were so tough for her. At least *she* was faithful to him. He always argued that he had not been unfaithful because he had never *actually* been with someone else. What she saw that day she walked into his study when he was he was doing the online prostitution was the same as being with someone else in her eyes. She couldn't see it any other way. He cheated on her through the act of pornography.

This was devastating enough, but what really drove her away was that he asked her to be like them and do the things they did. That so disgusted her that she could not look at him any longer without complete disdain. She left him, moving back to her parent's home in Colorado. After weeks of tears and anguish she sought out a lawyer. A call from this Pastor Simon was not going to change her mind. She was sure it was over, but something told her that she had to go, and give it one more try.

After getting off of the bus Jamee felt uneasy. This place was huge. People passed by her, all in a hurry to get to their destination. They were all so distant. Feeling terribly alone and lost she was glad to see the café where Simon told her to meet him. It gave her a sense of familiarity in this strange place. Jamee got something to drink and found a comfortable booth where she could see people coming in.

She sat patiently in this little café at the bus station, waiting for Simon to meet her there. So much was going on in her mind that she often drifted in and out of the moment. She took her book out of her bag and tried to read, but it was of no use. Concentrating on any one thing right now was too difficult. She looked around taking in the business of the restaurant. A young woman sat in the corner alone eating a sandwich, and every time Jamee looked over in that corner, this young woman was looking right back at her. It made Jamee uncomfortable. There was something about the woman that compelled Jamee to keep looking. She seemed lonely and sad. Jamee wondered if maybe her heart had been broken too.

Then, there was the table in front of her with the happy chatter of young moms, and the noisy activity of children, which actually made her smile. Another woman sat quietly hidden behind the screen of her pink laptop, and was obviously involved with the content on her computer. Life was happening all around her, and though she took notice, she still felt indifferent to it all. She wasn't too sure about this Simon guy. How did she know she could trust him?

She also worried about how she could be sure she was leaving with the right person. He told her he would pick her up here and gave her a brief description of himself. But still, she wondered, would she really know him? He told her he would approach her, thinking that was best considering the bus station was not the best place for a woman to be questioning men to see if they were the one who came to pick her up. She told him she would be wearing a blue and gray Adidas track jacket with gray track pants. Her bag was blue and gray Adidas, and she said she had a blue ball cap she could wear so that she might be more easily recognizable. She hoped it would go smoothly, but she was edgy about this whole meeting, wishing she had emailed him a picture.

As she sat there drinking her green tea, Jamee noticed a man come in the door, and he began walking over toward her as if he knew her. She wondered if it was Pastor Simon, but as he got closer she hoped not. He had a strange look on his face that troubled her, and made her uneasy.

Please don't be him, she thought, closing her eyes.

The man came closer and stopped at her table. He just stood there a moment and stared at her, but his eyes didn't stay in one place. They travelled up and down, covering every inch of her body. After he stood there a moment, the smell of alcohol began to invade her space. Now fear arose as she sensed the danger. Her eyes quickly shot around the room, and no one was paying attention.

"Are you looking for someone?" she asked after gaining courage to speak.

The man said nothing, but just shook his head.

"You should go now. I am waiting for someone."

Jamee was feeling threatened and needed to act. Quickly she began gathering her things. If he wasn't going to leave, then she would. He moved in closer to the table. Once again, Jamee's eyes darted all around the room, and her inspection revealed total apathy from others in the restaurant.

Can't they see?. Are they just ignoring this situation? What will I do? Surely no one will let anything happen to me in here.

Pulling her bag up off the floor, Jamee scooted to the edge of the booth. Just as he moved over to keep her from coming out she heard someone call her name.

"Jamee, is that you? I've been looking all over for you."

Jamee was relieved to see another person walking toward her. She didn't know if it was the pastor, nor did she care. As Simon got closer, Jamee's would-be assailant moved away and left.

"Looks like trouble was lurking," the Pastor said holding out his hand to her. "I'm Simon and I am very sorry you had to deal with that."

Jamee shook his hand. "I was getting a little worried."

"Well, you are safe now. Come on. My car is just out the door."

Jamee hesitated, and suddenly found it hard to move.

"He's not in the car," Simon said, sensing her uncertainty. "He is waiting at the apartment for you. Are you ready for this?"

Jamee just nodded, grabbed her bag, threw it over her shoulder and quietly followed the pastor out to his car. The ride from the bus station to the pastor's house was only about ten miles. The traffic stretched the drive to twenty minutes longer than it would normally take, but she didn't care. She was in no hurry to see Amos.

"Thanks for agreeing to come, Jamee," Simon said, trying to watch her long enough to get an idea of her frame of mind. At first, she just remained quiet. Except for a timid "You're welcome," she offered no more. Simon had eased into talking with her and didn't push. He figured she would talk if needed, but he didn't expect what was to come. Suddenly without prompting she just started talking.

"I hate him. I don't know why I even came here. He has never been truthful to me. When we met, I thought he was a Christian. But after we were married, he told me he never said he was a Christian, and it was my problem for just assuming it. Maybe he was right, but he talked all the right stuff. I just never thought to quiz him about his faith."

Simon figured he might gain more trust by letting her tell her story.

"How did you meet? Was it in Indiana?"

"No, not Indiana," Jamee said. "I am from Colorado. That's where we met. He was one of the newest musicians in the band that played at a conference I attended."

"What kind of conference was it?"

"It's called, *Living for One*. Ever hear of it?"

"I have," Simon said, quietly looking at Jamee. "I went to one myself. But that was before I graduated high school ten years ago."

"So that makes you about seven years older than me," Jamee said. "I wonder if it has changed much over the years."

"I don't think so. It was a program with contemporary music, a dynamic speaker and lots of prayer and testimony. It convinced me."

"You mean it worked?"

"Well, I am still a virgin if that's what you are asking."

Jamee blushed, and turned her head to look out the window. Simon was annoyed with himself to have been so blunt. He knew she had been hurt too much, and he should have been gentler.

"I'm sorry, Jamee. That was too outspoken of me. Forgive me?"

She shook her head, but continued to stare out the window. Trying to recover her confidence he began talking again.

"So, what was the memorabilia that you took from the conference that would remind you of your commitment? For five years in a row we were offered promise rings. They went over really big with the girls, but not so much with the guys, even though I have one."

"We had dog tags," Jamee answered. "They had inscribed on them, *Image of God*" as a reminder to us that we are made in His image, and that we are set apart for Him. I kept mine even after what happened with Kambo, but I gave them to Amos as a symbol of my purity in our marriage."

Silence again loomed. Simon knew Jamee was struggling and he tried to offer encouragement.

"What a concept. I think I would love to have my bride hand me such a gift. It would be an awesome wedding present."

"Yeah, Jamee said, I wish it could have been reciprocated. Our problem is as much my fault. I settled for much less than I wanted in a husband. I was in a relationship at the time of the concert, and I had hoped one day to marry him. His name is Kambo. We were so happy, but something strange happened after that concert, and it changed everything. Before I knew it he was gone, and nobody knew where he was. He just disappeared. After a while he finally called his mom to let her know he was okay, but he never revealed to anyone where he was. I kept thinking that one day he would come back to me. I wore my tags proudly, being the faithful girl who waited.

A year later, the Living for One Conference came back. I had already graduated high school and wanted to be a part, so I offered to help. It was an amazing event and the testimony of our speaker was sending kids to the front to pray like crazy. Then all of a sudden, there he was. He came up on the stage and asked to share his testimony."

Jamee began crying, feeling the pain all over again. Through the tears she choked out the rest of her story.

The one I waited for faithfully got up on that stage, told everyone there that he failed, and that he had come in contact with someone who had AIDS. So many people there knew us both. I hadn't done anything wrong, but I felt ashamed, and I was angry. He tried to talk to me, but I couldn't even look at him.

That's when I met Amos. He was playing in the band that night and he saw me crying, and was so sweet to comfort me. Well, that was the beginning of my relationship with Amos. We got married, moved to his hometown in Indiana, and the sweetness went away."

"How long ago was that?" Simon asked, trying not to focus on the things that would make her start to cry again.

"Five years last week. Look," she said as she straightened herself up and wiped her eyes. "I don't think this is going to work. I came because I knew I had to try. But I don't think he will come home."

"So, don't go home for a while. Stay here and regain your strength and maybe give Amos some time and space to accept Jesus as his Savior."

Jamee shrugged her shoulders and said nothing. She couldn't really make a commitment yet. She had to see what she was up against first.

When they arrived at Simon's apartment, Amos was inside, sitting on the couch with his laptop. As soon as he saw them come in, he quickly logged off. Jamee couldn't prove it, but was sure he wasn't looking at the weather report. It was a familiar scene. Amos jumped up, went over to Jamee and wrapped his arms around her. He bent over to kiss her, but she moved her face away to avoid his kiss, and stayed that way until he released her.

"Lord, we have a long way to go," Simon thought. "I need your help here." He silently prayed, and then busied himself getting them settled. Simon took Jamee's bag to the bedroom and showed her around the apartment.

"Make yourself at home," he said. "I am going to go and cook us some dinner."

Amos waited until Simon left the room before he said anything to Jamee.

"Well, nothing has changed, has it?"

"What do you mean, Amos? Is that directed at me?"

"I mean there is nothing here. I can't even give you a kiss. How can you expect me to *not* look elsewhere for my satisfaction?"

"How is it that can I expect that? Because you are my husband, that's how. Why don't I want you to kiss me? Because you make me feel like you are only using me to fulfill those depraved desires you learn about from your internet flings."

"Such strong language for my little Christian girl, isn't it? Why did you come, Jamee? Was it just to remind me of how unhappy I make you?"

"I came because I have to be able to say I did everything I possibly could to make our marriage work. I made a commitment to you, and whether I am happy at the moment or not, I have to try to make this work."

"Well, miss innocence, you haven't done everything, nor will you."

"What's that supposed to mean?"

"Well, maybe if you would acquiesce to my requests, I wouldn't look elsewhere."

"You are a sick man. Do you think I am stupid? Your requests are not normal, and if I gave in to them you would only drag me down a road to depravity and I am not going there, not for you or for anyone."

"You are just being a prude, Jamee," he said drawing closer to her.

"Don't come near me, Amos Desi. I hate you!"

Simon heard Jamee screaming and came to interrupt the fight. When he arrived he saw Amos and Jamee nearly toe to toe, and he became concerned for Jamee's well being. Surely her husband would never hurt her.

"Dinner is ready you guys, let's eat."

An uncomfortable silence ruled during dinner and Simon resisted trying to make conversation happen. Jamee insisted on helping Simon with the dishes after they finished eating, and Simon took the opportunity to ask Jamee if she would be in danger with him leaving the two of them alone.

"Jamee, has Amos ever physically hurt you?" He asked.

"No," Jamee whispered with a heavy sigh. "No, he has never physically hurt me—emotionally, mentally and spiritually, yes, but never physically."

"So, then you will be okay when I leave, right?"

"Leave! Where are you going?"

"I will be spending a lot of time at the church, and will be sleeping there while you two try to work on your marriage. I will spend some time with you both each day in counseling, but most of what you will need to work out will be done without me."

Jamee threw her towel down and ran out of the room. There was no place to run though, and she finally went into the bedroom and slammed the door.

This place is too small for us, she thought. *Sleeping arrangements will be rough. Where will I go to get away?*

She would have to endure, knowing she had to try to make it work. This is why she came. Maybe Amos was right. She wasn't very loving toward him. Maybe she should try to at least get close. Besides it was either that or she would have to choose to sleep on that small couch. This was not going to be easy.

Amos knocked on the door. "Jamee, can I come in?"

Jamee hesitated. "Jesus, I can't do this without you, but I believe that I can do all things through You. Please give me the strength."

She straightened her tee shirt, opened the door and stepped back so he could come in. As Amos walked through the door those feelings of disgust came rushing in, and she could barely resist them.

"*All* things through Christ," she whispered.

Amos took her hand, and as he did Simon walked up to the opened door.

"I am going to the church. If you need me you can call my cell phone."

He handed a business card to each of them and Jamee wondered why he had given them each one. It seems one would have been sufficient. Then, almost as if he had heard her thoughts he answered the question.

"One for each of you in case one of you loses a card, or in case one of you gets lost, and you need a friend to find your way back."

As he walked out Jamee's stomach turned. Could she do this?

"Lord, there is turmoil in my heart today," she prayed. "Take it and replace it with your peace, and cover the noise of confusion with sounds from heaven." Then Jamee uttered the words she said so often in situations that were difficult for her to handle.

"God's will, I want nothing more than what he wants, nothing less than His best and nothing else matters."

Burning Flame

Each day passed into the other, and no changes came. Jamee insisted that her husband show her love and respect, and he insisted she forget her fairytale dreams and give in to his requests. Finally, Amos no longer tried to resist the lure of the lust that raged within him. He was imbedded in this lifestyle, and he reasoned that it was no use to fight it. Again Jamee walked in on him, and saw that his lust for pornography had sunk to the depths of exploitation of children, and she wailed in anguish over what she had seen.

"I am done trying," he told Jamee. "This is who I am, and who I will always be."

Amos made no excuses. He didn't want to get rid of the pictures, or find a way out of the entanglement of beautiful women who could fulfill his needs. He figured he would be content with a life of unrestricted sex and unrestrained values. In a final moment of decision he allowed that liar, the devil, to convince him that what he did was natural—that he was made this way by God, and because he was made this way that he would go unpunished for his actions. He even found ways to justify the exploitation of children that he had begun to explore. The Adversary laughed because all his work had come to fruition. In this devilish moment of time, he had given the final push, and Amos Marcus Desi was both feet over the edge, and dug in to the darkest recesses of pornography.

"Sorry Jamee," Amos said. "I can't give this up, not even for you. This is my life, my destiny. You are better to go on and forget about me. Get those divorce papers together and file them. I will give you all you want, knowing you deserve so much more."

As he backed out the door of the preacher's apartment, Simon came up the walk behind him.

"Hey buddy, are you going somewhere?"

"I'm done here, Simon. I can't pretend any more. I know you wanted to help, but I can't stop."

Jamee was crying, leaning against the open door with her head hung. Her long curly hair was falling down in front of her face. Amos looked back at her, and then to Simon.

"See that she gets home safely, would you?"

Simon held out his hand.

"Amos, don't do this. The word of God, the truth of Jesus is already close to your heart. You know what you need to do. Just say yes to Him. He will free you. Let Him in. He will arise within you, and set you free. Don't do this, man. If you walk away now you may never come back"

"Forget it preacher, there is no word in me. There never was. Anyway, if it ever had been there, it is gone now. Maybe someday God will come back around, but for now, He is gone. He doesn't want to be around a perverted punk like me."

Simon moved in closer to Amos.

"Lord," he whispered. "Please don't let the enemy have him."

Tears were now welling up in Simon's eyes.

"Someday might not come, Amos. Come on we've been fighting this together for two weeks now. Your wife is here and wants to help. Don't let go now."

Amos turned and walked away from them as fast as he could.

"I don't want any help," he said, and walked away.

The wind made the temperature drop, and Amos tried to zip up to keep out the cold, but the zipper broke. In frustration he placed his hands in the pockets and drew his coat closer together. Rain began to fall and poured out from the heavens drenching him.

"Just what I needed," he thought. "As if it wasn't bad enough being cold, now I have to be cold and wet, with no place to go."

The clouds kept forming, and the sky got darker. Amos could see a storm coming. He just wanted to get inside to get out of the rain. He kept walking, and like a magnet he was drawn toward that place he had managed to avoid while staying with Simon.

"Just going there to get out of the rain," he reasoned.

For a moment he stood there looking at the sign that still hung by a single chain, and thought about his conversations with Simon. He saw the sign behind it, lit up and glowing red neon lights all around it. The wind blew harder, and the rain still poured down. A dark cloud hovered eerily over the place, and seeing this sent chills through Amos. But he ignored what he saw, as well as the hope that Simon had tried to instill in him for change, and he took hold of the door and opened it. The stench of cigarette smoke hit him immediately, and telltale smells of alcohol permeated the building. But it was warm and the rain and wind was no longer annoying him.

The bar was the main attraction where most people sat drinking and mingling. Even with the overt intimacy he saw over near the corner tables, he reasoned it was no different than any other bar he had been in before. In the scheme of things it looked pretty normal as far as bars go. Amos sat down on a stool, and ordered a beer. He looked around while waiting for his drink. There was a stairway behind the bar that led up to a hallway of doors. It kind of reminded him of the Old West Saloons he had seen in the movies. Every once in a while people would come out, and sometimes couples, and sometimes someone would come out alone.

"Never seen you around here before," the bartender said as he was wiping up the spilled beer from the counter. "Are you new to the area?"

"No," Amos answered. "Just passing through, looking for a place to get out of the rain before I leave the city."

Thunder bellowed outside, and could be heard over the music that was playing.

The bartender smiled. "They say a bad storm is coming. You should plan on packing it in here for a while. Take in a movie or something, if you know what I mean. And if you aren't here for that kind of business, then you probably better go back out in the rain."

Amos stopped instantly, and looked at the puny little man behind the bar that was belting out demands like he was strong and mighty. He thought he could easily take this guy out, but he knew there was someone else nearby that looked out for this place and this little man.

"How much?" Amos asked.

"$50 if you watch alone and $100 if we send up someone to keep you company.

Now his mind was reeling.

Company?

"Your choice," the bartender said shrugging his shoulders.

Amos didn't have much cash and pulled out the credit card. He knew it would show up on the statement, and that it would hurt Jamee, but there was no other way for him to get what he wanted.

"Do you take credit cards?"

"No doubt, buddy, so what will it be?"

He bit his bottom lip and thought a moment.

"I would like the company, and he handed the bartender Selene's business card."

"Is she here?"

The bartender rang up the credit card, and gave Amos a key.

"Yep, room 6 he said. You go ahead and I will send her up."

Amos grabbed his beer, and turned toward the stairway as someone else walked into the tavern. Looking outside of the opened door, he could see the storm was worsening. The wind was blowing stronger, and it was hard to see much out there at all. Amos blinked quickly, and looked again out the door. A tall black man stood in the entrance staring in.

"Chance, is that you?"

Amos ran to the door to see, but when he got there no one was outside.

"Must have been my imagination," he thought, and he headed up the stairs. Inside the room a cloud of cigarette smoke lingered from the occupants who were here before him. Two ashtrays, still full of cigarettes sat on the coffee table in front of the couch. One still held a smoldering butt. There was one window covered with black curtains that kept the light out. He went over to open the curtain and looked outside to see what the storm was doing. It was strangely calm. There was no wind, no rain, and not even the sound of a bird.

"Maybe it's the calm before the real storm," he said. He closed the curtain again, and turned back to the darkness. A large screen TV sat in front of a couch and underneath it was a selection of X-rated movies. He decided to choose one while he waited on his company to arrive.

Amos leaned back into the couch and got comfortable and watched as he waited. He heard the door open, and then suddenly a sound like that of a freight train resounded throughout the room. He jumped up, and turned to look toward the doorway. In the middle of that entrance stood a hideous looking creature. It looked barely human, with decayed skin hanging on dried and rotten bones. Her eyes were mere sockets, and her hair was dead strings that held on only in patches around her head. The freight-train sound got louder, and the room began to shake. Amos ran for the doorway, but was blocked by this ghoulish thing and could not escape. The noise got louder, and he covered his ears to keep from hearing it. As he screamed no one heard the sound of his voice over the brute force of the funnel cloud that ravaged through Fantasy Tavern, leveling it to the ground.

Recorded now, the records reveal. Gone—he's gone. There is no appeal. Entered he into the cave of Hell, knowing here that Satan fell. Treading spite all Heaven's plea. Now lost forever—eternity

R escue workers arrived after the storm had subsided. The entire corner of that street was ravished by the tornado. The ragged sign that advertised the old Adult Entertainment Center was torn into four pieces, and thrown to the four points of that intersection. Fantasy Tavern had collapsed. All that remained was rubble, and all that were inside perished. A hot burning flame belched up from underneath the debris, and the firefighters extinguished it before it had a chance to spread. Fantasy Tavern was destroyed. It was one year to the day that the Adult Entertainment Center had closed up.

Pastor Simon was there with Jamee, sifting through the debris looking for something that may have said Amos had been here. They had not heard from him, and all of her attempts to call him went straight to voicemail. It had been four days since the tornado hit, and other families waited and wondered. Crews came in to clean up and periodically found something that was not burned or destroyed, which told yet another family member that their loved one was buried in the pitiful grave. The area was roped off, and people were not allowed to go searching through the debris, but today the officials turned the other way and didn't say anything to those who came seeking answers.

Simon and Jamee were standing near the back part of the lot, and looking at all of the mess when Jamee saw something shiny poking through the heap. She went over and moved the debris away, and pulled it out grabbing for Simon's arm as she did. It was the dog tags she bought the night she and Kambo had gone to the conference together— The same one she had given to Amos.

"He was here," she whispered. She trembled as she picked it up from the rubble.

"Look, the dog tags I gave him when we were married." Jamee cried so loud that others stopped and watched. They understood what it meant. Not only had she found proof that her loved one was buried here, but also proof that he came to such a place as this.

Simon took the tags and cupped them in his hands. The inscription was clear on them, *Image of God,* and on the back Jamee's initials were inscribed. "He must have cared for you, sis. He just had a debt that he would not allow Christ to pay, and it kept getting deeper and deeper. You mustn't put any blame on yourself."

"I don't. I just wish we could have been a couple, and I wish I knew why God allowed my life to have all this hurt. Simon, why am I always getting hurt? Can't I have something good in life?"

Simon hugged Jamee and while he held her he prayed, "Peace, Father, give Jamee peace."

Changing the Picture

Jamee sat alone in the apartment, curled up in the white wicker chair that was tucked away in the corner of the living room. Simon had graciously moved into the church until she could get past the shock of what had happened. He tried to convince her not to travel alone, but instead to call her parents to come, and travel back with her. Confusion had already captured her, and she wasn't sure she could go back to Colorado. She didn't know what she would do.

"Where is my home now?" she whispered.

Feeling the cooling air that came in through the opened window, Jamee took the throw from the couch and curled back into the pocket in the chair. Someone knocked at the door, but she ignored it.

"Jamee, are you in there?" Simon asked as he placed the key into the lock. She still didn't answer, feeling she just simply didn't have the energy to even get up.

"Jamee, it's me, Simon. Is everything okay?"

She watched the door open slowly, and wondered why he tiptoed around her. Was he afraid of her? Did he think she was fragile? It didn't matter. Nothing mattered. She was destined to loneliness and maybe she *was* too fragile to handle anything. She sure couldn't handle a relationship with her husband without it killing him. She was convinced that she was more to blame for his death, believing she drove him to seek out the perverted lifestyle that finally led him to his grave.

Then there *he* was. Simon was every bit the gentleman, and tried to help her sort through all of this mess. She sure didn't know what to do with his kindness and courtesy. Simon peeked around the door and saw her sitting in the chair, looking despondent.

"Oh, Jamee, You are here. Sorry to just barge in, but I worry when you don't answer. How are you? I came to see if you might want to go for a walk or do something to get out of here, and get some fresh air. It would be good for you."

Jamee didn't answer. She turned her head away from him and stared at the wall.

Simon walked over to her, and pulled the ottoman in front of her so he could see her face, which was tear-stained and weary. Jamee shook her head and tossed her long hair in front of her face. She didn't want him looking at her. He sat there for a moment, not sure how to respond. He wanted to help, but just didn't know how. He gently took the strands of hair, and pulled them back behind her ear.

"Jamee," he whispered. "I called your parents. They are coming to be with you. It's not good that you are alone, and as a single man, it's not proper that I come in here as often as I do. I hope you don't mind. They will be here soon. I am leaving in just a few minutes to pick them up from the airport."

Jamee didn't react. She just sat there with her head bowed. Simon sighed and leaned his head back, and silently prayed. Now what, Lord? What can I do or say in this moment?"

"Jamee, can I pray for you?

She still did not look up at him, but nodded her head to say yes. Simon found that, even in prayer the words just did not come as he would have liked. He wanted to pray for healing and blessings and peace and so much more, but all he could pray was, "Lord, Jesus Christ, have mercy on Jamee."

She lifted her head and thanked him.

"That was perfect," she said. Her lip was quivering and her chest began heaving the deep sighs that lay within her, and she cried hard, throwing her arms around Simon's neck, and clinging to him in desperation. As she held on tightly and cried something stirred within him, and he felt he wanted to pull her in closely. Feelings he had not expected arose, and he felt like he never wanted to let her go. He almost relinquished his chivalry to the sudden emotion that had come over him, but instead he gently pushed her away, trying to be inconspicuous, and got up as if to get her a tissue. Then he noticed the picture on the wall and stopped. He stood there stunned in silence as he looked at the place where he had hung a plain art board with a simple pencil drawing on it. Now it was filled in with life and color and more pictures. He looked back at Jamee for a moment as her eyes blinked back the tears. She sniffed and took in a deep breath.

"Simon, I'm sorry. I know I shouldn't have."

"Wait!" He choked. "No, Jamee. It can't be. You drew the pictures on this canvas?"

"Oh Simon, please forgive me. I didn't mean to impose myself here. I draw when I am depressed or confused. I needed to draw. I am so sorry. I didn't have a canvas and this one was just there. It was so empty."

Simon turned back to the canvas where once was a simple penciled picture of Jesus with a single man in worship. Now it was a composite of color and life and people. It had become a painting of Jesus unlike he had ever seen. He ran his hand over the freshly chalked canvas. It was beautiful, yet disturbing. It was like a sonata that played out his life. The face of the Lord embodied myriad emotions. Peace, joy, anguish, and more. Suddenly he felt every emotion defined in the lines on the face of Jesus. When he pulled his hand back from the canvas red chalk clung to his fingers, and he rubbed his hands together letting the redness cover them. He looked at the painting again and saw two women praying behind a church that looked like his church.

"Jamee, you drew all this?"

"I . . . I, well, yes, I am afraid I did."

Simon pointed to the church.

"Jamee, this looks like my church."

"I know, she said. "There is something about your church that needed to be captured in the canvas. I could see it just as if I were standing there."

"And the women praying," Simon asked. "Who are they?"

Jamee jerked her head upward, sighing deeply.

"One of them is me," she said looking directly at him.

"But I don't know who the other is. I just felt there was someone else who has prayed for your church other than me. So I drew another."

"You are praying for my church?"

"Of course I am! Well, it has helped to take my mind off of everything. I pray so I won't mope."

"The other woman in the painting looks a lot like my mother," Simon told Jamee. "She was a praying woman—a good woman who worked hard all her life, and died young." Now he was fighting back tears. "I started this piece for her."

Jamee was overcome now with regret.

"Oh no, Simon, I can't believe I just ruined it for you. I didn't mean to."

"Jamee, stop. You don't understand, and I don't know if I could tell you right now the significance of what you have just done."

"Please forgive me, Simon."

"Finish it!" he interrupted again.

"What?" Jamee was puzzled. "I don't understand. You *want* me to do more on it? That doesn't make any sense."

"Yes. I want you to draw more. Then I will know for sure."

"Know what, Simon?"

"I can't tell you now, and besides I need to go get your parents from the airport. If there are still images that you feel need to be on this canvas, finish it while I am gone. He began walking toward the door. Will you be okay? It will take me about two hours to pick them up, and get back here.

"I will be fine." Jamee bowed her head and shook it back and forth. "I am so sorry about the canvas."

"Don't be. I believe that God does work all things together for good to those who love him and are called according to his purpose. So don't be sorry."

On the way to the airport Simon called out to God. "This is not what I had expected. Lord, I thought you would give me someone who was more like me. I am not sure this is what I want. Lord, I don't understand."

Simon waited for the Lord, but there was no answer. Maybe it was a mistake. How could it be that Jamee would be the one he would marry? This is not how he had imagined meeting his bride.

"Lord! No! This is not what I want. Jamee is a beautiful person, but she is, she is . . . Lord, she is *tainted*."

"So are you Simon." The Lord spoke to him for the first time ever in an audible voice. Then there was silence, and the Lord continued to speak to his heart.

"You, Simon, born out of wedlock, and into the arms of a girl of sixteen, are as the rest of creation—tainted by the sin of Adam, scarred by iniquity and marred by sin. And you, like Jamee, are redeemed by the blood of the Lamb, and made into a new creation."

Simon was overwhelmed, and had to pull over to collect himself. This was too close to pain and suffering. It was far too close to remembering his mother's pain. He didn't know how he would handle it, but he gave it to God.

"Lord, she didn't draw the veil into the picture. If I return and the veil is on that canvas, I will acquiesce with no questions asked. I will trust you in this."

Jamee wasn't so sure she was looking forward to seeing her parents just yet. They begged her not to marry Amos, but she didn't listen. Her relationship with them had been strained, and she wasn't sure how they would react to coming out here for this.

As she thought about the Christian life, and about parents and the things they do for the love of their children, she remembered God sending His Son, Jesus. She thought of the verse from Matthew 27:51,

And, behold, the veil of the temple was torn in two from the top to the bottom.

She remembered from her studies that this was the veil between the holy place and the holiest of holies. It was the veil that only got moved once each year on the Day of Atonement to allow the high priest to enter the sanctuary that enshrined the presence of God. No one could enter but the priest. And on the day Christ died the veil was rent to signify access for all into the presence of God.

She thought about this and all that Christ gave for her. If she never gained anything on this earth, she had Jesus. As Jamee looked at the picture she saw the message of Christ all over it, but the one thing that was missing was the redemption. The access now given to enter into the presence of God was not clearly defined in the art. So, she took out her chalks and began to draw the veil in front of the opened door on the church. Then having completed this she felt a sense of peace, and she rested.

It seemed no time before the door had opened and Jamee's parents came in with Simon. He stood back as they entered, went straight to their daughter and embraced her. They held each other for a long time and then began to talk. Simon looked up to see the painting, and was not surprised to see the veil had been drawn in.

"Jamee," he said. "I am going to go to the church, and will leave you and your parents here alone to talk for a while. Call if you need anything. I will bring something to eat when I return. Jamee nodded,

When Warriors Fall

but she wondered if he noticed the picture. She wanted to tell him she finished it, but her parents were there, and she needed the time with them.

When Simon returned he saw that suitcases were packed, and had all been placed in the living room. Jamee and her parents were in the kitchen drinking a cup of tea and talking.

"Did you make some decisions, Jamee?"

"Yes, Simon. We are leaving on the next flight out, and I will be returning with my parents."

Jamee's dad stood up and walked over to where Simon was standing. "We want to thank you for the care you have extended to our daughter. We thought the sooner we got her home the quicker she could begin her healing process. We have to leave at 6:00 to get to the airport on time."

Simon looked at his watch. It was 4:00 now.

"I brought some chicken. Will you all eat with me? Then I can take you to the airport."

He was feeling pretty subdued and did not feel much like socializing, but this was necessary.

"There is plenty of time to eat," Jamee said. "I will get some plates out."

They ate for the most part in silence until Jamee asked Simon about the painting.

"I finished it," she said. "Did you see? I hope it was what you had hoped."

"It is perfect, Jamee. It is just what I had expected."

Jamee's parents looked quizzically at each other, then back at Jamee. She shrugged her shoulders at them as if to say, "I don't know either."

"My mother was sixteen years old when she got pregnant with me," Simon began with a testimony that would change the course of his life and Jamee's.

"Her story was a life marked by pain. My dad left before I was even born and we never saw him again. My mother gave her life to Jesus, but there were still daily struggles of being a single parent, and making the best for us on what little she had. It was especially hard overcoming the emotional condition my father left her in, but she always found time for two things. One was for prayer, and the other was to teach me how to be a Christ follower. She was an artist, and loved pastels. it was her favorite means of expression on canvas. He paused a moment, and let that thought rest in their minds.

"Jamee," he continued. "The original sketch on the canvas was my attempt to draw just like her, and though I could come up with a pretty decent sketch, it was a labor for me. I obviously was not as gifted in this as she was. But she was always so proud of that canvas and my little contribution."

Jamee's parents knew about the canvas. She had told them how she probably upset him by drawing more on it and not really thinking about the implications of doing so.

"So how can we make this right?" her father asked.

"It's already right, replied Simon. Please let me finish."

"My mother found out she had cancer and she died five years ago. Before she died she said that the woman I would marry would complete me. She said that God had given her a vision showing her that this woman would finish this canvas as a symbol of God entering in, bringing beauty into my plain and simple world. She said this woman would finish this piece with the story of our lives."

Jamee's heart was pounding. This was too much for her to take in, and Simon knew it would be. He knew he had to keep talking and finish before she went dashing out of the room.

"I was stunned when I saw you had nearly completed the picture that my mother told me would be drawn, and when I left I told the Lord, that there was one thing missing, and if you added it while I was gone, then I would simply trust Him."

"The veil?" Jamee asked.

"Simon nodded, "Yes, the veil."

Jamee's father began to interject his thoughts, but Simon cut him off.

"Jamee, Mr. and Mrs. Adams, I don't expect any kind of response right now, and I think it best for now that nothing more is said. I just need to take you all to the airport. Mr. Adams, I would like to stay in touch with you, and when you and your wife and Jamee feel it is right, I will begin to properly court Jamee."

"What if I say it's not right?" Jamee objected.

"That's not in my hands, Jamee. It's in God's hands."

Jamee sat back in her chair and breathed deeply. There was much confusion. She was still feeling grief and pain, yet something stirred in her of the possibilities. She shrugged it off. If it was of God, then she would be able to revisit it later. But for now, she wanted no relationships. For now, she only wanted Colorado and the comforts of home.

Jamee's father sighed deeply and then spoke directly to Simon. "My greatest concern right now is to protect my daughter, and this is more than I can internalize. It *is* best that no more is said at this time."

Then he took a business card out of his wallet and gave it to Simon.

"You may call *me*, but not my daughter."

"Dad!" Jamee objected.

"Jamee, please trust me on this. I know you are a grown woman, and I respect that. We will talk more about this, but for now, let me take care of you."

Jamee simply nodded in acquiescence.

Simon remained subdued as he took them to the airport and said the good-byes. The past few weeks had been a whirlwind. He had not known how much his life would change as a result of listening to God and caring for the souls of Amos and Jamee. He was glad for the parting time as well. There was much to think about and he needed the time.

To the Warrior Fighting Pornography

Pornography is a dangerous fire that has spread into the very heart of American society insomuch that it is deemed a part of the culture in which we live. It is an exploitation of human sexuality at any and every level that it presents itself. Its producers are seeing monetary results to the tune of $10 billion dollars every year. The demon of perversion has no scruples and cares not what or who it destroys in order to promote the fast-growing industry.

Internet has obviously made porn more accessible. Simply entering the word porn on an Internet search engine produces over one billion hits. The acceptance of this industry by society has made the lines even more blurred than they have ever been before. We find that Christians are not immune to the lure of porn. It has found its way into the church and is moving through the hearts and minds of God's people at breakneck speed, bringing some statistic results over the sixty percent mark. Many don't realize the vast numbers of people caught in the trap of porn because it is hidden in the dark. Virtual infidelity is on the rise, and some of God's people get swept up in the tail of this dragon, losing themselves in the midst of it all.

Pornography eats away at the intelligence of the individual, and eventually circumvents the reasoning part of the brain to the point that the mind gives way to a habit. Then the mechanical part takes over and an addiction is formed. Porn destroys the ability to control one's carnal and base instincts. It severs right thinking from the man or woman of God. It ultimately kills the soul and renders man to the level of an animal.

If you are caught on this battlefield, it is likely that no one knows—yet. Remember, if you gave your heart to Jesus, you are a warrior of God. You are saved by grace to do good works that God has prepared for you. You are on mission for the King of kings. If the enemy has you surrounded, call out for reinforcement. If he has imprisoned you, fight for your freedom! Fight back by calling on the name of the LORD. Here are some steps to take to be freed from the bondage of pornography:

1. Remember that the enemy works in secret, and darkness hides him. Your first step is the hardest because you will have to expose the enemy and tell someone about your addiction. Consider this when you are working up the courage to tell another person: The enemy has used pornography to entrap you. You are a victim. This by no means excuses the sin. You must confess It. You are a child of God. He will forgive you. Freedom begins with confession to God and then to another.
   If we confess our sin he is faithful and just to forgive us our sin and cleanse us of all unrighteousness.[8]
   Therefore confess your sins to each other and pray for each other so that you may be healed. The prayer of a righteous man is powerful and effective.[9]
2. Realize that your addiction to porn is not based on truth but on fantasy. It is a false and distorted picture. Pornography is like a drug that demands continuous use and takes more each time to achieve the anticipated high.
3. Call this what it is—sin. Don't let the enemy control your mind, and cause you to justify this sin any longer. Announce that he is a liar, and Jesus is the truth.
4. Seek godly professional help.
5. Above all, fight. You are a soldier of Christ. Fight to be freed from the encampment of the enemy. His stronghold is not impenetrable. Christ is able.

PART 2

The Death of My People

Death is invading the church. The people of Yahweh, born again in the name of His Son, Jesus, are being swept into the closets and corners of an insidious plot devised by the prince of deception. They are being killed, one by one, because they have bought into his lies, and stepped into his traps. There are many ways that death is occurring, but three are prevalent in the pages ahead. These are: physical death, emotional death and spiritual death.

The physical death is abortion, and it has more spiritual implications than the average churchgoer realizes. Women in Christian churches are having abortions, and, as a result of this sin in their lives, most of them are suffering spiritually. As we will see in the life of Roni Simone there is a great spiritual battle ensuing for the minds of young men and women today. The propaganda is put out by pro-abortionists that advocates the killing of the innocent. It is a lie that comes from the mouth of Satan. These lies are tickling the ears of Christians, deceiving them, and bringing God's people under oppression and bondage.

As you will see there are two voices calling out to us here. Concerning life, we have the representation from two characters—the mother and the child, and in essence they represent one.

Even in the case of abortion, that natural unity (the connection between mother and child) cannot be separated here on these pages, nor should they be separated in the premature death that advocates call pro-choice. There is no choice in the laws of nature, or in the laws of God. If you destroy the child, by nature of unity destruction knocks at the mother's door as well. For the mother, death can come as an emotional death, and as we will see in the life of Damiria and Mariel, it alone has the potential to completely destroy. Though this emotional death does not physically destroy, it is death nonetheless—a death unto eternal destruction if there is not a powerful God-intervention.

Another evil that causes an emotional death is gossip. It preys on the weak and broken-hearted and is compounded by wagging tongues that lack discretion. It comes from people that care little for the heart and soul of a person. It presents itself as righteousness, but is in reality a harsh word sown in envy, strife and greed. Gossip is a destroyer that grows in the mouths of church-goers who have found someone to point at instead of themselves. The mindset of the gossiper is that the one who falls hard into areas of sin such as sexual immorality, pornography or abortion has committed such a grievous sin that they can no longer lift their heads up. And because these are considered the unspeakable sins, gossiping fingers point to them in a most obvious way, and thus detract from the one who is pointing. In other words if I can point to one whose sin is more appalling than mine, then I can point away from that which I don't want others to see as sin in me. To gossip about another person is merely to cover-up for one's own disillusionment with sin that lives within. Gossip is deadly. It kills emotionally.

Finally there is bitterness, which is a deadly weed in the church, for it robs people of the fullness of life that is offered in John 10:10. It enters a life in many ways, but always stems from having taken our eyes off of the Lord, Jesus Christ and putting them on our circumstances. Left to its own devices bitterness can bring about spiritual death whereby the believer can belong to God but live out his life in complete lack. I believe it was the weed of bitterness that ultimately prevented the Israelites from entering the Promised Land and caused their forty years of disappointment and bereavement.

As we will look at these deaths in the lives of those we follow in part two, it is my prayer that if you see yourself in any of these that you will remember that the intention here is not to condemn, but to open a door for healing by exposing the truth of death in the church. Please approach this second part with openness for healing in your own life, as well as in the lives of those around you who may need a touch of the Great Physician's hand. Remember that forgiveness heals and love covers a multitude of sin. Sin must be exposed so the enemy can no longer set up camp in our lives, but don't leave compassion behind.

Roni Simone

SHOUT FOR JOY BECAUSE HE HEARS

Shout joyfully to the LORD, all the earth; Break forth and sing for joy and sing praises. I was crying to the LORD with my voice, and He answered me from His holy mountain. (Psalms 98:4)

Breath of God

Where did the flower go?
That lay breathing in my hand
Colors of joy and wings of green exploding sweet aroma

How did those colors bloom?
Reds, purples, and golden crinkles
Touching every branch and flower whispering songs of mystery

How did this sonnet sing?
A story deep within me
Breath of God, compelling light caressing life's progression

How His touch imbues me
Though golden colors whisper
A fading flower in His hand, exploding colors of joy

Dance of the Gods

As Roni Simone sat in the coffee shop waiting for her boyfriend, Jouda, to arrive, unseen entities of demonic forces were gathering and hovering in the room next to her. She shivered and felt a sense of fear, but didn't know why. She picked through her short hair, and went to find a table where she and her boyfriend could have some privacy. As she waited she could still sense an unsettling spirit that gave her reason to be afraid. It made no sense. Everything around her appeared to look normal, but she was uneasy. She tried to shrug the feeling off and tried to think of something else as she waited. She let her mind wander to the conversation she had with the woman who had helped her at the clinic and things she shared with her about Jesus.

All the while the demons waited. Soon the time would come that they would call out to their reinforcements, and begin to press in and work against the smoldering wick that Roni held in her. They knew that she had been talking to *that Christian* girl, and they were determined to shackle Roni's mind with such shame, that she would remain bound, and not ever follow after Jesus. Their intent was to crush her before she had a chance to say yes to the Holy One. Their devilish activity was destruction, and she was the target. They wanted to close the door so that she would not walk into the Light, and in the process, they could offer the sacrifice of a human child to the principalities that ruled them. The sacrifice was an added incentive for this demonic horde because if they were to win, they could take out the person and sacrifice yet another life to their rulers in authority.

Roni waited quietly. Her cappuccino sat steaming in front of her and she stirred it as she looked around the room at the people who sat sipping coffee and engaging in conversation. Some of the couples looked happy and she wished that she and Jouda could be that happy. It seemed all they did lately was find anything and everything to argue about.

Roni was barely eighteen years old and alone—except for him. Her parents were killed in a car wreck right after she began dating Jouda two years ago. After that she lived with her older sister, but recently moved in with Jouda, against her sister's advice. Their homes were five miles apart, but they didn't see each other much at all. She felt it was that her sister had rejected her, but her friends denied this and said it was because her boyfriend controlled her life. She knew she had some faithful friends, but she avoided them because she had grown weary of hearing them always telling her she should walk away from him, and live her life without being under his control. She just couldn't let go because she always felt he needed her. And now, it seemed *he* was really all she had. He had in so many ways become her savior. She adored him, and now she struggled to understand why their relationship was so messed up.

Jouda's father lived in Haiti and had managed to get a job on a cruise ship where he often served for months at a time as a cabin steward. His mother, a wealthy Scandinavian beauty was on a cruise when she met Jouda's father. Their relationship lasted one week and they never saw each other after that. Jouda was born nine months and two weeks later. His mother named him Jouda, which is Haitian for traitor, because his birth uncovered her indiscretion. She eventually gave full custody of him to a couple who brought him back to America. Jouda lived with both adoptive parents until his mother finally left his father after enduring years of abuse. When he and his mother moved to Mississippi he brought with him a broken and distorted childhood. Meeting Roni was a distraction from the pain that he carried with him daily, but she was becoming more of a burden to him now.

The coffee shop was an old refurbished house that sat in the middle of the town square. Roni sometimes thought the place seemed creepy, but she liked the coffee and Jouda always wanted to come here so she just ignored all those feelings. She sat near the large glass window so she could see when he was coming. From where she sat she could see the entryway into the next room. She didn't like going in there because it had only the tall tables and a couple of couches that were uncomfortable.

She didn't like the way it was decorated either. It was darker than the other rooms. The pictures on the wall were painted by the owner of the coffee shop, and they disturbed her. They were distorted pictures of women, one having a very beautiful body scantily dressed, but the face was blurred and unrecognizable. Another was of a woman whose face was looking down at her body that was not connected. All the limbs were disconnected and floating off to the side. The one that was the most disturbing was that of a woman lifting the baby in her hands up to the sky. She tried to tell herself that perhaps it represented a dedication to God, but the fire in the background didn't fit with that thought. The pictures and the room repulsed her, but it wasn't just that room, the entire shop seemed antagonistic.

In a hidden place the demons continued to gather. Roni couldn't see them but they could see her. A fiendish council had been called to gather at this coffee shop to prey upon the souls that could be stolen and given to them for spiritual derision.

Drums bellowed out into the darkness to the tune of a death that could not be heard by human ears. But in the realm of hidden things, it was a loud malevolent drone that summoned the dance of the gods. Ashtoreth, Molech, Baal and numerous demons of lust were being summoned with each beat of this devilish cadence. A demonic ritual would soon take place that would call out hell's combatants to wage war against the purity of life. Unknown to Roni, she would be a key target. Though unseen and unheard it was felt. Roni didn't know why, but fear came upon her again. She felt an evil presence, and kept thinking it was something about that room.

All Roni could see was the entrance to that room and the corner of a tall table sticking out just past the door jam. Every once in a while she noticed the person sitting at the table when he leaned back in his chair. She never saw his face, just a tattooed arm. She sat there, staring at the doorway, lost in thought about that room, wondering who was in there. Was it the owner? She didn't like him, though he and Jouda got along pretty well. Mesmerized by the unknown, she let her mind wander, and was afraid to stay here. She wished Jouda would hurry. This place was creepy.

She had been so busy looking in the other room and daydreaming that she didn't see Jouda come up the walkway to the shop. The bell on the door clanged as it opened, and it startled her. She looked over at the door and was surprised to see Jouda. He was standing there sternly, arms crossed in front of him, and looking over at her in disgust.

Now what have I done, she thought.

He walked over to the table and pulled out a chair.

"This better be good," he said, opening his smart phone to log on to the Internet. "What's up with having to meet you here, anyway?"

Roni flushed making her pale skin look more chafed than colored. She did not want to tell him this news, knowing he wouldn't like it. The doctor told her she was about six weeks along, and she knew that with her petite frame she would be showing soon. She had no choice. She had to tell him. She reached for his hand hoping he would respond to her like he used to do, but Jouda continued to look at his phone. He didn't make eye contact with her at all. He just continued to text.

Where are you, man? Jouda typed on hid phone.

"Jouda," Roni said. "I have something I want to tell you."

"I'm listening," he answered, still not making contact.

"What is it?"

As she began to talk, a text message came in for him, and he shifted his attention from her to the phone.

Just around the corner from you, the text read. *I saw you come in. Why are you here?*

Jouda looked around the corner through the doorway and saw the edge of the table and the computer. Then Darayan looked around the corner and Jouda tried to be inconspicuous when he acknowledged that he saw him.

"Do you know the person in there?" Roni asked

"Not really."

Meeting Roni, he continued to text. *She says she has something important to discuss with me.*

"I have seen him around," he said finally acknowledging Roni's question. Laying his phone down, Jouda's thick eyebrows closed together as one when he looked at her.

"So, what is it you want to talk about that is so important?"

Roni shifted in her seat. She was afraid of the reaction she would get from him. And the longer she hesitated the more irritated he got.

"What is it, already? Are you leaving me? What?"

"Jouda, I am pregnant," she said looking straight at him not wanting to miss a single reaction. She feared anger, yet hoped for acceptance.

Jouda said nothing. He grabbed his phone again.

"Pregnant," he typed, and hit send.

Darayan, still sitting in the other room responded immediately.

"No babies in my clan."

A question mark was all that Jouda sent back, and he waited so he could be clear. He needed to know exactly what Darayan was saying to him. This guy was like a brother. Jouda had to admit he had some strange ways and tended to be controlling of their group that he called the clan, but Jouda felt compelled to listen to what he said. He just couldn't resist him, and if the truth was known, Jouda had come to where he would do anything Darayan told him to do.

"Jouda," Roni said as she watched him looking at his phone like it had all the answers he needed. She was trying to hold back her frustrations at him.

"Jouda, did you hear me? I am pregnant with your baby. Can't you stop texting and say something to me?"

"I heard you," he said. "Just give me a minute to think; will you?"

The phone's vibration interrupted the tension between them and in silence Jouda read what was sent by text from Darayan.

"ABORT!"

Jouda did not hesitate. He snapped the phone into its case and put it in his pocket.

"I don't want a baby."

As he said this Darayan walked through the doorway of the other room, and was heading out of the coffee shop. His dark presence sent chills through her. She had never met him, and didn't know that Jouda knew him. Nor did she have a clue that he just pronounced death on her baby. All she knew was what she felt as he passed through the room, and it was a terrible sense of evil.

"So, I am on my own, is that what you are telling me? This is your child too!"

"But," Jouda said pausing and leaning forward face to face with Roni. "I don't want a baby, and they make these things easy now. So do what you have to do."

Jouda seemed not to notice the tears rolling down Roni's face. Her hands were shaking and lips quivering as she tried to speak, and he seemed not to care at all.

"You want me to get an abortion? So, what if I choose not to do what *you* want?"

Jouda looked around the coffee shop to see if anyone was around, then grabbed Roni's neck and squeezed just enough to make her gag.

"Then I will strangle him the first chance I get, and tell the cops you did it. Now, do you get the message? I don't want a baby! I really don't think I want you either, but I might reconsider that part once you get rid of the extra weight.

Roni felt nauseous and ran to the bathroom with little time left before she got sick. She wasn't sure if she was sick from the pregnancy or from seeing this foul side of Jouda. Kneeling there over the bathroom stool, she cried and wished she had never come to meet him here. She stayed for what seemed like a long time in the bathroom. The nausea had gone, but the fear remained. His words echoed in her head, "I will strangle him, strangle him . . . strangle him."

"Oh God," she screamed. "Where are you? Do you care about me? Do you really exist? How can you let this happen to me?"

Roni's scream exploded through the bathroom and out into the coffee shop, and to her surprise no one came to see what was going on. It was eerily quiet. She wondered if Jouda would be still at the table waiting for her. She had never seen him act like this before. She finally got up and washed her face, looking in the mirror and wishing her eyes were not so red. She opened the bathroom door and peaked out looking at the table where they sat. Her cappuccino cup was still there, but Jouda was gone.

Roni's face was splotched with red. Her eyes were still wet from crying, and she felt even sicker now that Jouda was gone. She sat down at the table, and then saw a note sitting beside Jouda's cup. She reached for it, and then pulled back. Afraid of what it might say she hesitated to read it. The tears began to stream again as she held that piece of paper in her hand. She knew it would not be good, but she opened it anyway and began reading. It read:

I DON'T WANT A BABY. GET AN ABORTION! DON'T MAKE ME FORCE THIS ISSUE.

Hope Deferred

Hope deferred makes the heart sick, but a desire fulfilled is a tree of life. Proverbs 13:12

Roni shook hard as she held her stomach and cried. The coffee shop was silent except for the sound of her sobs. No one seemed to notice, or care that she was in distress. She was alone and afraid. Thoughts of having a happy healthy baby ran through her mind as she held the note in her hand, but those thoughts were persistently interrupted by the gruesome picture of what Jouda might do. She thought she could leave town to have the baby, but she knew she wouldn't make it far with two dollars in her wallet. Everything seemed so hopeless. Roni grabbed her purse and headed out, but stopped short just outside the door. Where would she go? Would it be safe to go home? Would Jouda do something to hurt her?

She began to walk toward her sister's house. It was eleven blocks away, and the walk there was tiring. She stood outside, just in front of her sister's yard, looking at the house, and straining to see inside. Then she sat under that old, large maple tree that she always had loved as a kid and quietly continued to watch. This was where she grew up. It was home.

After her parents died she begged her sister, Kate to move into this house. It took many months of convincing, but Kate finally agreed. It seemed, though, that as soon as the key had unlocked the door, the fleeting good life of home was lost again. Shortly after they moved in to the old home, Roni met Jouda and things fell apart after that. Roni remembered that day. She had felt that her world had collapsed and nothing could be worse. Her situation now, was worse than ever. She needed her sister, but they had parted in a bad way. It had become so bad that Kate would not return her phone calls. Roni knew Kate had grown weary of her calls begging for money.

Roni took a deep breath. "What am I afraid of anyway? She is my sister, and I know she loves me.

But will she love you after you tell her, whispered the antagonist in the silence of her soul.

"No matter how Kate feels, I need her," Roni said, feeling her stomach turn as she began to step forward toward the house.

"Just go on and knock," she whispered. "Don't make yourself sick over this. Just do it!"

She tried to calm herself, but couldn't contain the turning anxiety inside of her. The queasiness erupted, and she vomited everything that was left in her stomach. Finally, she gathered the nerve to go up to the door and knock. Silence followed, and she knocked again—this time longer and louder, but no one answered.

"Please, Kate, I need you. Please let me come in."

Roni knocked one more time. She tried to peek through the window to find any sign of activity in the house, but when she saw nothing, her shoulders dropped, and she bundled up sitting on the step of the porch. More than ever she was alone. No one was there to help her—no one.

She stood back up with new resolve and tried one more time, knocking and crying out.

"Kate! Please answer, Kate, I need you." She kept calling out her sister's name, hoping there would be an answer, but there was none.

She probably doesn't want to help me anyway, Roni thought as she walked away feeling defeated.

Again the demons gathered. Followers of Set, the god of chaos were again on the prowl. They began to congregate in the principalities' whirlwind of confusion that was stirring itself up in the presence of this disheartened young woman. Lying demons, frantic demons, demons of despair and defeat amassed as Set called a gathering for the purpose of destruction in the life of this one that God had already chosen as His own. Their weapons aimed at her emotions in attempt to kill her longing for restoration and reconnection into God's domain of light and truth. They knew their target was vulnerable, and that their aim to deceive was unstoppable. They merely whispered lies, and her vulnerability caused her to believe them. Encircling her with clouds of anarchy and a tempest of pretext they led her mind astray in an attempt to imprison her for life. They were convinced that once they were done with her she would no longer even desire to call on the name of *Him*.

"Abandoned!" whispered the demon Rejection.

"It's hopeless," said the demon, Despair.

"Give up," murmured Defeat

"God doesn't care," sneered Malevolence

"You aren't strong enough," cried Pathetic

Roni was crying, breathing heavily as she walked away from that door. She felt abandoned and lost. She was alone and it seemed no one cared, not even God. With nowhere else to go, she headed back to her apartment hoping Jouda would not be there.

He typically did not come home on Fridays. She never knew where he was and now she didn't care. She only wished he would not come home, at least for tonight so she could have some time to think about what she would do.

As Roni came through the door she took a deep breath. His car was parked on the street, but he often left on Fridays with a car full of really creepy people. She never dared go after him because she was afraid to even look at these friends of his. It was quiet inside. That was a good sign. Jouda always had the music up way too loud. She walked through the apartment and sighed relief that he wasn't there. She eased up on the bed and laid her head down on the only pillow they had and slept, until the opening door awakened her at midnight. She stiffened as he walked toward the room, but to her surprise he came and calmly sat next to her on the bed.

"Are you doing alright?" He asked as he gently brushed his hands through her hair.

This was like the Jouda she had met two years ago. He was gentler toward her, and always had treated her with kindness. He hadn't been this way for a while though and she wondered what he was up to. Still she couldn't help but relent to his touch.

"Not really," she said hoping he might change his mind. "I am really tired from all the worrying. You are home unusually early for a Friday," she said keeping her eyes downward. Is everything okay?"

"I have to tell you something. That's why I am home,"

"What is it Jouda, are you in trouble?"

"No, I have a job to do this weekend and it will bring us in lots of money. So, I am leaving and won't be back until Monday."

"What kind of job?" Roni asked timidly, hoping he wouldn't get mad that she asked.

"Not to worry, it's safe. It's best that you don't know anything."

Jouda continued massaging her neck as he spoke to her, and felt her relaxing.

"So, tell me what you are worrying about."

"Our baby, Jouda—this is *our* baby. How can I kill it?"

The silence stiffened Roni, and she feared what might be coming. Suddenly he squeezed the back of her neck, pinching it hard, and pulling at her hair.

"Jouda, that hurts! Let go! What are you doing?"

The silence became more exaggerated as his grip intensified on her neck. She couldn't hear anything. Even her own breathing was muted. His phone rang, and he let go of her neck to answer it.

"Yes, leaving now," she heard him say. She recoiled as he pocketed his cell phone. She knew he wasn't finished with her yet. Roni looked at the door, and though her mind was saying run, she just sat there looking at the chipped paint that hung off of the trim. She felt her stomach turn as she watched the cockroach crawl effortlessly across the door and head toward to the kitchen. As Jouda gently ran his finger down the side of her face she pulled away anticipating the worst. Without notice he grabbed her chin turning it abruptly toward his face.

"I want that *thing* in you gone when I return. Do you get it? If you do what I say, you get the treatment I gave you when I came in, but if you don't you will be hurting much worse than this."

He jerked her head as he let go.

"And don't worry about my work. I am paying the bills, right?"

He stood and stared at her a minute, saying nothing. She felt his eyes could violate her soul. She wished he would leave, and was relieved when he turned to leave. As he walked away she saw a bandana hanging from his back pocket with the picture of a skeleton on it. Emblazoned across that black bandana was the inscription MHM. She was curious what it meant, but didn't think too long about it. She was just glad to see him go. He didn't pack a bag. He didn't say good-bye. He just walked out. And as soon as the door shut behind him she broke down and cried. Monday would be a day she would dread to come.

Jouda tried not to reason why he was so set on being the antagonist in Roni's life. He was a man who was too easily taken by the things of pleasure, and he knew this about himself. That is why he relied so heavily on the drugs. They were a source of pleasure for him, as well as a sedative for his aching heart. He saw the soft places deep inside of himself, and could not allow any of those feelings to surface, because as soon as they did he would lose it all—the access to drugs, his connection with Darayan, and possibly even his life. It was not wise to make Darayan angry, and make him to turn away. Jouda needed what Darayan had, but deep inside he hated what this man represented.

Darayan was ruthless. He was calloused to the sweet and simple things of life. He especially hated the name of Jesus. He was a cruel opponent to anyone that opposed him, and he left no plunder when he went in for the defeat of another. Though he was only twenty-three, he looked old and mean. A sinister figure, he loomed over his brood that he called, *The Clan*.

At first, His ways were disturbing to Jouda, but Darayan had something he wanted. The drugs kept bringing him back around until the voice inside that cried out for righteousness was hushed. Eventually, Jouda started to become like Darayan—ruthless, uncaring and menacing. It was this callousness that silenced the small voice inside that was desperately seeking recognition, especially concerning his own child, on whom he had already pronounced a death sentence. That small voice was faint, but he recognized it. It was like a cry in the dark. He even heard it in his sleep when he dreamed, but he dare not take heed to it. he was afraid that if he did, it would drown out the voice of power forever. So, he followed Darayan, and silenced any other voice that was raised up against this leader. Jouda knew that when Monday came he would have to take action if Roni did not do what she was supposed to do. The scenario he had imagined never developed because Jouda ended up following Darayan into a trap, and found himself in another place he had not expected.

Monday morning arrived and with it came the news that Jouda had been arrested in a burglary attempt. Roni postponed making that dreaded appointment as soon as she heard the news. She waited to hear more about his release. She thought he might call. But when the call never came, she wondered if this was the end of him. She hoped it was.

She sat back in her chair and began to make plans, setting her eyes on Jouda's secret place in the wall behind the picture. He didn't know she knew about it, but she watched him put money there before. Roni moved the picture and stuck her hand in the hole where his money was hidden. It wasn't much, but it would be enough to see her through for a few months. She hoped that Jouda wouldn't miss it when he came back—if he came back. She would use this for rent, and as far as food, there were always places to go to get more food if she needed to do that.

Days and then weeks had passed that she had not heard from Jouda. She didn't know anything. Maybe he was still in jail, or maybe he didn't care about being around her any more, and just decided not to come back. Either way she was glad, and she determined to move forward with her life to find a way to make things good for her baby. She was not sure yet how that would all take place, but for once, life looked a little lighter.

From the Valley of Affliction

And there I will give her vineyards, and make the Valley of Achor a door of hope. (Hosea 2:15)

Roni needed to get out for some fresh air, and decided to go for a walk. Sometimes walking helped to clear her thinking and she hoped she would be able to think through what she could do next, and make some plans. As she walked past the apartment complex office, she noticed a help wanted sign in the window. She stopped and looked at the sign for a long time and finally decided to inquire about it. Even if Jouda came back, she reasoned it would be good to have a job. Maybe he wouldn't be so mad at her if she brought in an income as well. She was now four months and beginning to show, and wondered if she should hide it from the manager when she applied. She decided she wouldn't mention the pregnancy.

Her stomach turned at the noxious smell coming from the cigar smoke that was skulking out one side of his mouth, while he held the cigar in the other corner. He didn't even look up at her, but puffed away at that awful smelling cigar as he inquired of her need.

"What can I do for you, young lady?"

Well, at least he acknowledged she was a young lady. That's more than she ever got from Jouda. She didn't know if she would make it through that cigar though, and hoped this would go quickly.

"Hi Mr. Satler, I have come to ask about the help wanted notice you have posted on the door. Could I fill out an application?"

As the manager turned in his chair, she watched his struggle to move around. He didn't seem to have a lot of energy, and his belly was certainly a hindrance to quicker movement.

What an odd shape, she thought.

He was very thin in the upper half of his body, and from the waist down he went to an extreme in width. His thin face and arms seemed to be in proportion with the rest of the upper half, but something happened below the waist. She had never seen weight gain like this before. She found herself staring as he stood to his feet, and then quickly looked to the floor as if not to notice. Still puffing on that cigar he went over to the file cabinet without saying a word, took out an application and pushed the piece of paper on the counter top that was in front of his desk.

"Fill this out," he said. "Then we can talk."

Roni completed the application as quickly as she could and handed it back to him.

"I'm done, Mr. Satler. Should I wait, or will you call me back after you have had a chance to go over my application?"

He didn't answer her question directly, but began asking his own questions.

"Never worked before huh?"

"No, Sir."

"Can you be on your feet all day, cleaning for four days straight?"

"Yes, Sir."

"I see you are just barely eighteen years old. Have you got a social security card and another ID?"

"Yes, Sir."

"Will it make you nauseous to clean up bathrooms that are left unattended?"

"Pardon me," she asked a bit puzzled with the question. Then she saw his eyes go from her belly, and then back up to meet her eyes.

"Oh, Yes, I can do it with no problem."

"How far along are you?"

"About four months."

"Been to see a doctor yet?"

"No," she said looking at the floor.

"Well, you will have to take care of that right away because I want a physical before you start so I know you are able to work."

"I have the job?"

"Yes," he said with a hint of compassion in his voice. I wondered what you would do. I mean, I saw that Jouda had been arrested. So this will help, right?"

"Oh, thank you Mr. Satler! I . . ."

He cut her off and spoke a little more sternly.

"This isn't charity, girl. You have to work four days cleaning. You tell me each week which day you need off, and that's your only day. Your Doctor appointments have to be on your day off, you understand?"

"Yes, Sir."

"Your rent comes off the top of your check each week. Is that acceptable?"

"Yes."

"That will give you about $100.00 each week after taxes for food and other needs. Will that be sufficient?"

"Yes," she said, now smiling. "I think that will be good."

"Alright, then, today is Monday. I want you to start a week from today. Does that give you enough time to get that physical?"

"I think so."

He saw the hesitation and knew she didn't have a clue how to begin doing this.

"Go to the health department. You don't need to make an appointment. You can just go as a walk-in. They will tell you what to do next. And tell them you need a physical to start a job, and that a pregnancy test is required. They can get you directed right. Go on now and I will see you on Monday. Bring me the results of the physical when you come in."

"Do I come back here to the office?"

"Yeah, you will need to check in here every Monday morning to get your weekly schedule for cleaning. Don't forget that each week you will let me know what day you need off. Monday is not an option, got it?

"Yes, Sir, and thanks again," Roni said smiling. Her smile was sweet and it just made her landlord smile as well.

"Go on, out with you," he said trying not to smile too much. "I am not your daddy, now just go on and get yourself ready to work. I will see you at 8:00 on Monday morning. Don't be late!"

Roni left skipping. She had a sense of freedom that she had not felt in a long time. She wanted to be able to give her baby a fair chance, and now she felt there was hope. She did not plan to keep the baby, but hoped that Jouda would stay away at least long enough so that she could give birth and adopt her child out to a good family. Then, at least he couldn't kill the baby *or her*.

Gerry Satler finished the last of his coffee before leaving the office. He wondered if the girl would show up today. He hoped she would. He Never did like Jouda. He believed the sweet person in Roni was covered up by the heartlessness of that guy.

"Funny," He said to himself. "The cruelty of one person can be powerfully dominating in another person's life. How did this young woman hold up under that kind of pressure? For that matter, how did she even get to be involved in his life? Why did she make such a choice—stupid girl?"

At the very moment of chiding of Roni's lack of common sense, this brusque and fiercely independent man lost himself in a time when he felt his world would never be good. He had allowed himself to emotionally reenter a world where alcohol dominated his life; and the reliving of it made his heart ache and he cried in spite of himself.

"Snap out of it, Gerry," he chided himself. "You have to get going and can't be seen as a sniveling baby. Those days are gone. You have been made new."

Being such large man, it took some work to arise from where he was sitting, and get ready to go. As soon as he got up, he took the cigar he had just lit, and knelt down to the floor snubbing it out on the ceramic tile in front of the rug.

"Lord, I know this is not what you want. I am weak, but you are strong. Help me to be free of this bondage. You took away the desire for alcohol, you are helping me to be free of the desire to eat everything In sight, and You can help me to be free of this as well."

As quickly as he knelt down, he got up and went to work again. He took hold of the application that he was just given.

"Roni Simone," he said out loud. "May God show Himself to you in a real way, and I pray that He will give you everything you need."

With that prayer, he grabbed his hat and walked out the door, not knowing how God would use him to answer that simple prayer he had brought on behalf of this lost and lonely girl.

As the next few months passed he watched her seem to come to life. She worked hard, and without fail impressed him with a strong a determined character. He asked her many times to come to his church, but she never showed up. He gave her space and time, but he did not give up asking, and at some point, would bring it up again. He always remained professional and seemed a stern old boss, but deep inside he genuinely cared about her well-being.

One day, he thought. *She will say yes to Jesus, Lord, let it be soon.*

Roni was beginning to feel tired more often, and her feet always hurt at the end of the day. She was not going to let that stop her though. She was living independently, and beginning to feel secure in her life and her job. As she walked to the newly vacated apartment, she thought of how much she enjoyed working for Mr. Satler. She could see right through his pretense of austerity. He was tender and as gentle as a lamb in her eyes. He always tried to make her think he was rough, but she knew better.

Roni also enjoyed the paycheck. It gave her enough for food and a few other little luxuries like an occasional movie. She liked being able to take care of herself, and she really was glad to show Mr. Satler that she was a responsible person. So, if she had to waddle to work to earn his respect, then that is what she would do. She reveled for a moment in all the things going well in her life right now. So many things she enjoyed that Jouda had prevented before. But more than anything she could think of, she enjoyed her freedom from Jouda. In the months she had of this freedom, she felt as though her soul was coming alive again. This was better than being with him. There was no yelling, no belittling, and no abuse. It was a wonderful life. He was gone, and she rejoiced. Roni was even beginning to pray again, and thought she might go this Sunday to Mr. Satler's church.

No one knew how long Jouda would be gone. She had tried to see him once, but he refused to give permission to allow her into the prison as a visitor. Another time she went by the coffee shop and had a cup of coffee to sit a while and see if she could learn anything. She did find out that he would likely spend some time awaiting trial.

The timing for her was crucial knowing he could serve a long sentence or be set free sooner. Roni already knew she would have to start planning on how to avoid getting back together. She knew she did not want that. She also knew how over-powering he was, and that she would have to plan and be smart about how to get out from under his grip. In just two short months a baby would arrive, and she nudged at the possibilities of keeping her child.

Could she raise this little girl by herself? Could she manage to keep Jouda away from her so she could live a good life? Roni shook it off. It was an impossible dream, yet a dream that brought a sense of meaning and purpose to her. Still she discounted it. There was no time for day dreaming while her work for the day was still ahead of her.

Before Roni unlocked the door to the apartment that Mr. Satler had sent her to clean today, she could smell the horrible stench. It turned her stomach, and she wondered how she was going to clean this one. When she walked in, the smell overpowered her, and she ran immediately back outside vomiting every bit of the breakfast she had that morning. Reaching for her bag she grabbed the bottle of water for a drink. The smell of garbage was foul, and she wondered how anyone could have lived like this. She wondered if she could continue this job, but she was determined. She had to do this because in a small way this was a step to a better life for her and for her baby. She grabbed a scarf from her bag and wrapped it around her mouth and nose like a mask. She breathed deeply and entered the apartment.

"Oh Dear Lord," she said in exasperation. "This one is going to be a challenge. I will need your help, God."

The kitchen had food all over the counters. Flies and maggots had covered what looked like chicken that was sitting on the table. Dog feces were on the floor, and to her surprise it had even been stepped in. Opened cans of tuna fish and baked beans were left there. Trash was overflowing and the place was destroyed by holes kicked in the walls. One door was barely hanging on one hinge. Roni set down her cleaning supplies, and did an inspection of the remainder of the apartment before beginning the cleaning. She inspected every room to assess how long it would take her. She walked through using the management's inspection sheet to list the needed repairs.

Writing covered the bathroom walls like graffiti found on the walls in subway stations. Words ran together and dried with the drips of the paint that splattered each expression of profanity and slander that was written there. Roni was recording on her list to paint the bathroom wall when she noticed the initials written in red, and inscribed there on the wall was a rough drawing of a skull and initials were written across it in a calligraphic design that she had seen before. MHM—It was this same thing that was written on that bandana she saw in Jouda's pocket the night he had left. On the floor, underneath the graffiti covered wall was a notebook. Roni picked it up, and as she opened it she saw it was someone's journal. Reading some of the entries she wondered why this had been left behind. Did this person want it to be found, or did they even know it was here? There was so much written in the first couple of pages—things like outlines for violence and crimes that were being planned. Roni felt compelled to let someone else know. She left immediately, and took it to Mr. Satler. As he sat in the office chair seemingly unaffected by yet another leftover from a bad renter, she read the first page to him.

The words were enough to make Mr. Satler stand up out of his chair and reach for the book.

"I have just been initiated into the clan of Malach HaMavet. I had to attend a death party and then write about my experience there."

The entry went on to detail the events of the party which included the killing of a dog. The writer went on to say how detestable it was to him, but he understood it was necessary to keep out any unwanted members from this clan that was recognized by its initials MHM.

"After all," he said. "I follow the ways of Malach HaMavet. I may not understand, but they are ways that give the power to our clan. I must follow without question."

"Give me that book, girl," Mr. Satler said holding his hand out.

"This is not something you need to be internalizing. I will take care of it from here. You are not to go back to that apartment. I will get it cleaned another way."

Roni handed him the book and just stood there in front of him. She sensed that he had already encountered such things, and maybe knew something already about this clan.

"What is it?" he asked. "Is there more?"

"That clan . . ." she stammered. "Those initials were on a bandana that Jouda was wearing the night he left and got arrested. I want to know who this is he follows. What is it I am up against? What do you know about them, Mr. Satler? Tell me, I need to know this."

Gerry shook his head back and forth.

"It may be best if you don't know."

"Then how can I protect myself or this baby if I don't know?"

"Alright, alright, I do know about these people. I try to screen so this kind doesn't get into my apartments, but here is evidence of one, and now you tell me Jouda was involved too. They get better at cover up."

"So who are *they*?"

Mr. Satler leaned his head all the way back, and he took a deep breath before answering.

"*They* are a very dangerous cult gang. The person they say they follow does not exist—well not in this realm anyway. MHM is the initials for the Hebrew words Malach HaMavet, which mean angel of death. This gang has not been in existence long, but in a short time, they have wrecked lives, destroyed relationships and have put fear into the hearts of many a good people. Their focus is on death and destruction. They write about it, their music and art reflects it, and they party about it. They are calloused and brutal. The most they could ever be charged with as a group is killing animals, but their leader, whose name is Darayan has been busted for violent assault, and on top of that he is a drug lord. I'm telling you the man is ruthless. If Jouda is connected with him this is bad news, and you had better be gone far away by the time he gets out of jail."

Roni took a deep breath and prayed that God would deliver this baby before Jouda could get to it. Now she feared what he said he would do was possible and he might very well try to kill this child and her.

"Mr. Satler? Will Jesus protect us?"

This burley man sat there wondering how to answer such a question.

"Do you know Jesus?" He asked.

"Well, I know a little about him. But I want to know Him more."

"What does that mean to you, Roni? Do you know about having a relationship with Jesus?"

Tears were welling up in her.

"Yes, my parents were Christians. They used to always tell us how important it was to have a relationship with Jesus, but I always argued that there was plenty of time to make that decision. I was just a kid, what did I know? Then all of a sudden, God took them from me. That's why I am asking if Jesus protect us—me and my baby. I'm asking because I don't see how he protected me from losing my parents. Then, I lost the relationship with my sister. Can He keep me from being hurt by evil people? I figured I must not know Him well enough, because I couldn't really answer this question. I want to know Him more, Mr. Satler. Can I come to church with you this Sunday? Please let me go with you. I am too scared to go in by myself."

Gerry looked tenderly at Roni as she pleaded with him. In such a short time this girl had become like a daughter to him, and he felt he wanted to protect her as much as he could. He wanted to take her in and be a parent, but he always kept at a distance.

"Roni," he said with the gentlest look she had ever seen in his eyes. Know this: You can do anything through Christ, because He gives you strength to do it. He *will* protect you."

Gerry took a deep breath and a moment of doubt flashed through his brain as he thought about all the, *what ifs,* that could happen. But he pressed on.

"Roni, I want you to go to church, and you can come with me if that's what you want, but that is not what initially will help you to know Him. Oh it will help your relationship to grow with Him, but you have to have the relationship first. Do you have that?"

"I don't know," she said "How can I tell if I do?"

Mr. Satler went to his desk and grabbed his Bible, and as he took it into his hand a heavenly multitude began to gather in that small office, because they knew that a lost child was about to come home. God's angels gathered. Unseen and unheard they watched as he took her through the word of God to a place of salvation. Cherubim stood guard to fight off the enemy's hordes that would bring every attempt to prevent this moment from happening.

As they looked at the words written in the Bible, prayers were rising to the Almighty God from people who had already been praying for Roni. Two people from church who had been asked to pray for her suddenly found themselves compelled to go to a quiet place and plead for her salvation. They understood what was happening without even knowing the circumstance for which they prayed.

Another prayed, but she didn't know why. Kate was in the middle of cleaning her house and suddenly felt compelled to pray for her sister. She had not heard from her in such a long time and felt bad that she had quit taking her calls. She wished she knew what her sister was doing, and how she was. But at the moment she only knew she needed to pray. So, there in her kitchen she knelt before God, and asked that he would protect her sister from evil.

"Roni, do you know you are a sinner who needs Jesus?"

"Yes," she said. Her voice was quivering as she tried hard not to cry. Mr. Satler didn't quit. He kept pushing through. This was her time. Today was the day of her salvation.

"Do you believe that Jesus died for you to set you free from the penalty of sin, and to bring you a blessed hope of eternal life with Him?"

"Yes."

"Roni, do you accept Jesus as your Lord and Savior; and will you receive the free gift of salvation that He has for you?

Roni could only shake her head yes. Her tears were flowing fast and she was desperately trying to wipe them away. Mr. Satler placed his hand on her shoulder.

"Roni, I want you to say a prayer and ask Jesus to forgive you, and to come into your life to be your Lord."

"You want me to pray out loud?" Roni asked, blinking back the tears. "I can't remember the last time I prayed out loud."

"Yes, dear, I think you should pray out loud. Don't worry about me. It's just between you and God."

Roni took a deep breath and to Gerry's surprise, she knelt down, right there in the office and prayed.

"Lord, I have done so many wrong things. I am a sinner. Please forgive me and come into my life. Lord save me and help me to know you more. I do want to know you more. And Lord, would you protect me and my baby, and help me to go see my sister?"

She rose to her feet and together they said, "Amen!"

"Now, Miss Roni, you can say you know Jesus as your Savior, and you can come to church with me so you can learn more about Him. For now, though, get your purse. We are going to see your sister."

"But, Mr. Satler, I can't!" Roni began to object.

"What if she won't have anything to do with me? What if she rejects me? I am so afraid that she won't love me and . . ."

"Hush, Roni," Mr. Satler said, grabbing his hat. "We are going to her house. If she rejects you, and I don't think she will, then we will recalculate our moves. But, we have to go. Hopefully you can stay with her."

"What, are you kicking me out of my apartment?"

"You know that you can't stay there. Jouda will be outraged if he gets out and finds you still pregnant. He didn't want the baby, right?"

Roni sat quietly. She did not want to answer.

"Didn't you say he wanted you to get an abortion? Didn't he threaten to kill this baby if you gave birth to it?"

"Yes," Roni said. "Yes, he did, but I was hoping the baby would come before he got out, and I could put it up for adoption."

"And then what? You would wait for him to come back and get you pregnant again?"

"No way, Mr. Satler, Why would you think that? Especially since I just gave my life to Jesus? How could I even think about doing this all over again?"

"Then, it is as I said. You need to get out of that apartment. Look, if he comes back here it is best if he doesn't find you anywhere near—not living here or working here."

"You are firing me too?"

"Roni, get your purse, and let's go to your sister's house. I want what is best for you. If your sister will take you in, that will offer some safety for you. I will help you with finances until you can get on your feet again. You are going to have that baby soon, and you need to take it easy now. But mostly you need to get away from here. I am not going anywhere. I will pick you up for church, and keep in touch. This is best, so, no argument now. Let's go."

They sat quietly in his car. Roni didn't say anything. She desperately wanted to regain a relationship with her sister, and at the same time she wanted to stay near this sweet man who had become like her father.

Mr. Satler could feel the emotion rambling around in his stomach. He knew that Roni needed to be somewhere safe, and all he could think about was her protection. He hoped she understood. He was not throwing her away, but sending her toward healing, restoration and hope.

She will see soon enough, he thought.

"Roni, how do I get there?" He asked quietly.

Roni gave directions, and Gerry took the route slowly, giving ample time to pray together. It was too soon for Roni when they drew closer to the house. Her stomach began to jump with anxiety as she saw all the familiar landmarks that stirred memories and reminded her of just how near to the home they were. She worried about her sister seeing her like this—so full with child.

"God, I really need you." She prayed. "Help me to know what is best, and to accept what you choose for me. Help me to do what you want."

When they pulled up to the house, that big old tree was there as usual to greet Roni. Somehow that tree was a welcome sight and made her feel like she was home; still she sat immobile in the car, afraid to go up to the house. The car rumbled as it idled, and the noise of its purring was all that she heard in the midst of this moment of expectation.

Gerry turned off the ignition and paused.

"Let me go before you and pave the way."

Roni nodded. That worked for her. At least if her sister had bad things to say about her she wouldn't have to hear them. She watched as Mr. Satler walked up to the house, and her insides leaped up into her throat as the door opened. Kate looked so beautiful. Her hair had grown longer and it lay so smoothly on her shoulders. Roni wanted so desperately to run out of that car and up to the porch in hopes that Kate would embrace her. They stood talking for the longest time, and then Roni saw the door shut and Kate disappeared behind it, sending Roni's hopes deep into a well of rejection. Gerry came and opened the door and got into the car. He just sat there a moment and waited.

"Well, what did she say?" Roni asked. "Does she hate me, and never want to see me again? What all did you say to her? Please tell me."

"I just told her your situation. She asked me to wait here a moment. So, that's what we are going to do."

Kate opened the door and came walking toward them. She was carrying a blanket in her hand. Kate came to Roni's door and opened it. She bent down and reached inside hugging her sister.

"Welcome home, Roni," she said with tears streaming down her cheeks. "I wanted to get something before you came in. But let me explain first."

Kate sat on the edge of the SUV's side runner and tucked her head inside the front seat right next to Roni.

"Roni, after I quit taking your calls, I felt so awful. I cried day and night, and prayed that God would show me some hope. One night as I prayed, the Lord told me to get out Mama's gingham throw that I had tucked away in a memory box. He said I should lay it on the bed in your old bedroom, and that every night before I went to bed, I was to go in, and pray for your return. He said that when you returned I was to wrap it around you before you came into the house. The Lord told me that this would be a sign to you of His covering and protection."

Kate smiled, and wiped away the tears now forming in Roni's eyes.

"Welcome home," she said as she wrapped the quilted throw around her sister, then poked her head back in the car.

"Mr. Satler, thank you. Roni can stay here the night and we can go get her things later. How soon do you want her to pack up the apartment?"

"Take your time," he said. "It can wait for now."

Mr. Satler watched as the two of them headed toward the house. He felt the joy of this reunion and the loss of the daily presence of this young beautiful spirit.

He rolled down the passenger window as they walked up to the house.

"Roni," he called out. "This Sunday, at 9:00—I will pick you up right here. Okay?"

Roni gave him an affirmative nod. Then she turned back around to finish that wonderful walk up to the door that led her back home. As she opened the door she looked back to find that Mr. Satler was still there watching and waving. His smile was so big that it seemed to stand out above everything else. She was too far away to see the tears streaming down his cheeks, but it was better that she saw only the smile, as it built her confidence in the choice of coming home.

Kate and Roni walked together as they headed down the hallway toward Roni's old bedroom. The entire house was different inside. Kate had redecorated and made it look more modern and much brighter than Roni had remembered.

"The house looks nice, Kate. You've changed everything, and made it look so welcoming. I really like what you have done here. I feel like I am coming back to my roots, yet it is all new."

Kate stopped a moment and turned toward Roni taking hold of her sister's shoulders with both hands.

"Roni, I hope you like your room, but if you don't we can change it. When I redid it I made the room speak to me about the hope of you coming back. So, that is why it is decorated the way it is. I am going to let you go in by yourself so your reaction to it can be without my presence to influence you. Remember it can be changed easily, and it won't hurt my feelings if you want it changed. You are here now, and that is all that matters."

Roni headed toward the room, pulling her purse up on her shoulder, and hanging on to it as if it provided a sense of security for her. When she opened the door she was taken back at the instant sense of peace that came flowing from that room. Her eyes were immediately taken to the large print on the wall. It was a copy of Rembrandt's painting of The Prodigal. It drew her in and she began to sense the love in that room. Everything about it spoke volumes of a God who loved her and who was glad she was home.

She took her time looking around. She didn't want to miss anything. The walls were soft glowing amber that hinted of peach colored tones. The bedroom suite was the same that was hers before she left. It was an antique set that had weathered the years and remained like new through all the wear and tear of her childhood. The mattress on it was new. It was the double pile pillow top, and it looked so much more comfortable than what she had been sleeping on in her apartment. A new quilted comforter that was simply adorned in brown and bronzed colors covered the bed with home-spun warmth. The older lighting had been replaced with amber glass and two sconces were added to the walls on each side of the window, which was covered by an elegant balloon shade. A rocking chair had been added to the corner of the room and there was a large cedar chest that had not been there before. It sat under the picture of the prodigal, and on top of it were pictures of Roni and her parents.

Roni walked over toward the chest to open it, but was so overtaken by the picture of *The Prodigal* that she stopped to examine it before she opened the chest. She saw the Father lovingly placing a hand on his son and she was suddenly overwhelmed with the knowledge that God, her Father had been lovingly and longingly waiting for her to come back home, and ultimately to come to Him. She knelt down on the floor in front of that chest and under the picture, and thanked God for such a provision, for such a hope and so much love.

As Roni prayed there was a tiny light that poked through the darkest corner of that room and shined brightly down upon her head. Though it shone brightly it went unnoticed by her. As she gave thanks to the Lord for her deliverance another light was added, and then another. The heavenly host began to gather one by one, each coming in to dispel the darkness that wanted to close in on her in this moment of return and renewal. Ministering angels came in and filled that room until there was no darkness left. Many of these Heavenly Beings came just to see the beauty of God as he hovered over Roni while she humbled herself before Him. They always longed to see such things as this. For the angels of God knew that He was always creating, and they understood the magnificence of His Word as it began to sweep people off their feet, and into a harmonious adventure with the Lord. Unlike their evil counterparts they reveled in the movement of God over a person who was submitted to His ways, and they cried out for more of the glory of God to be revealed in a person's life as they sang unto to Him, "Holy, Holy, Holy are you Lord!"

The morning light came through the window to awaken Roni. She sat up in the bed and felt refreshed. For the first time in a while she felt secure. She knew that Mr. Satler was always looking out for her, and now she was here safely secured with family. She pushed back the lingering thought that Jouda could return without notice.

The smell of coffee brewing drew her out of her bed and toward that wonderful fragrance. She knew that Kate only brewed the best coffee and usually from freshly ground coffee beans. Her sister sat in the kitchen at the table reading her Bible and sipping a cup of coffee. Roni came up from behind her and kissed the back of her head.

"Are the coffee cups still in the same place?"

"And should you be drinking coffee, little sister?"

"Well, I have been all along, but I have tried to cut down. I usually only have one cup in the morning. Besides, who are you to say anything? I think you are the one who introduced me to espressos and lattes and such."

They both laughed and Kate got up and hugged her sister.

"I have missed you, and the laughter and the joking around that we do. I am really happy that you are home."

"In some ways it feels like I never left," Roni said as she poured creamer in her coffee. "You made it so easy to return. I thank God for you."

"And that means God is in your life, Roni?"

"Yes, just yesterday, before we came here, Mr. Satler helped me to pray to have a relationship with Jesus. I rejected the Lord for so long because of Mom and Dad's death. But God put me into the hands of a very caring person who changed all that. Mr. Satler is like a father to me in so many ways."

Kate sat silent for a while. "There will never be any one like our daddy, but I think Mr. Satler is probably a very good choice of a father figure. So, tell me what are we having, a boy or a girl?"

"A girl," Roni replied dropping her head a bit.

"And does she have name yet?"

"I have given her a name, Kate, but I am not keeping her. Her name is Abiona. It means born for a journey."

Tears began to uncover Kate's disappointment. "Why are you giving her up for adoption? I can help you with whatever you need."

"It's not that, Kate. I want her to live, to be secure and safe from harm. And I don't ever want her to know or meet her father."

Roni began to tell Kate all that had happened, and how Jouda began to change, and how he had insisted on the abortion, threatening to kill the baby if she gave birth to it. She also told her how they had discovered Jouda's connection with this cult, and how it had made her feel even more afraid for her baby's life.

"If I want Abiona to live and to have a chance in life I have to do this," Roni spoke quickly, flushing out her own emotions with her story. "I love my baby. In the time I have carried her she has become so special to me, and I want the very best for her."

"I understand," was all that Kate said. "I will stand beside you whatever you do."

A Very Present help

God is in the midst of her; she shall not be moved;
God will help her when morning dawns. Ps. 46:5

Jouda readied himself in the confines of his cell. He had done everything possible to ensure an early release from this jail cell. Still awaiting trial he knew that the potential was there for a long term imprisonment. He had done all the things he thought necessary to present himself as the poor mixed-up kid who just got himself in with some bad company. He had asked for counselors and even pastors to come in to talk to him, and he knew all the right things to say to convince them that he had the *good boy* in him. He really did not care to talk to anyone, but if he was going to get out he had to pretend to be getting help. He even pretended to accept Jesus as his Savior, so that the pastor might give a good word for him in due time.

His plan was laid out with such finesse that all the manipulation could not be detected as a false appearance. He had the picture in his mind of how he should look, and he painted it well enough to convince many around him that he could reform. In the months that he had been in this jail cell, hoping for a breakthrough for his release, he devised his schemes. He trusted Darayan to take care of any financial needs that were looming. He thought of Roni. He really didn't want to see her when he got out, but he knew he had to find her, because he did not want a kid dragging him down in life. He figured she would be waiting for him anyway and that if she had done what he asked that maybe he would keep her around a while longer, but not too long. There were plans being made even now for big jobs in Florida, and he planned to go alone. He would play Roni until it was time to go, and then just leave.

There was a bit of a twinge in his heart when he thought of how they had first met, but he tried not to think too much about that. With every tender thought, there was always a sharpness that came upon him that poked at such affectionate thinking, and he dismissed it quickly. He could not afford to go soft.

A couple of times he got out pen and paper to write her a note that spoke to her with gentleness, but each time he ended up crumpling the paper and throwing it away. He was oblivious to the battle that raged each time he began a letter. In a longer than usual moment of compassion he held on to the thoughts of those beginning moments in their relationship. He thought of her hands rubbing the temples of his head, and somehow managing to caress away the pain of a migraine headache. He pondered whether it was her gentle touch or the prayer she whispered for him as she massaged. He felt his heart beginning to melt at the thought of those early days, but what he did not feel was the disturbance that was gathering around him as he began to pen yet another letter that spoke of the deep affection he once had felt for her.

He had barely written the salutation, when suddenly it felt as though the pen was yanked from his hand and it dropped to the table. He sat still for a moment, and then picked the pen up again. As he began to write again, he felt a strong hot wind rush past him, and again the pen was mysteriously removed from his hand, and thrown across the room.

"What in Heaven's name was that?" He exclaimed.

He quickly arose and looked around. The cell was quiet. He went to the corner of the room where the pen had landed and grabbed it up again. As soon as he sat down and began to write again he heard Darayan call out to him.

"Not Heaven's name Judas."

Laughter belted out and sounded as if it was just outside the door.

"Darayan, quit playing games with me."

Jouda turned to look at the paper on the desk. All he had managed to write was *My Dearest Roni.*

"Judas!" the voice came again, softly, in a whisper, as it entered the cell this time and echoed off all four walls.

It was no doubt Darayan's voice. Whenever Darayan tried to make a point to Jouda about the dangers of caring for people he always spoke to him softly, calling him Judas, emphasizing the *s* at the end of his name. It had to be Darayan because no one else called him that name. His heart pounded. The voice was calling to him, but no one was there. Jouda stepped back standing clumsily in one corner of the room with his eyes flashing all over that cell, searching every corner, though he didn't know what he was looking for.

"What?" Jouda answered. "Where are you?" His heart was beating hard. Then it beat all the harder when he thought he heard a baby crying. Jouda dropped to his knees, pen falling from his hand and he covered he ears.

"Stop it! Stop! Stop! Stop!"

The guard came near.

"What's going on in there? Are you going nuts on us?"

Jouda's face was flushed. He didn't see the guard standing there at the door. He just stared past him, and went back once again to pick up the pen. When he bent over to get it he heard the baby crying again, and then that voice like Darayan's calling out to him.

"Judas!"

There was no more noise. It was quiet. But, Satan's hordes were working diligently to keep Jouda's mind immersed in depravity. Jouda's thoughts turned to abortion, and the desire for any tenderness began to leave him.

"No babies in my clan. The voice called out to him. No babies, no place for all that love. Got it, Judas?"

Jouda ignored the voice and moved back to his desk. He took paper out and began to think about what to say. But the demons haunted him, and continued to press in on him, until he threw the pen himself, and ripped the paper to shreds, screaming and laughing uncontrollably. Then he realized the guard was still watching, and the young Haitian regained his composure. He turned to look at the guard who stood looking at him.

"Sorry," Jouda said. I was just reliving some bad news from home. I am okay now."

"Well alright then," the guard said matter-of-factly, "You wouldn't want to mess things up for tomorrow, now would you? They think tomorrow's hearing will be in your favor? If I were you, I'd not do too much that will mess that up. Your lawyer is here to see you. That's why I am here, so let's go."

Jouda resisted the urge to jump up and down. He quietly got up and stuck his hands through the opening in the door so the guard could cuff him and get him ready to take to the waiting room to talk to his lawyer. His day would be here soon. He was sure of it. As he walked out the door and headed toward the reception room, he thought he heard that voice again.

"Judas," the voice whispered. "Remember, don't go soft on me."
He turned quickly to look back.
"Forget something?" The guard asked.
"No, I'm good."
The disturbing voice was quickly forgotten. But his haunting had only just begun.

Hidden Love

That which we love is held loosely in our hands
Tomorrow comes and takes us down another road
And we wonder if we have loved selfishly.

Old friend, Bygone, seems to catch up with us
And remind us of those rocky crags
Where again we meet the sting of yesterday

That which we love wants to journey our way
Yet we turn love aside to hide, to hide, to hide
Yet never to forget what could have been

Roni stood in front of the full length mirror in her bedroom, examining the uneven tilt of her belly as her baby girl thrust herself completely to one side. Kate walked by and saw that Roni was pushing gently at a large bump sticking out, and she was laughing.

"Want to play a game, huh?" She laughed again as she pushed back at the little foot that was extended out in an obvious stretch.

Kate tried to be quiet, and not disturb this moment between mother and daughter, but she couldn't help herself, and began to laugh too.

Roni turned her exposed belly toward her sister.

"See that foot? My dear little Abiona is persistent."

Kate walked in the room and placed a hand on that tiny protrusion, and Abiona pulled in quickly as if she knew it was not her mother.

"You will have to get used to Aunt Kate, dear," she said and then stopped, suddenly realizing that Abiona would never know her Aunt.

Roni's large smile was suddenly gone.

"I am sorry, Roni. It was a slip of the tongue." Kate paused a moment. "You haven't reconsidered, have you?"

Roni shook her head. "It has to be this way, Kate. It is the only way I know of for Abiona to be safe. There is no other way."

"Just how bad is Jouda? Do you really think he would hurt her?"

Roni sat on the bed, and motioned for her sister to come and sit down. She began to share with her sister all the awful things that had taken place in her relationship with Jouda, and his involvement with the gang. She talked about the times he had hit her, and the threat he had made on the baby's life.

"I just can't take a chance."

"You wouldn't go back to him, would you?"

"Not a chance, but I am afraid he would find me, and kill my baby. I know it's hard. Believe me as hard as it is on you, Kate, it is more so for me. I have fallen in love with this life in me, and I would love to keep her. In almost two months she will arrive, and I don't know when Jouda will get out. This has to be done."

Roni stood up and hugged her sister.

"I need some fresh air. I am going for a short walk."

"Want me to go with you."

"Thanks, but I really need some time to think and pray."

Roni left the house and began walking and praying. She walked to the nearby park, and sat on the swing for a while. This was where she and Jouda used to meet before everything turned sour, and she moved out of her home, and in with him. She started to swing, closing her eyes while she went back and forth. As the breeze blew through her hair, she began to envision her pushing her little girl on that swing. She could hear the laughter, and imagined her calling out, *Mommy, push me higher.*

For a moment Roni felt she should not let her little girl go. Maybe it could be possible to keep her. Maybe they could get away and not be found. Roni let her mind wander as she began to slow down. Then, suddenly she felt someone grab the swing from behind her, and as it wretched back and forth she tried to hang on. Finally the swing stopped, and she jumped off to see who was behind her. But before she could turn around she was on the ground. She had been pushed hard, and landed sprawled out on her belly with her arms out in front of her. Pain scorched the tips of her hands, and her knee felt like it twisted behind her. She crouched upward on all fours trying to regain her stance when she saw Jouda standing over her, almost daring her to get up again.

"Dear God! She cried. It's him." Then she screamed. "My baby, please not my baby!"

Roni struggled to her knees, and as she pushed herself up, Jouda grabbed her by the hair, and pulled until she was standing. He turned her to face him. As Roni looked at him she felt sick. He looked so evil. His head had been shaven, and she noticed burn marks on his head. They looked like cigarette burns. His eyes were hollow, and dark circles hung beneath them in swollen pockets outlined by the dark creases. His hands looked like he had grabbed barbed wire, and someone pulled it against his skin. These cuts were obviously infected while there were others that had begun to scab over. He looked pathetic.

What things has he been into while in prison, she thought. In a moment she flashed back to times they had done outlandish things that seemed to have some dark spiritual overtones. She recoiled at the thought.

"No babies," he said. "I told you no babies," he repeated as he flung the back of his hand against her face landing his knuckles just under her right eye. The blow was so hard that she fell to her knees again. Grabbing Roni by the arm he dragged her to his car.

Roni fought him as much as she could, but she was worried about the baby.

"Where are you taking me?"

"You have an appointment, and you won't be late because I am taking you there."

He shoved her in the car, got in and drove off quickly. It took about thirty minutes until he finally stopped the car in front of the abortion center.

"I already called for you," he said staring at her with hatred in his eyes.

Roni was crying and Jouda looked around to see if there was anyone who would notice them. Then he took out a gun, and placed it on top of her belly. He pulled the trigger on an empty chamber. The click of the moving gear made her jump, and she cried all the harder.

"Now go do what you are supposed to do. When I see you again, if that baby isn't gone I am going shoot it out, and kill you too."

Jouda pushed her out of the car. He watched as she walked up, and opened the door. He did not leave the front until he saw her talking to someone at the desk. She turned around twice, and saw he was still there.

"God, where are you," she cried. It looked like there was no way out, but still she kept crying out to God, asking him to help her.

"Are you alright," the receptionist asked. "Can I get you a glass of water or something? Maybe you should sit down for a minute."

Roni sat in the waiting room until finally a nurse came out to talk to her.

"What is your name, and how can we help you?"

"Roni Simone," she said crying, "but please I really don't want to do this."

"I know," the nurse said hushing her. "Come on, let's go back to a waiting room so we can talk, and get you away from all the eyes out here."

Roni thought she seemed nice enough. Maybe she could help her figure out what to do. The nurse took Roni back to a counseling room, and had her sit in the chair until she returned. While she waited Roni tried to call Kate, but got no answer. Kate's voice mail came on, but Roni couldn't bring herself to leave a message. What would she say anyway? So many thoughts were swirling in her head right now. What would she do? If she went back home would she be putting Kate in danger. Would Jouda be waiting outside?

The nurse walked in, and began checking Roni's vitals.

"Hi, my name is Rhoda. I see you made an appointment for termination of the pregnancy. I will be one of the nurses working on your case. In all there is a team of three. It will be the doctor, me and a nurse's aide. We just need to check your vitals, and have you to sign some paper work. Then, we can begin the procedure."

"But I didn't make the appointment. My boyfriend did. I don't think I really want to do this, but I am afraid if I don't . . ." Her voice trailed off and she felt she couldn't finish the thought. She just dropped her head and began crying again.

The nurse took Roni's chin and lifted her head.

"It will be just fine. It will be done before you know it. Sometimes this is the best choice, and you have to try not to listen to shame. Just do what you came to do, and try to have faith in yourself that this is the right thing for you."

Roni acquiesced, and signed the paper work. The nurse finished the vitals, then escorted her into a sterile procedure room.

Mr. Satler was busy with financial paperwork, and thought he heard a baby wailing outside his window. He got up to look, but when he got there all was quiet. There was no baby. He thought maybe he heard a cat or something, and went back to work. When he sat down he heard it again. This time he bowed his head and asked, "What is it, Lord."

He sat quietly a moment, and felt compelled to pray for Roni and the baby. He got down on his knees to intercede for both of them, and found himself in the midst of a mighty spiritual battle on her behalf. When he finally felt it was okay to stop he called a couple of friends whom he had asked to pray for her, and urged them to pray.

Another had heard the call to prayer, and knelt immediately before the Lord. Dr. Asher was working in his lab doing some research, when his call to prayer came. He didn't know the name but he understood right away that a young girl was in trouble, and needed the Lord to intervene. As he prayed his wife came in, and knelt down in front of him.

"The strangest thing just happened to me," she said. "I was outside pulling weeds up from around the flowers at the fence, and someone in an old pickup truck pulled up, rolled down his window and said, "Excuse me Ma'am."

"I looked up from the flower bed, and saw a young man behind the wheel. He was very polite, and quite innocent looking.

"What is it, son," I asked?

He said, "I am supposed to tell you to pray for Abby."

"Who told you?"

"Don't know who he was," the young man said, "but I saw him when I gassed up a couple of blocks back. He asked if I was passing this way. He said you would be out pulling weeds, and I was to give you that message."

Dr Asher took his wife's hands, bowed his head, and began to pray. He knew that he did not need to know specifics, but prayed none-the-less that the Lord would reveal anything that he needed to know in order to intercede for this stranger. As he began to pray he sensed danger and evil surrounding her. So he began praying through Psalm 18 for a young woman named, Abby, asking God to rescue her out of danger, to devour the work of the enemy in her life, and help her in her time of need.

Roni lay on the exam table wondering how everything that had seemed to be going so right had turned out this way. She and her baby girl had made it safely to this point, and now she was here on this table waiting for the doctor to come in and perform what they called a partial birth abortion. Roni thought back to when her baby had first kicked. She had then made a promise to her to give her life. She talked to her as if she was right in front of her, and told her she would find parents for her that would love and care for her all of her life.

When the team walked into the sterile room of the clinic Roni began to panic. Her heart was pounding, and she was sweating profusely. Her mind was racing trying to unscramble this mess and find a way out of here before it was too late. The nurse came over to inject her with something. She didn't know what it was, but she saw the needle.

"Wait," she said. "What is that? Wait a minute, please. I am not sure I want to do this. Please wait!" She was hyperventilating and beginning to struggle.

"Just hold on, Honey," the nurse said. "It will be fine, but you have to calm down. "It's just because it is your first time, that's all. Once you go through it you won't think it so bad."

"First time?" Roni asked. "Good Lord, are there people who do this many times? Oh, God, help me," she cried out as the nurse injected a sedative into her arm. She watched as that needle went in and the hand of that woman who was behind the needle was suddenly like something out of a horror show. All she could see was the brown age marks on her hands and the accentuated veins that told her age, and these were growing larger as she watched them. Roni shook her head to try to clear up this warped picture, but when she looked up at the nurse's face all she could see was a blank where her face should have been.

"God help me!" She screamed as they began to move quickly, putting her feet in the stirrups. She felt helpless.

"God, I am so sorry! Forgive me! She cried all the louder. "Forgive me and save my baby. God, please help me!"

"Doctor, the patient's heart rate is 160 and rising. What should we do?"

Roni heard those words, but the nurse's voice was as if it came from a tunnel.

The gray haired woman was stroking her arm.

"Calm down, now, just calm down."

"Please let me go. I don't want to do this. Please, I want my baby to live."

"It's too late. The Doctor has already begun."

Roni looked down over the draped white sheet that covered her knees and saw what looked like demons dancing around the doctor's head. There were so many faces in front of her, and they were grouped together, encircled in each other's way like a ball of thorns, poking and screaming at each other as they fought to be on the top part of the circle. Some she could see so clearly. One appeared at first to be the face of a girl, who was gentle and mild looking. As it got closer she saw what looked like tears, but then quickly realized it was blood pouring out from the eyes.

Roni screamed again at the sight of these hideous faces all gnarled and horned. She tried, but couldn't make out the doctor's face. His appearance was hollowed out, empty, and void of any emotion or substance. She glanced at the table next to him and saw what looked like scissors. Shrieks of terror now escaped from her. The demons, the horror, and those horrid scissors—it was all too much.

"No! She screamed again as she took her feet from the stirrups, and kicked off the sheet. No, no, no, I won't let you do this! I can leave now if I want to, and you cannot stop me."

She jumped off the table and grabbed the sheet to wrap around her. They both attempted to get her back on the table, and put her feet back in the stirrups, but she struggled fiercely. She jumped off the table and was looking for the door. Roni looked like a person who was running for her life from a fierce opponent. Panic filled her eyes as they darted around the room looking for an escape.

"Quickly, stop her!" The doctor yelled at the nurse. She has probably already caused enough panic in the waiting room with all of her screaming. If she goes running out of here like that it will cause chaos out there.

The nurse managed to grab Roni's hands.

"Let go of me!" Roni wailed. "I want to leave and you are holding me against my will. Let me go now!"

"I will," the nurse said still holding tightly to both of Roni's hands. "I will let go of your hands and not make you do anything you don't want to do, but I want you to promise you won't run, and that you will calmly listen to me. If after that you want to go, then you can. Do you understand me?"

"Fine," Roni said. "But if I see any indication that you are forcing me again I will scream murder. Do *you* understand?"

The nurse nodded an agreement, and let go of Roni's hands. She was able to calmly talk to her enough and keep her from running out. They sat together on the table as the nurse explained her options.

"You can go if you want, but the doctor has already begun the procedure, which means for you the best course of action would be to finish now".

"No!" Roni snapped. "I want to go. I want to go now!"

"Finally, the nurse conceded. But you do realize you are leave against medical discretion?"

"I don't care. I just want to go, and I want to go *now*!"

Finally the nurse complied.

"Let me get your clothes. Do you have a ride home?"

Roni just shook her head. Who would give her a ride? Then she thought of Mr. Satler, and gave the number to the nurse. To Roni's relief he came quickly to get her. She moved slowly getting dressed because she was so weary from the struggle. She kept wondering what the doctor had done so far. Nothing was explained to her. They just left her here to get dressed. The nurse said there would be a full report in the file, and on her follow up paperwork. She supposed she would read it there. She didn't want to ask any questions. She was too afraid.

The door opened and Roni jumped.

"Your ride is here," the nurse said. "We sent him to the back door so you wouldn't have so far to walk."

"Right," Roni thought. "You just don't want me to go out the front." Roni didn't care how she got out, or what door she used. She just wanted out. The nurse took her to the door in a wheel chair, and stopped near one of the other exam rooms to run back and grab the aftercare report. Roni saw a young girl, about her age sitting up on a table. She was crying. Another nurse was patting her arm.

"It's all over now, Dear." Roni heard her say. "You can go home soon, and start all over with your life. You did well."

Roni thought, *Start over? Did well? How is that? Is it because she didn't struggle? Is it because she acted on something that maybe was forced on her? And how does one start over after bringing a death sentence on her child without the ghost of this place haunting her all the days of her life?*

Roni was sorry for this girl, and as she looked into the room, she prayed for her. The nurse saw Roni peering in, and shut the door.

"Okay, now we have everything," Roni's nurse said and, took her to Mr. Satler, who was waiting at the end of the hall.

"Are you her guardian?" The nurse asked.

Mr. Satler's eyes were all over this place. He wasn't going to offer much information. He knew that he didn't need to. Roni was an adult, and could make choices of her own free will. He was just coming to help.

"No," he said.

"Well," the nurse countered. "Miss Simone, is leaving against medical advice, and has signed a waiver releasing us from any further liability with her or the child. The procedure was incomplete."

"Fine," he said, "Roni, let's go." Mr. Satler looked at her downcast face, and gently stroked her eye that he saw was bruised."

"Did this happen here?"

"No," she said as the tears fell. "Jouda is back. He got out of jail and . . ."

"Shush, no more needs to be said."

He took her arm and led her out the door.

Roni couldn't help but notice that his eyes were on her as she took her place in the front seat with him. This wonderful man had cared so much for her, and she felt ashamed that he had to come here, to see her like this and to know what she had done. She never imagined he would know about all this. She thought she would have to follow through with this secretly, and tell him something to cover it all up.

"Roni, what were you thinking? You had come a long way. Your walk with Christ was becoming so dynamic. What could have urged you here?"

She turned her head to look out the window away from him.

"Fear makes us do all kinds of things."

That fear was still in her. Where did she think she was going to go? Jouda would always find her, and maybe the next time he would kill her? That moment was a standstill for her. What would she do? Where would she go? Would she ever be free from this insanity? Then, suddenly she shrieked as pain struck her, and made her double over.

Gerry Satler's large arm came across to her side as he stopped the car immediately at the sound of her scream.

"Are you okay, Roni? What is it? What did they do in there?"

"I tried to stop them," cried Roni; "but they started the procedure anyway. They wouldn't quit until I fought them so hard they had to let me go."

Another pain came and then more until they were coming one after another. Mr. Satler turned the car in the other direction, and headed for the hospital. By the time they had arrived, Roni could not walk, and he ran in to get help.

"She's in labor," he said breathing hard. "It's too soon."

When Warriors Fall

In no time the medical personnel were out the emergency room door, and in the car helping Roni out onto a gurney. Mr. Satler was behind them. He cared about Roni, and wanted the best for her. He was not leaving her now, not after all that has happened. He was having difficulty breathing as he hurried through the corridors with them, but he managed to keep up anyway.

Roni reached for him.

"My baby, will she live?"

"She?" he asked with a smile. "You never told me it was a girl."

Roni squealed again and bent over with pain.

Mr. Satler hushed her and took hold of her hand.

"Gonna be okay, dear girl, Just hold on a bit longer. It will be okay."

Abiona's Choice

And now says the Lord who formed me in the womb to be His servant, To bring Jacob back to Him, so that Israel might be gathered to Him (For I am honored in the sight of the Lord, and God is my strength), He says it is too small a thing that you should be My servant, to raise up the tribes of Jacob and restore the preserved ones of Israel; I will also make you a light of the nations, so that my salvation shall reach the ends of the earth. Isaiah 49:5-6

This passage is the second of Isaiah's servant songs. It is a song depicting the freedom and redemption offered to God's people. It is one that speaks in a prophetic voice of the one called to deliver God's message, and also of the One who would come to bring the final sacrifice for the redemption of mankind.

It is applied to the life of Abiona because of the nature of the battle that has ensued since the beginning of time. Just as Israel had enemies who wanted to besiege her, so did Abiona have an enemy who wanted to snuff out her light before she ever had a chance to see it.

Some liberty, in application only, has been taken with this passage to merely emphasize that God will lift up whom He chooses, and nothing or no one can stand against Him. It is not meant to take away from the purity of the prophetic voice which points to Jesus Christ as our Savior, rather it is to point us toward being lights, and helping others to be the lights He called us to be unto the ends of the earth.

Born for a Journey

She awoke again from the same nightmare that always left her feeling helpless and agitated. As usual she jumped out of bed and stood on wobbly feet before she was even fully awake. Then she sat back down on the bed inhaling and exhaling slowly to get her breathing back in rhythm again. As she sat there catching her breath and calming herself down, she recounted the dream, wanting to make sure she covered every bit of it. There could be something she was missing, and she couldn't afford to let the smallest detail slip by her. She had to understand this thing that visited her so often in the night, and know why she could not shake it.

Abiona grabbed her pen and paper and began to write the things that were in her dream. She always did this. In fact, her diary was full of the same dream written each time she dreamed it with the date at the top. There were not too many variations, but she was compelled every time to write it out. Today's entry was no different.

Monday, April 5, 2011

I was awakened at 6:45 a.m. by the dream. It is always an invasion to my soul. I cannot figure out why it keeps coming to me, but it comes at least three times every week. Sometimes I relive this nightmare every night.

I always start out in a safe place. It is comfortable and warm, and I am satisfied. I always feel like I am floating and just relaxing, and then something loud invades the peace and quiet. No matter where I move I am hurting. There is no escape from it. Then, suddenly something has hold of me, and it feels like it is trying to rip at me, and pull me apart. There is such an overpowering sense of being pulled away from safety—a horrible pulling, pulling, pulling until finally, I am left in this hollow void of intense pain, and feel I am slowly weakening. Then there is darkness, and more floating.

Finally, I enter another place that is cold. There is more pain and noise. Frightened, I cry out, trying to scream, but cannot. I seem to have no voice at all. There are people all around me, and they are probing me, poking me and sticking sharp needles into my arms and legs. My breathing is labored, and again I try to cry our but cannot. A woman's hand reaches for me, and the diamond on her ring reflects the cold metal around me, creating a rainbow over my head. These hands wrap me in warmth, and surround me.

I know why I have these dreams. I believe I am only remembering the terror of the attempt to take me from my mother's womb, but I must be missing something or they wouldn't keep coming. There must be something more I need to know.

As Abiona wrote again about the dream in her journal, she was looking for something different—a new element that would help her understand what she needed to know. This time as she entered the dream she also wrote a request to God.

Dear Jesus, I had that dream again, and I want you to help me understand why it keeps coming to me. I can't get rid of it so please help me to know what is not yet uncovered.

Then she sat quietly. When the words came she began to write out her thoughts to God in poetic form, with each stanza falling naturally into place for her.

No Hiding Place

Mama can you hear me, a voice had echoed long
I'm helpless here without you, Mama,
Something just went wrong
That drone is in my dream
A distant sound forlorn
I hear a heart beat pulse then fade.
I fear it is my own

My world was quiet mama, now noise is all around
An enemy thrust its weapon in,
No hiding place is found
It tries to pull me out of comfort,
Into a world of fear
Make them stop, protect me!
Mama, can you hear?

A hand reaches out for me, one so kind and warm
The woman now is holding me.
She's hidden me from harm
Mama can you hear me
God says He used her hand
To keep me from destruction,
Mama, do you understand

Mama, I am safe now, and Jesus loves me so
Because of Him I forgive you,
Mama, I wanted you to know

After reading the poem she had penned, she knelt down and prayed a prayer that had become a ritual for her:

"There is victory in Jesus. I may have been hated from the time of my conception, by those who were supposed to love me, but I am loved by God. He is eternally my Father, and will not abandon me."

Abiona was small. She only weighed 90 pounds and stood barely reached 5 feet 2 inches in height. She was very pale, with albino blonde hair that had more white tones than the golden. She had blonde eyelashes and eyebrows. The few freckles that spotted her nose were darker than the typical brownish red freckle. Though her skin was pale, she still had an earthy look that adorned her with a simple beauty.

A senior in high school she was nearing graduation date, and was still trying to decide on colleges. She figured she had probably waited too long, but it didn't matter. She was in no hurry. Abiona thought differently than most seventeen year old girls. She wasn't anxious to get away from home, and didn't mind saying so to her friends. In fact, they often teased her about being a mama's girl. That's because her mother always called her just that—Mama's Girl. Abiona didn't mind the nickname because it was a term of endearment by her mother, but she was proud of her real name. It meant born for a journey, and she determined that as she set out on a new journey in college, that her journey would be worthy of the calling God had placed in her life.

Usually prompt and diligently on time, Abiona was caught off guard when she heard her mother coming up the stairs.

"Abiona," she called. "Abiona, it's time to go to church."

Abiona jumped off of her bed.

"Church, oh no! Where did the morning go? I can't believe I have sat her for two hours not doing anything but daydreaming. What was I thinking?"

The door opened and her mother was standing there looking somewhat surprised that Abiona was still in her pajamas.

"Abby, are you not feeling well? Why aren't you dressed? Should I call the doctor?"

"No, Mom, I am doing alright."

Abiona got up and walked over to her dresser.

"Sorry, I have been daydreaming. I can be ready in ten minutes."

Skylor walked over to her daughter and put her hands on her shoulders.

When Warriors Fall

"The dream again, Isn't it?"

"Yes, I . . ."

Abiona stopped because what she saw stirred her heart. The diamond in her mother's ring reflected off of the silver tray on her dresser, and it created the most beautiful rainbow. Instantly Abiona ran to the journal she had recorded in this morning.

"How did I miss it," she said shaking.

"Miss what, dear. What are you looking for?"

"I think I found the missing piece, mom. The rainbow of your ring reminded me that the person who comforted me when I was born had a diamond that created a rainbow. I never saw that before, but this time it was there in my dream. The diamond on her hand created the beautiful rainbow just like yours did." Her voice trailed off a bit.

"Mom?"

"Abiona, when I told you that we had adopted you, and that you were an abortion survivor, I had always hoped that would be enough. But I see plainly that there is more that I need to say now. We need to sit down."

"What about church?" Abiona asked.

"We'll just go to the next service. I think we need to have this conversation now."

They sat on the edge of the bed as Skylor began to unfold the rest of Abiona's story.

"When you were born, I was not a Christian, nor was I married. I was fresh out of nursing school and could only find part time work at the hospital in obstetrics. It was a job that was strictly an on-call position and I didn't get called in that much. So, to supplement my income, I took a job at the local abortion center. I needed desperately to work, but it seemed nothing steady was available for me except this abortion clinic. They hired me even though I refused to be a part of the abortion procedure. I was not a Christian then, but I just could not bear to be a part of such a thing. The position was for a nurse in after care for the women who came in, and somehow that justified it in my mind.

The day I saw your mother come in my heart broke. She was so young and vulnerable."

"Wait!" said Abiona. "You know my mother? Do you know where she is now?"

"Yes, I knew her, and no I don't know where she is, and I do need to finish."

Abiona nodded and buried her face in the pillow as her mother finished.

"Anyway," Skylor continued. "Your mom was too far along to be having that procedure but they attempted it anyway. I remember going into the restroom and crying as I saw them take your mom into the procedure room. I went to check on your mom to take her vital signs, and when I went into the room she begged me to help her. She said she didn't want to do this, but couldn't leave that place and still be pregnant, because she was sure her boyfriend would kill her. I ignored her pleas. I thought, *what could I do?*"

That didn't set well with me. I believed abortion was wrong, but I chose to do nothing to help your mom. I just told her I needed to collect her personal belongings before the procedure, and put them in a safe place. I hate to admit it, but I chose to turn my head and allow what would happen in the next hour, because I was too selfish and too afraid to help.

After hearing a lot of commotion and screaming I was told that the procedure had failed, and that your mom was leaving. I went to get her personal possessions. Your mama dressed. She was crying profusely, and said not one word to me. She waited on someone to pick her up, and then left with him. She left still pregnant with you. Before the procedure went too far she made them quit. She couldn't go through with it.

This ring was part of her personal effects, but it fell out of the bag. I put it in my pocket and determined to look her up, and give her the ring back myself.

I knew the abortion was not successful, and that your mom had asked to leave against medical advice. That was when I too left that place. I left that job, and what I thought was a step for my career that day."

Skylor stopped talking and began crying as she remembered those days. She needed to stop a moment to be able to speak again.

"I'm sorry, mama, you can stop now if you need to."

"No, I should finish."

Skylor cleared her throat and continued.

"As God would have it, fifteen minutes after I left that clinic I received a call from the hospital where I worked part time. They had two delivery nurses out sick and needed me there right away. So I went. When I arrived, I checked in, and it was then that I saw your mother. I soon learned that the abortion attempt and the trauma from the clinic had caused her to go into labor, and I was to assist with the after care in your delivery."

Skylor began playing with the ring on her finger as she relived the moment she was sharing with Abiona.

"As I waited for you to come into this world, I remembered I had stuck that ring in my pocket, and took it out to look at it for a moment. I remember thinking how beautiful it was and wondered, if there was something special about it. Then, the announcement came for IC Unit. That was my cue. Unconsciously I placed the ring on my finger.

I came in that room, forgetting the ring was still on my finger, and picked you up off that cold tray where they were poking and prepping you as they would any premature baby. I wrapped you in a warm blanket and whispered in your ear that you would be okay. Then I went home, still in possession of that ring.

Later I learned that your mom's landlord, Mr. Satler, took the two of you to a place called *Wonderful Life Ministries*. She had to be in a safe place because your father wanted you dead, and she needed to hide herself and you."

Skylor watched Abiona as she explained this part. It had to be a hard blow to know that your father wanted you dead, but Abiona didn't seem to internalize it at all.

"I know that is not comforting information."

"Oh, you mean that my dad wanted me dead," Abby asked without even blinking an eye. "That's really not new news, mom. Abortion has murder written all over it."

Skylor watched Abiona carefully. Taking a deep breath she continued.

"The man who ran the ministry was Doctor Asher, a retired family practitioner who had committed his life and work to helping young women like your mom to heal, and get back on their feet. He and his wife had helped to stabilize your mother's health, but more than that they gave her a new start in life.

Being a Preemie you had to stay in the hospital a while longer, and then came to stay with your mom at the ministry house. Both of you stayed there almost six months. I came daily to help them monitor your progress. I initially went there to give this ring, back and to see you again, but I found the people there were wonderful, so I kept coming back offering my services. I remember being amazed from the very beginning about this man and woman and their ministry, because they had prayed for you by name before they even knew you. When you came in with your mom, Dr. Asher had asked if she had named you.

She told him she had named you Abby, and the full name was Abiona because it meant one who is born for a journey. And when she said that the doctor stopped what he was doing, and turned to look at his wife. Then his wife took your hand, and told you all would be well. She told you that Lord had gone ahead of you, and they knew this because God had led them to pray for a girl named Abby before she came to them. This drew me in, and I wanted to know more about a God who cared so much for an unborn child."

"That makes me feel pretty special right now," Abiona said interrupting her mother.

"You know," Skylor said, "As I watched them care for you and your mom, it drew me even more to Christ and I became a Christian. I became engaged during that time to your dad, who served at the ministry house."

"Yeah," said Abiona. "I know about the ministry house and how you met dad there, but why didn't you ever tell me all this?"

Skylor didn't answer her question directly, but continued to tell the whole story.

"Your mom, Roni Simone, wanted to put you up for adoption because she felt the shame of trying to abort you and didn't think she could ever look you in the eye when you grew up. Mostly, though it was because she feared for your life. She asked if I would be your mother, since you were already attached to me. So, as soon as your dad and I married we adopted you. Your mom left town after that and I don't know where she went. But before she left she asked that I would someday give you this ring. She wanted me to tell you how sorry she was, and that she loved you very much."

Abiona's tears were falling silently on the pillow as she held it close to her heart."

"And what about my dad, do you know where he is? Does he still want me dead?"

Skylor paused a long moment. "Abby, your father is dead. He was killed in a drive by shooting just shortly after we adopted you. He will never be able to harm you."

Skylor took the ring off of her finger, and held it out to her daughter.

"Abby, I found out that the ring belonged to Roni's mother—your grandmother. Roni got it after her mom was killed in a car wreck. She felt you should have it. I guess I was waiting for the right time to tell you all of this, and give you the ring. And it seems the time is now. Do you want it?"

Abiona took the ring. "She really did love me, didn't she?"

Diverging Paths

A TALE OF TWO MOTHERS

Damiria

Gentle Girl

He will redeem my soul in peace from the battle which is against me, for they are many who strive with me. Psalm 55:18 (NASB)

Mariel

For She is Bitter

Death and destruction are never satisfied, and neither are human eyes. Proverbs 27:20

Cries behind the Veil

Damiria was gentle and soft spoken. She never interjected an opinion other than when asked, and she tried hard to go unnoticed whenever she entered a room. Her short black hair hung longer on one side, and fell so often into her eyes, that she just let it hang there. She was comfortable with it covering her eyes. At nineteen she felt old and ugly, and those feelings crippled her. Most of the time, she just wanted to hide. She tried to keep behind an unseen door those things that were too painful to share with anyone, but keeping them buried was killing her.

"Honestly," she said to the counselor. "I don't know which is worse—hiding these feelings or bringing them out. How do you reconcile killing your own child? It was just always easier for me to hide and pretend it never happened. I have tried to reason that it was not a baby, but I know better. When I was a kid, I always dreamed of that perfect home with a husband who loved me. I wanted a big family, but now it seems I have ruined that. Who would want me now?"

The counselor leaned forward in her chair.

"I want to recommend a recovery home for you, Damiria. I am concerned about your eating disorder. Pain that you have not dealt with is taking a toll on you, and I am not sure you can mend on your own. I think you need to act soon. You look frail, and the direction you are heading will lead you right into the doors of a hospital emergency room. This recovery home will help you with some of these things I can't touch. They have helped many young women recover from the trauma of abortion, plus they can walk you through this problem you have with eating. I am going to have my secretary give you their information when you leave. Will you contact them?"

Damiria sniffed and wiped her nose with the palm of her hand.

"Okay, I will," she said. Then, she left the counselor's office, and did not even stop at the front desk to pick up the information. She knew, even as she promised to contact this home, that she would not do it. She didn't really want to change her eating habits. She could not control the cries that often came in the middle of the night, but eating was one thing she *could* control. She was too thin, and she knew it was her own fault, which is why she sought out a counselor. She didn't understand herself. She wanted help, but at the same time she didn't want to change. This issue she had with food was no stranger to her. She knew it was a problem, but thought that maybe she deserved it.

Anorexia, she thought. *How in the world did I get here?*

This was something she didn't want her parents to know. They didn't need another thing to be ashamed of concerning her life. Still, she realized that they probably knew something. How could they not know? She was so thin and sickly looking. She figured they didn't want to ask because if she told them she had an eating disorder that they would not be able to handle it.

She took her time getting home and found herself daydreaming way too much during that long drive. She had passed by her favorite coffee shop, and had no memory of the drive up to this point. No one to talk to, and no one to share the day with left her feeling alone again. She was glad that she did not live with her parents anymore, but she hated being alone. As she entered her apartment she wished life was different. The silence was too much for her to bear. She turned on the TV to get some sound that would fill up the room, and take the edge off of the stillness. She passed by the kitchen, and went straight to the leather couch in the living room to stretch out and relax. The drone of the TV hummed as she drifted off to sleep. Sleep was the only thing that felt right to her, except times like now when she had the nightmare.

The dream haunted her again. She heard a baby crying and got up to go to him. As she neared the nursery the cries got louder, and when she opened the door she saw a baby boy in his bed with a purple veil dangling in front of him. The veil looked like a silk curtain, and it blew as if there was a gentle breeze entering in behind it. Above the veil, on the wall, there was a portrait of the dead body of Jesus as he was being taken down from the cross. An inscription was written in gold at the bottom of the picture that said, He *was led like a lamb to the slaughter but he opened not his mouth*. As always, desperation arose in the midst of that dream and urged her toward the veil to get to that crying baby, but when she pulled back the curtain she woke up.

Her heart pounded with anxiety, and she reached for her anxiety medication that was on the table beside her and washed it down with the half empty glass of wine left from the night before.

"God, why won't You help me!" she cried as she grabbed the bottle, and took another pill. She continued pushing the pills down her throat until the bottle was empty.

"There, God, I did it. Everyone keeps telling me that you love me, and that you died for me. So, I guess if you think I am worth anything, then you will come and save me. If you don't, then I will be with my baby at last. Maybe now I can get behind that veil."

She went to the refrigerator and took out the wine bottle. Not bothering to even pour it in a glass, she drank the remainder of the wine.

"Maybe I will pass out before I die, and not feel anything. I just don't want to feel anything anymore."

Damiria pulled back the long side of her hair and tucked it behind her ear as she wrote her note.

Don't really want to die. I just want my baby back. God help me! - Damiria

She folded the note, and shoved it under the door to her apartment, so that it lay out in the hallway. She was having trouble breathing, and went back over to the couch to lie down.

"So this is it. No one will see that in time. I am just going to die. She felt weak, and then became confused and disoriented. The fear of dying began to make her panic, and she jumped up off of the couch. Staggering, she opened the door, grabbed the note from the floor, and ran out to the street. Holding the note in her hand she screamed, "Does anybody care about me?" Then she passed out falling in a heap on the ground.

In that place between life and death Damiria once again heard the baby crying. She walked toward the sound of that cry and saw the crib behind the veil and an oil painting of Christ being taken from the cross. She watched her own movement, as if seeing from outside of herself, as she moved toward the crib. With each step drawing closer the terror began to overtake her. She saw him, her baby was standing up in the crib, and his arms were outstretched. He was crying, and she began moving toward him to take him out of the bed to comfort him, but she couldn't move. Demons came in poking and picking at her, grabbing her hair and dragging her away so she could no longer see the picture of Christ. A ray of light came down from heaven looking like a life line being tossed to her in the midst of this deadly array of turmoil. She grabbed hold of it, but struggled to keep it in her hand. She fought off arrows that were aimed at her heart, and demonic hands that reached out to grab her. She screamed all the while, desperately trying to hold on to the cord of light as her oppressors closed in to take her into the dark world. Then, suddenly the noise and the clamor ceased as the fight within her gave way and she began to let go of the light. Succumbing to the darkness she found herself drifting toward a dark figure, whose hands were opened, and inside of them were the drugs.

"No!" she cried out. "God have mercy on me. I am sorry, please rescue me!"

Darkness kept pressing in, and surrounded her until she no longer saw anything but ugly creatures glaring at her through shadows of despair, grief and emptiness. The dark figure grabbed her arm. She couldn't see its form except for the hand that took hold of her. It was filled with sores that looked like burns that opened into festering cavities, but no blood was in them. She screamed as the sinister spirit drug her toward a black veil that hung dormant in front of a raging fire. As they drew closer the fire got hot, and she began to hear the sound of chanting. It was a mantra that droned out the ancient names of the gods of death and Hades.

"No, No, No!" She screamed. "Lord, I want to change, please come in and help me. Save me from that thing behind that curtain. I promise I will serve you. Just help me."

They drew her closer to the edge, and she felt the fire spitting out from behind the curtain. The smell of her own singeing hair filled her nostrils, as sizzling flames lapped up the air near her head. Now on her knees, with her face to the floor she cried out in anguish.

"Jesus, have mercy on me!" She cried out the name of Jesus over and over again.

Suddenly she saw the shadow of the cross of Christ emerge above her. It surmounted that dark figure that was pulling at her, and blood from that cross began to drip onto her head and covering her, and spilling onto the shadows that were pulling her into the flames. At this, the enemy was compelled to let go.

"She's back," the paramedic said, "now let's get her stabilized and to the hospital so we can get the drugs out of her system"

He touched his partner's shoulder. "Thanks for praying, it made a difference for this one."

Damiria woke up in the hospital, and quietly looked around the room. The gray walls were accented with medical charts, and a white board listing the names of the attending staff. The beep of the monitors sounded distant, and the IV Drip felt cold entering in through her hand. When she saw Abiona she gasped.

"Are you an angel? Am I in heaven" she asked? "Is my baby here?"

Abiona did not show her amusement that this young woman had thought she was an angel. She sensed the gravity of the thought process that was taking place and wanted to enter into this woman's life unobtrusively. She was careful not to do or say anything that would push her away.

"Damiria, my name is Abiona. I am here to help get you through this. You are in the hospital ICU."

"Hospital, why am I . . . ?"

She remembered that final thought before unconsciousness.

"Somebody does care," she said looking up at the ceiling.

"Yes," Abiona said. "Someone does love you. You just rest for now. I will be here until you are awake enough, and are able to talk. There is so much good ahead for you."

"Good, for me?"

Abiona took a heated blanket that the nurse's aide had brought in, and covered Damiria with it. She began tucking her in, trying to comfort her with songs of hope. Damiria wrestled her arm free from underneath the covers, and grabbed Abiona's arm.

Wide-eyed and panic-stricken, she squeezed painfully hard. Abiona winced, but did not let on that it hurt, because she sensed something coming. She was afraid if she did anything that Damiria would not talk.

"I was in Hell!" Damiria's look was intense and she searched Abiona's face to see her response, but Abiona didn't budge.

Damiria peered intensely into Abiona's eyes.

"Did you hear me? I said I was in Hell."

"I heard you, dear," Abiona said smiling. "I was just trying to determine if you were saying this in the literal sense or not."

"Believe me it was literal. I was in the very grips of Hell. It was frightening. Darkness was all around me, trying to pull me away from the light. Please tell me. What do you know about Hell?"

Abiona thought for a minute how to respond. She wanted this young woman to rest, and to not talk about things that would stir her emotions so much.

"I know Hell is a real place where a person is tormented, and separated from God for eternity. I know about Hell, but I would rather tell you about Heaven right now. Could I do that instead?"

Damiria nodded an affirmation so Abiona continued.

"Heaven is a place where there are no more tears. It is place where you don't have to fear darkness, and don't need external lights, because Jesus is there. He is all the light you need. It is a place where we will live in peace and unity with the Lord, Jesus Christ."

"I know about Heaven," Damiria interjected. "My parents brought me up in church. The church taught me so much. There were so many people there that loved the Lord, and taught me to love Him as well. Those first thirteen years of my life were so wonderful. I wish I could go back"

"What happened after thirteen years," Abiona asked.

"I got pregnant. There was a new family who came in to our church. Their son was sixteen and I couldn't resist him. She took a deep breath and finished. I was angry because people only saw me as the deacon's daughter and not as a person. I just messed up, that's all. Only one time and I got pregnant. Of course, as far as my parents were concerned no one could know that that the *deacon's* daughter had stepped so far out of line. So my parents insisted that I get an abortion. I was just too young and really had no argument. So I did it. I went to the clinic, and got an abortion."

Damiria waited to see how Abiona would react, but she just listened. There was no outward response, but inside Abiona was screaming, because she hated what this had done to Damiria's life. She had to fight back the strong emotion that stirred from being a product of the lie that says abortion is acceptable. Abby's countdown for peace began, and before she responded to the pain in this girl's heart, she silently prayed a quick prayer asking for wisdom.

"We will talk more in the days to come, but for now, let's pray for peace and forgiveness so that you can rest, and gain momentum for change. Have you ever asked God to forgive you for this?"

"No, why would He forgive me? I am not worth His time."

"He can and will forgive you if you ask Him. Have you ever asked Him to be your Savior?"

"No," Damiria said as she reached for the tissue box on the bed tray beside her. "I have always felt like I wasn't worth saving."

"Well," Abiona said, tucking in the blanket around her, "Let's just pray about that. You are worth saving, and I will ask the Lord to show you how much he loves you. For now just get some rest. Sleep, Damiria, we will talk later."

Abiona prayed, and then headed over to turn off the light.

"Leave it on," Damiria said.

Abiona kept the light on and quietly turned to leave.

"I will be back tomorrow," she said. "Please rest and don't worry."

Damiria was hesitant to close her eyes. The fear of reliving that time in between death and life unnerved her. The thought that she would again see her baby, and not be able to reach him made her anxious.

"What is it?" Abiona asked.

"I don't know how to let this go. There is something missing, something I need to do now, but I don't know what that is. Can you help me? Please don't go yet."

Abiona realized that for Damiria today was the day of her salvation, and she took her by the hand and said, "Just pray what I pray."

Damiria nodded her head. "Alright, I will."

And in the next few moments they prayed a prayer of forgiveness and repentance, and Damiria accepted Christ as her Savior.

"Could we do one more thing?" Abiona asked. "It might be a little painful at first, but I think in the end it will be a great benefit for you, and help you to rest."

"What is it?"

Abiona but pressed on.

"Before I go, I would like for you to name your baby."

"Name him! Why?"

"It will help you to make his life and death more personal, and enable you to grieve properly. Trust me. This will be of great benefit for you."

Damiria stammered as she tried to speak through her pain.

"Well, there is a name that I love. It is an African name that means *one who forgives*. I saw it in a story I just read about a man who tried to live out the meaning of this name in his life. The name is Mohari. Do you think it's a good one?"

"I think it is perfect," Abiona said. "Mohari is a good name. Now try to rest. We will talk more in the days ahead."

Silence in the Dark

Mariel sat on the exam table waiting for the doctor to come in and give her the final exam that would determine if she could leave yet. She felt nauseous. She couldn't believe that they actually made her look at the baby and all the parts to confirm that everything had been extracted. That picture kept coming back to her. Her child lay on a sterile table in front of her, dead and dismembered. She began rocking back and forth on the table holding her arms up as if cuddling a small baby. She rocked and cried, and then began screaming. Her screams brought two nurses running toward the room.

"Not again," the older nurse said as she opened the door to the room. "I have already had to endure too many of these cases today. I sure hope this is not going to be another one."

Mariel sat on the exam table, the fingertips of her hands were pressed into her temples and she continued rocking and screaming. Nurse Rhoda nodded to the aide to go to the other side of the exam table. It was a precaution they often took with potential crisis cases. As they both came toward the head of the table Mariel rocked more furiously, and screamed louder than before. Rhoda took hold of her hand, patting the top of it.

"It's okay," she said trying to calm her. But Mariel kept rocking and screaming.

"Look at him," she cried.

"Who," asked Rhoda? "Who is it you want me to look at?"

"My baby, Perdu, look at him lying there. He is losing blood, and his arm is missing. Can you find it? Please help my son?"

Rhoda nodded again to the aide. "Wait here with her, and don't let her get up. I am going to get the doctor so he can prescribe a sedative."

While she was gone Mariel had quit screaming, but her trauma remained. She scooped up the tissue paper that covered the exam table, and fluffed it up as she would a blanket. Then, she gathered the paper into her arms, and began to rock back and forth singing lullabies.

"This is my son," she said looking up from the paper she had bunched into her arms. "I named him Perdu. What do you think? Do you like it?"

"It's a nice name," the aide said looking at the door, and hoping the nurse and the doctor would enter soon. This was beginning to get too creepy, and she was ready to call it a day. There was too much mayhem for one day.

When Rhoda came in Mariel had taken the wadded up paper that only a few minutes ago stood to represent her child, and had thrown it toward the door.

"I'm an idiot," Mariel yelled as she stood up daring the nurse to tell her to sit back down. She stood for a few minutes. Then she quietly sat in the chair across from the exam table. Rhoda went over to her, patted her head, and sat there for a minute before she spoke. When she felt that the time was right she began to help Mariel up out of the chair, and back onto the exam table.

"The doctor wants you to rest, and he has ordered some medicine that will help. Can we do that for you now?"

"I guess," Mariel responded bitterly.

Rhoda gave her an injection, and had her lay back on the table.

"Your ride is here and waiting for you in the lobby. Do you want him to come back here with you?"

Mariel said nothing. She just lay there staring at the ceiling.

Rhoda again looked across at the aide who nodded as if she already knew what she was to do. She grabbed a warm blanket and laid it gently across Mariel covering her up to her neck.

"When you feel ready just let us know," Rhoda said. "We will get you dressed, and call for the wheel chair to take you to the door. Then you can leave. We will call and check on you in a couple of days. I will leave your home care instructions in your folder. Be sure to take it home."

Mariel laid her head back onto the exam table and stared at the light above her. That last word spoken by the nurse repeated in her brain. The sedative was beginning to take effect, but there was still the wrestling of her spirit that would not let her go. She watched as shadows were cast toward the darker side of the room where a small light hung over the instrument table. Just before dropping into a deep sleep she swore she saw a cradle being rocked in that corner, and she simply turned her head away.

"I don't want to see anymore," she whispered as she covered her head. "I have seen enough. Please, don't make me look at anything else."

After an hour had passed Rhoda came in to try to wake Mariel. Her ride had been waiting, and there were no more patients in the clinic. She figured that Mariel would leave drowsy, but she needed to get her up and going.

"Mariel, you need to wake up, Dear. Your ride is here, and waiting to take you home. Come on, now, let's sit you up and get you ready. You should be able to travel now without any difficulty."

Mariel opened her eyes, but she was distant. She stared off to the other side of the room, as if something there held her attention. She said nothing, but just sat on the table.

"I am going to get your wheel chair. Can you sit here by yourself while I go get it, or should I call for the aide?"

"I am fine," Mariel droned.

Rhoda hesitated. This was probably the most severe case she had ever seen. It was not something that she had dealt with on her own before, and she wasn't sure about this girl. She considered calling in the aide, but instead left her alone to go get the wheel chair.

"I want you to just sit there till I return, okay? I want to help you off the table, so just wait there for me. I won't be long."

Rhoda hurried to get the chair, and when she returned she found Mariel just as she had left her, unemotional and very detached. She wondered if this girl had brought with her a lot of psychological baggage. Rhoda reflected that when she came in for the abortion she was very quiet and timid, but she reasoned she had seen many young women who were timid and reserved, although none had reacted like this. Many were so young that timidity was almost expected. A stab of regret pierced her. How young some of these women were! A fleeting thought ran through her that so many of them need direction in life, and this usually stiff-necked nurse felt the sting of teaching them how to use every possible means to destroy the people in your life.

Rhoda took a deep breath. She was feeling the heartache arising. She hurried out of the room and leaned against the closed door to collect her emotions. She surmised that she was the head nurse and could not be seen with any display of emotional unease. Straightening her posture she pressed her hair back away from her forehead and struggled to take another deep breath, but the anxiety was too much. The years of this kind of work was taking a toll on her, and until now she was unaware of it.

"Lord, what am I doing to these girls?"

Rhoda looked down the hallway back and forth hoping no one would come by at this moment, but then suddenly she called out for help as she felt things begin to take a turn for the worse. Her heart was racing and she was hyperventilating. She felt like she would pass out. Rhoda grabbed her chest, and screamed out in pain as the choking sensation gripped her with fear.

The aide was coming down the hall with the clothes for Mariel when she saw Rhoda in distress. Calling for the doctor, she dropped the clothes and ran to call an ambulance. Rhoda's distress did not subside and fear was beginning to take over. She screamed out for help just as the paramedics arrived.

As they were preparing to take her to the ambulance, the clinic doctor covered her with one of their warm blankets to help ease the chills and shaking.

"Was it a heart attack?" the aide asked him.

"No, I don't think so," the doctor said as he watched them take her out the doors. "I've seen this before. I think it was a panic attack. It looked like a pretty bad one too. She may not be coming back to work again. Let's get the patient sent home and call it a day."

The aide grabbed the clothes and opened the door to the room, only to find the room was empty. The supply cabinet had been ransacked, and emptied, with gauze, scissors and tape scattered all over the floor. A baby blanket had been stuffed in an empty box with a pair of medical shears sticking inside of it.

"Doctor, doctor!" the aide called out running down the hallway. "She is gone, she is gone. The patient is gone!"

Silent Cries

Silent cries make their way,
Down the hallways of despair
They leave the souls of innocent babes
And pierce the heart that snuffed their lives

To the Warrior Fighting Abortion

Those Who Have Seen the Veil

Where can I begin to enter in for the one who has experienced abortion? I lost two children to miscarriage. One was a boy, which was actually my second miscarriage. I was sixteen weeks when I lost him and I mourned greatly over his loss. I named him Benjamin, which means *beloved son*.

The first one was the most devastating because I felt that I was responsible. I was sixteen, and about six weeks pregnant when it happened. Although I was scared, I had every intention of keeping the baby, but I was a young teenager who had been wounded from an early age. I thought I had the capacity to love, but I lacked the heart of sacrifice it took to genuinely love this child. As a result, I lost my baby due to reckless behavior. A night out, and a bottle of gin is what I believed destroyed my first child. Two days after drinking too much, and stumbling and falling, I sat on the couch in my living room in intense pain as I waited for the passing of my child. My father, who was inebriated, sat beside me telling me that we would keep the baby, but because of his drunken state he had no idea that the baby was not going to make it. The more he cried about my being pregnant, the more disdain I felt for having done such a reckless thing that caused me to miscarry. I felt I had killed my child. I immediately shoved the emotions somewhere deep inside, but they eventually emerged again in my life, and nearly crippled my ability to love others and love God. Years later I named this child. It was the beginning of healing for me in doing this. I named him Mohari—the one who forgives.

If you are reading this and have had an abortion, let me say that even with my personal experience, I cannot pretend to know your pain. The angst created by the severing of mother and child in any instance can be almost unbearable. And to know it was by your own hand, and personal choice creates a whole new set of emotions.

If you are fighting with the pain of having an abortion I would encourage you to do all you can to bring restoration to your heart, soul and mind. It begins in the heart with a relationship with Jesus Christ. Only He can take all the brokenness of your heart, and restore you. If you have never had that relationship now is the time to ask Jesus to forgive you and to turn away from old ways. Let Him give you His ways.

If you are a Christian who has had an abortion, don't let the enemy tell you that you are finished. Let Jesus pick up the brokenness, and give you a new start, but don't stop there. Dig deep and find out what it is that pulled you away from Him, and begin to work there for change.

Receive the forgiveness, and forgive yourself. This is the beginning of restoring your soul. That inner presence of the Holy Spirit can rejuvenate you. Call out for a fresh outpouring, and allow the Lord to change you from the inside out. Feed on the words of the Psalmist for a while as you strengthen yourself in God's word.

Finally, when you feel the healing is there for you, begin to seek the counsel of the Lord to discover those things that need to be renewed in your thinking. Destructive thoughts of any kind can lead you away from Jesus at any time. So they need to go. Your mind is the battlefield where the enemy encamps against you. You must be strategic in your fight for restoration. Know your enemy, and how he plays in your thinking. Know your mind, your fears, thoughts and temptations, and as you fight, take a battle buddy with you. Let someone know the battles you face, and pray.

Prayer is a mighty weapon in the hand of any warrior. Pray God's word, because then your weapon becomes alive in the power and might of God.

To the warrior, who may be just entering this battle of the mind: Don't allow the enemy to isolate you, and hem you into place where you hear only his lies. Your child is fearfully and wonderfully made. Don't give in to fear. Instead give way to God.

Reaneva Ashanti

STRUGGLES WITH PEOPLE

Two men went up into the temple to pray, one a Pharisee and the other a tax collector. The Pharisee, standing by himself, prayed thus: 'God, I thank you that I am not like other men, extortioners, unjust, adulterers, or even like this tax collector. I fast twice a week; I give tithes of all that I get. Luke 18:10-12

Little Foxes

Little foxes spoil the fruit
Now ripening on the vine
I'll meet my Lord in midst the vineyard
And together we chase them out
The spoilers of my life

Little foxes who bring to ruin
Allow no blossom to bear its fruit
I'll tuck my budding shoot in His vineyard
And He will hide me from them
The spoilers of my life

Little foxes run about
Mouths agape for my demise
I'll take the hand of my Beloved
And he will bring to ruin the foxes
The spoilers of my life

Catch the foxes for us, the little foxes that spoil the vineyards, for our vineyards are in blossom. Songs of Solomon 2:15

Not Like Her

It was a new day for Damiria. She was told that her recovery was complete, and she was finally leaving rehabilitation. She was excited about entering into a new life where there was freedom and peace, but there was also a bit of fear of the unknown. She was able to face it by the help of her friend, Abby. In gratitude, Damiria looked up to the heavens, and once again thanked God for Abiona, who came at a time when she desperately needed someone. She walked out of the doors of the Oakland Heights Christian Center for Women's Mental Health, and saw Abby waiting in the parking lot for her.

There were many emotional impasses that Damiria had to work through in order to be released, and she had struggled through them all. In many cases she realized that she had pressed through only by the grace of God. There were still other things she had yet to work through, but the center felt that these things were not life-threatening and needed to be worked out over time, and in the process of everyday life.

Two really difficult tasks lay ahead of her. One was to talk openly to her parents about insisting she have an abortion, and to seek a heart of forgiveness concerning them. She felt that she was able to forgive them for the most part, but there was still some animosity that their greatest concern was to cover up the sin of their daughter. She wanted them to care more for her welfare, and the welfare of this child who was now forever gone from them.

She did not want to move back home, but was not ready to be on her own either. Abiona had told her about a place called *Wonderful Life Ministries* where she could live until she was able to find a job, and get on her feet again, Damiria decided this was the better option for her as she was reintegrating into a normal life.

The second task was to go back to her parents' church for a while. She didn't completely understand why her therapist kept insisting this should be part of her transition back into the real world. She would have preferred to just start over somewhere else, and forget the horror of that time in her life. She reasoned that so far everything her counselors had her walk through had enabled her to reach this place of healing in Christ. So she would do what they asked.

As Damiria walked toward the parking lot she noticed the sun shining through the trees, and spreading rays over the place where Abby stood waiting for her. She delighted in the beauty of the day, and was amused at how much of that beauty seemed to hover over her friend. She thought maybe it was because Abby meant so much to her. Yet, she knew there was a touch of God on her life, and she was thankful to have such a friend.

Abby hugged Damiria, and pulled back the hair from her eyes.

"You look great," she said. "It is really good to see you looking so fresh and healthy."

Damiria sighed and smiled timidly.

"I gained some weight in there."

"Yes, you have, and it looks good on you. Get in. We will go get some lunch before I take you to the ministry house."

Abby knew that Damiria was to continue applying normal eating habits. The counselors told her it would be helpful to go out to eat once in a while, so it would begin to normalize eating around other people, which was something she had avoided.

"Good, I'm hungry," Damiria said. "I am anxious to move on with my life, so let's get going."

> *"But at my stumbling they rejoiced and gathered; they gathered together against me; wretches whom I did not know tore at me without ceasing; like profane mockers at a feast, they gnash at me with their teeth Let them be put to shame and disappointed altogether who rejoice at my calamity! Let them be clothed with shame and dishonor who magnify themselves against me!" Psalm 35:15-16*

Reaneva sat in the restaurant with her husband in silence. She stirred and poked at her salad wondering how to bring up the discontentment she was feeling in the marriage. She didn't talk at all, but she continued to look into her coffee cup and every once in a while she sighed to let her husband know she was not very happy.

"What's wrong," he asked, bending his head down to be able to look at her face.

"Oh, it's nothing really. I'm okay, Will."

"Right," he answered. "As sure as my name is Wilfred, you are not okay. I have heard those sighs way too many times. So, there are two choices here. Either we talk about what is bothering you, or you need to quit sighing."

"Fine, I will quit sighing then," she said, but she sighed one last time. Reaneva picked up her coffee, sipping it, and ignoring her husband. Her eyes were surfing the restaurant as she drank her coffee. It was an obvious way to avoid him. She didn't want to look at him, but all the while she desired that he would see her. Even though she wanted to ignore him, she edged in closer when she saw Damiria walk in with Abiona.

"Oh my word, I never thought I would see *her* again!"

Wilfred looked up, and knowing immediately who she was talking about, he tried to change the subject before the tittle-tattle began.

"So, how is your salad? You are picking a bit at it. Was it not very good?"

Reaneva ignored his questions.

"Don't you know who she is?"

"Neva," he pleaded. "Don't go there. Gossip doesn't look good on you. It isn't worth the price you will pay in the long run."

"Price *I* will pay? I am not the one who got pregnant when she was thirteen. And she was the deacon's daughter too. What a disgrace it must have been for them."

As Reaneva stared at Damiria, she ignored the twinge in her heart, and the small voice that whispered, *Judge not.* She continued the negative slander in spite of it.

"I mean, look at her coming in here like she has never done anything wrong—smiling, laughing and chattering away with her friend. Who is that person with her anyway? I have never seen her before."

Wilfred stopped her.

"Oh, and you have never done anything wrong in your Christian life, huh? Come on now, change the subject. Don't you have enough things to talk about without passing judgment on someone else, and using their downfalls as a means to make you feel better about yourself?"

Reaneva continued, "Ha, downfalls? I think you mean sin, don't you? I just think she should be ashamed of herself." As Reaneva spoke more words of scandal, a heavenly host was awakened. The blast of the shofar was blown by the mighty angels of God, and a pronouncement was spoken by authorities above.

> *"Stop judging so that you will not be judged. Otherwise, you will be judged by the same standard you use to judge others. The standards you use for others will be applied to you. So why do you see the piece of sawdust in another believer's eye and not notice the wooden beam in your own eye? How can you say to another believer, 'Let me take the piece of sawdust out of your eye,' when you have a beam in your own eye? You hypocrite! First remove the beam from your own eye. Then you will see clearly to remove the piece of sawdust from another believer's eye.* [10]

"She's been gone a while you know? I heard that she has been in rehab. In fact, I was told that she tried to kill herself. How can you be a Christian and go so low? To me it is unheard of. You either trust Christ or you don't."

Reaneva continued her barrage, shaking her head, as her tongue kept wagging. As she was still going on about Damiria's life, she once again paused as the Holy Spirit nudged her, but once again she ignored the urging of God. As she continued her offense against Damiria, she sank lower into the selfish and insensitive person that she had never wanted to become.

Unbeknownst to her malice was seeping into her heart taking her to deeper, cruel level of dissatisfaction. And the angels in the heavenlies turned away as they saw the birth of evil being produced in her heart. Knowing that the Lord would judge the wicked with their own words, this angelic host trembled in fear. Their voices reverberated in the high places and they echoed the words of the Mighty God. *The good person out of the good treasure of his heart produces good, and the evil person out of his evil treasure produces evil, for out of the abundance of the heart his mouth speaks.* [11]

Wilfred cut in to her wagging tongue.

"Reaneva," he said sharply, "remember from where *you* came? You did not have such a perfect past. How can you pass judgment?"

Reaneva stopped for a moment and stared at Wilfred.

"Just whose side are you on Will?"

"Neva, what do you mean whose side am I on? This is not something the two of you are battling out. It's just you. Honestly speaking, you have a problem and it is getting worse. Your gossiping tongue wags more and more, and frankly I am tired of living with it. Just stop it okay? I don't want to hear any more."

"Fine, then why don't you just leave me since you are so perfect? Then you wouldn't have to listen to me anymore—not that you ever did any way. All I was trying to communicate is how thankful I am that I am *not like her*. I may have come from a dysfunctional background, but that was not my fault. And I am *not* like her. I paid back my debt to society for the wrong I did. How can she ever pay back taking the life of her child. I'm just saying."

Wilfred stood up.

"I am leaving. When you come home tonight, we need to talk about finding ways to have couple conversations without talking about someone else. This is having too much impact on our relationship, and it needs to be resolved."

"*If* I come home," Reaneva said. "We will talk."

She had wished she hadn't spoken so abruptly, but it was too late she thought. So she continued, now taking her battle with the tongue to another level.

"You must feel sympathy for her because you are just like her, flashing your sin in front of God and everybody."

"Reaneva, that was over five years ago. My sin has been forgiven by God. I have confessed the anger problem I had, and have forsaken that way of life. What do you think I should do, walk around the rest of my life with my head hung down? When God forgives us, he forgets, and restores us. I have joy in what He has done, and maybe she has been restored, and found that joy as well. I no longer have that sin as you say. He has thrown it away, and forgotten it."

"Well I still remember," she said bitterly. "I will never forget. When I take my last breath, I will despise you, and her and others like you."

At that moment a loud and powerful voice thundered from above with a final verdict. Unforgiveness had taken her over the edge, and she heard nothing but her own rambling voice when the gavel was laid down in the heavenlies. *A fool's mouth is his ruin, and his lips are a snare* to his soul. *The words of a whisperer are like delicious morsels; they go down into the inner parts of the body.*[12]

After Wilfred left Reaneva sitting at the table, he heard it. He wasn't sure what the distant noise was, but he heard something that sounded like the muffled rumbling of an earthquake in its early moments of birthing terror. But he didn't look back. He just walked out the door. And in a world unseen an unleashing of menacing entities fled from Hell's door rushing in to work on the heart and mind of Reaneva Ashanti, who was now on her own. Without the voice and the covering of her husband, she would succumb to the pulling down of her soul.

Abiona paused before the meal and looked at Damiria.

"Would you pray and ask God for the blessing?"

"Me? I don't know if I am worthy to ask for a blessing. Are you sure?"

"I am sure," Abiona said seriously. "Why *not* you? You have been redeemed, and made new by the blood of Christ. You are His."

Damiria bowed her head, and Abiona followed. When Damiria began speaking Abiona cried at the joy of what God had done in this young woman's life. Damiria's voice was soft and tender, and those who were near their little corner of the restaurant were compelled to a moment of silence to listen as Damiria gave thanks to God.

"Lord, I am not worthy to call on your name, except by the blood you have shed for me. That blood has allowed a sinner like me to be able to access the very heights of Heaven with You. By your grace and mercy I am sustained, and I pray your continued grace and mercy to be extended to me, and to my friend, Abby. Today we give thanks for the greatest thing you have done in rescuing me as well as the simplest thing of being able to share a meal. Please bless this time, Jesus. Amen."

> *But the tax collector, standing far off, would not even lift up his eyes to heaven, but beat his breast, saying, 'God, be merciful to me, a sinner!' I tell you, this man went down to his house justified, rather than the other. For everyone who exalts himself will be humbled, but the one who humbles himself will be exalted." Luke 18:13-14*

I Love Her But...

Damiria went to talk with her parents before taking any other steps. She wanted to be able to share her testimony, and needed to let them know ahead of time her intentions. She felt as though nothing could stop her now. She had never had such a sense of freedom and well-being, and thought that if Christ could do that for her, then there must be others out there that needed Him as much as she had needed Him. She just did not want her parents to be surprised if the things she said came back to them.

As she entered the house she was amazed at how much she remembered and loved that familiar smell. Even in her rebellion, this home had certain things that comforted her, and there was something very comforting about the scent of home. It was fresh and clean, and it made her feel alive.

She had good parents who wanted to do the right thing, and live good lives before God. She believed in her heart that they were just as side-tracked about the pregnancy as she had been, and felt caught in the middle of something that they were not spiritually prepared to handle. Still, there was a hint of bitterness that tried to rise up within her, and she needed to prevent that seed from growing.

Damiria's parents sat quietly at the table, with their hands folded and eyes fixed completely on their daughter as she began to speak.

"Mom, Dad," she said, looking at each one. "First I want to ask you to forgive me for stepping outside of your covering, and going off into rebellion. I know that I hurt you. I have repented of that before God, and asked His forgiveness. I would now like to have your forgiveness and blessings, and it would mean a lot to me to be able to restore our relationship."

A long silence followed. Damiria's dad began tapping his fingers on the table, and her mom just kept shifting in her seat, trying to find a comfortable spot. It was the same thing that Damiria always saw just before her daddy spoke without kindness. These were signals that daddy's words were not going to be so gracious.

"Well, it's too far removed to be thinking about that now, wouldn't you say? It's gone by, and I say let it stay gone by."

Damiria looked up to demand eye contact with her father. His face was stern. His eyes were full of tears that he refused release, and his voice was strained. It was as she had remembered it to be on the day she told them she was pregnant.

"Mom, what do you think?"

"Sweetie, you know I have never strayed too far from what your daddy thinks. I like to support him, and make sure I am helping him more than hindering him. She turned to her husband, and smiled meekly.

"Honey, you know this to be true. I am usually right there with you, but this time I have to differ. It needs to be brought to the surface, and we *all* need the healing that we are only going to find by speaking the truth in love."

"*All*? You think we *all* need healing? I don't know about you, but I am okay."

Damiria began to hang her head. The shame was all coming back again, yet she knew she had to relive this in order to find closure. She started to say something but her mother spoke quickly.

"Really," she asked? "I have wondered all these years about that. How can a man of God be okay with killing a child, especially his own grandchild? I am not saying we had to raise the baby, but I am telling you now, that my heart has ached all these years to tell my grandbaby I am sorry. Now I have that chance to ask forgiveness."

Damiria lifted her head.

"Momma, I had no idea how much you were hurting over this. I always thought that . . . well I thought you didn't care."

"What's done is done, her dad interrupted. You were rebellious, and the sin is yours alone. Damiria, I love you but . . ."

"What," Damiria asked? "You love me but what?"

Her dad was so hardened at this moment.

"I love you, but I don't think I can deal with all the scandal," he said. "You have to deal with it on your own. It's between you and God. Leave us out of it."

He paused to keep his words from stuttering.

"And that pregnancy," he said becoming more irritated, "never became a baby. So, where, will you tell me, is this grandchild?"

Damiria jumped up from her seat after hearing her dad's brusque and uncaring behavior, and she reacted with a boldness she had never had with him before.

"That child, *your* grandchild's name is Mohari, and he is in Heaven."

Damiria's dad stiffened. Something she said made him suddenly break down, and he began to sob and cry bitterly. Damiria was puzzled, and didn't know what it was that made this conversation turn so quickly, and bring such a torrent of great conviction on her dad.

He couldn't look at either his wife or his daughter, but covered his face and cried out to the Lord. "Oh God, my God, she is right. God forgive me. I have sinned greatly, and there is no turning back from my sin. How can a man kill his own flesh and blood? Lord in heaven, have mercy, and forgive me."

Damiria reached for her father's hand.

"There is no turning back, Daddy. You are right. What is done is done, and we can't undo it. But we can ask the Lord to forgive us. We can forgive each other, and we can move forward. 1 John 1:9 says that if we confess our sin He is faithful and just to forgive our sin and cleanse us from all unrighteousness. Can we make an altar of prayer here and lay all those hurts down?"

"Damiria, forgive me," I wronged you."

"I forgive you," she said.

He paused a moment, and then got up from the table.

"There is something I need to show you. Then you will understand what has happened here today. Just wait here a moment."

Damiria's dad left the room, and she looked over at her mom. Shrugging her shoulders and lifting the palms of her hands up she said, "I don't know what he is doing. I guess we will both have to wait."

He returned with a jar in his hand filled with rocks, and dumped them out on the table. Each rock had something written on it. Some said had the words *trust, hope* and *wait*. Others had dates written on them. As he began searching through the rocks for a certain one he shared his heart.

"I know you must have thought many times that I am a man who has never been close to God, because I have acted a lot out of pride and arrogance. But I do love the Lord. When I knew you were pregnant, I feared the gossiping mouths that would ruin my standing in the church.

I dreaded the thought of my daughter being spoken of as one who fell. But I think even more than you, I had fallen because I served a god of pride.

In spite of that pride there have been many times in my life I have encountered God in ways that are powerful and meaningful—you know, life changing ways. When those times came I would grab a stone, and write a date on it or a word I felt He was telling me."

He began crying again, and had to take a minute to regain his composure.

"When we found out that you tried to commit suicide, I fasted and prayed, and I had an encounter with God. He woke me up out of a dead sleep, and told me that one day I would face Him to account for my pride. I never thought then it had to do with the baby. I was still so stubborn that I convinced myself that making you get an abortion was right even in God's eyes. I knew right then that I needed Him to change my heart, because it had become so crusty. I begged Jesus that when that day of reckoning came, that He would stand in front of me, and close my case by grace and mercy. I said if he would do that I would lay down all things for Him, even my position in the church if that is what He wanted."

He looked at Damiria for a long time.

"When did you name the baby?"

"I named him when I was in the hospital."

Damiria's father could almost feel the pride cracking and falling off of him. It was a special moment, and a very difficult moment. He knew that time of reckoning before God had come in this very hour, and he prayed, "Lord, change my heart now."

He breathed deeply, "Mohari—it means one who forgives. Doesn't it?"

"Well, yeah," Damiria said. How do you know that? It's not one of those names you hear every day."

He opened his hand to reveal the rock he had been hunting for, and on it written in black magic marker was the name *Mohari*.

Damiria gasped. "What is this?"

"After wrestling with God that night He woke me up, I asked Him for a word so that when my accounting came I would know. This is what he gave me. I wrote it down, and then looked it up to find that it was an African name that meant one who forgives."

Then Damiria's father pulled out three other stones. Keeping one for himself, he gave one to his wife and one to his daughter.

"This is a great day," he said. "I have come under God's judgment and lived. Let's take a minute and write a word on our stones, and we will set these apart for our grandchildren to know how great our God is."

When they were all finished Damiria's mom grabbed a wooden box off of the kitchen shelf. We can put them in here for now, and keep them separate for a time.

One by one they put their stones in the box, and they added the one special stone that spoke peace back into their lives. As they placed the four stones in box they said out loud the word that God had given them for this day.

"Mercy"
"Hope"
"Favor"
"Mohari"

Just a Prayer—Excuses for Gossip

Damiria sat in the beauty shop waiting her turn. She had decided that she did not need to hide her eyes any more. If there was any way that people could see in her eyes the joy that she now had in Christ she wanted that to happen. It was a statement to her that she was not defeated any more. She wanted to be able to look into the mirror every day, and see a new look that would remind her that she could stand strong. In some ways she wanted to be able to look in the mirror, and see beauty whenever the temptation from the enemy came to deceive her into thinking otherwise. She knew times would come that she would want to starve herself because of such lies, and she thought this would help. It wasn't the outward beauty she wanted to change so much as the way she saw herself. Making this a new day to include a new look, she thought, would be a reminder for her.

She started her day with prayer and reading in Corinthians about being a new creation. She prayed that the Lord would continue to shape her in this newness of life, and that He would let His glory crown her. She believed by faith that He would do it.

"So, what are we doing to your hair today, honey," the beautician asked.

Damiria sat up straight in the chair, and looked into the mirror as she spoke to help her overcome her fear of speaking openly. She wanted to share the power of God working in her life with the beautician. She took a deep breath and began telling her story, using it to define how she now wanted to look.

"I have worn my hair in my eyes since I was thirteen because I was ashamed of having an abortion, and I didn't want anyone to see me. I wanted to hide from the world, because I was afraid people would somehow be able to look into my eyes, and see what I had done, and hate me. I hid my eyes so no one could look inside of me. So the first thing I want is a new cut that will show off my eyes."

"Okay," the beautician said pursing her lips, and looking around at the other stations to see if the other customers were listening. She had heard a lot of beauty parlor buzz, but in all her time of working at the beauty shop, she had never been told something that quickened her heart so much.

"We can fix that," she said acting as if she was not moved by what Damiria had just said. "Did you look at some pictures we have? Do you have any ideas as to what style?"

"No," Damiria said shrugging her shoulder. "I will leave that up to you, but there is something else that I know I want. Can you add some highlights at the top of my head making them run down like streaks of sunlight?

"Well, your hair is very black. I can add just hints of golden blonde and strawberry red, but you don't want too much of that. Let's do that, and then if you feel you want more we can weave in some of the golden tinsel starting it from the top."

"Perfect. Let's do it."

"That will make a drastic change. I think it will look good, but it might take a while for you to get used to it. Is that okay?"

"Drastic is good," Damiria said smiling. "It is exactly what I want because that is what has taken place in me. You see, I have recently come out of rehabilitation. I took too many pills, and I nearly died. While I was in the hospital, God sent someone to me to show me how much he much He loved me, and my life has never been the same. I have been drastically changed, and I want this new look to remind me that Jesus makes all things new. The light of Christ has shined into my life, and when I look in the mirror, I want to be reminded of that great light. That's why I want the highlights. I want others to see my eyes so they can see the joy He has placed in me. I am going back to my old church on Sunday, and I want people to see a different Damiria, both inside and out."

Everyone was listening. All were moved by her testimony, but one listened with anticipation of telling someone else. She stopped what she was doing so she could get all the information, and she couldn't wait to share what she had learned today.

Hedda lived with her Grandfather, Ronal, who was on the deacon's board at their church when Damiria got pregnant. She wondered if her grandfather knew about all this, and if it would make any difference now all these years later, especially since Damiria's father was selected again by the nomination committee to serve as the chairman of the board. She was too curious about how much Damiria's father covered up. As she sat waiting for her grandfather to pick her up, she leaned in so she could hear more.

"Excuse me," Hedda boldly interrupted. "I couldn't help but over hear your conversation. Can I ask you a question?"

"Watch this one," the beautician whispered.

Damiria ignored the warning.

"Of course," she answered. "What is it."

"Does the church know?"

Damiria was taken aback by the question. "Does the church know what?

"Do they know about your sin?"

Wow! This girl is bold, Damiria thought.

She looked more closely at the girl as the beautician sorted strands of hair to color.

"Do I know you?" Damiria asked,

"Well, you probably don't remember, but we were in Sunday school class together. I always wondered what happened to you—why you quit coming to class, and why you quit talking to people. Now I know."

Damiria felt peace rush through her. She wasn't afraid of the truth.

"Well, I guess you do. Now I have a question for you. What will you do with it?" Strength and an unusual sense of confidence filled Damiria as she continued to address this topic with this girl. She looked at her, and saw pain.

"Forgive me for not knowing you. What is your name?"

"Hedda Jackson," the girl replied. "I am Nolan's granddaughter."

Now the memories came. There was only one Hedda, and from what she remembered, Damiria hoped she was a changed person.

"Hedda, you lived with your grandfather back then, right?"

"Yes, my daddy went to jail, and I went to live with my grandfather. When I went there, they told him that he should resign as deacon. Let me correct that. Your *father* told him he should resign as deacon to keep the church from scandal. I only know that because I could hear them talking from my grandfather's office."

"I am sorry about that. But it wasn't my sin that caused it."

"Maybe not," she said, "but I think it was unfair that your stuff got all covered up while mine was served up as the main course for the church."

"Believe me," Damiria said, "It is better to go through it than to shove it in the closet, and live your life in fear that it will pop out when you least expect it. Did your daddy ever get to come home?"

Ignoring Damiria's question, Hedda stood audaciously in front of her as if Damiria owed her something.

"So, you never answered my question. Did you tell the church?"

The beautician stopped combing for a minute and chided Hedda.

"C'mon Hedda, do you have to be like that?"

I'm sorry, honey," the beautician said to Damiria. "Don't worry about all that."

"It's okay," she answered, turning her attention back to Hedda.

"No, I haven't told the church, but I am certain you will," Damiria said as straightforward, yet as kindly as she could.

Damiria wasn't sure where this inner strength was coming from. It had to have been God helping her get through. She figured there would be times like this whenever she decided to share her story, but she never imagined how God would come through to help her. Damiria maintained her composure. She didn't feel anger or resentment, or even shame. She only felt sorry for Hedda, believing she was never able to deal with her own grief, and maybe needed a friend like she had found in Abby.

Hedda's grandfather pulled up and honked. She turned to look back his way, and then looked back at Damiria again. She ran out to the truck, and got in to head back to their little country home.

"Looking good," her grandfather said. "But you always look good. How was your day in town?"

"It was okay."

They rode in silence all the way home and Hedda said nothing about the conversation at the beauty shop. She spent the weekend pouting, and secretly wishing she could get away from this place. It haunted her—always having to look at pitiful expressions on people's faces. People felt sorry for her, and felt that her legacy would always be that of *Poor Hedda*. Even now she fought the thoughts that haunted her.

There goes poor Hedda, whose daddy left and never came back.

Her grandfather knocked on the door.

"Are you okay? Can I come in?"

"Yeah, you can come in."

Hedda sat in the chair by her computer. This seemed the perfect time so she approached her grandfather.

"Can we pray about something?"

"Sure, is it this thing that has been bothering you?"

"Well, sort of. I saw Damiria in the beauty shop the other day. And I want to pray for her and her family."

"So what does she want us to pray for?"

"She didn't ask me to pray. But I want to pray about the fact that she had an abortion, and that her family covered it up so her daddy could still be a deacon."

"Her grandfather looked at her gently. "You know we are having a board meeting in the morning, don't you?"

"Yes, I know. That's all the more reason to pray about this, right?"

"Hedda, I hope you learn this lesson well now. Gossip is the most destructive force in the church."

"Grandpa, I was just . . ."

"You were just spreading something you heard, because you are still angry. Hedda, there are two things that can destroy the life of a believer. One is resentment, and the other is gossip. Both lead to a spiritually void life, and what the gossiper doesn't realize is that while his loose tongue is bent on another person's ruin, it is often the one that can't stop talking about other people that comes to ruin."

"But, I thought you should know," she said, "that's all."

"I do know. He confessed it a long time ago to me. He didn't tell the whole church, but he did tell me. I was the one that suggested he be our chairman of the board. He had not told the church because he felt he couldn't add more shame to his daughter. When she confronted him about this, he asked her for permission to share it with the church staff and the elections committee. He asked them for a vote of confidence before the final decision came to make him chairman, and they gave it unanimously."

Hedda hung her head. "I'm sorry."

Hedda's grandfather sat for a minute calculating the right thing to say. He rubbed his chin, scratching through his beard, as was his habit when he was thinking.

"I have to go pretty soon, but I want to say something. Will you listen?"

Hedda nodded her agreement.

"Hedda, things have not always been easy for you, but we tried to cover for you as much as we could when you were growing up. You are no longer a little girl, and you have to realize the consequences of life are more than a momentary infraction. Some things you choose have the potential to cling to you all your life. So, it's better to deal with these infringements when they come, so that they won't entrap you later."

"Grandpa, what are you getting at?"

"Well, according to Psalm 1 there are two paths to choose. If you choose to walk in the counsel of the wicked, walk in the path of the mocker or sit in the seat of the scoffer then you will not be able stand up in the judgment. But, it clearly says if you choose not to go this way that you will be like a tree planted by streams of water, and that everything you do will prosper. The sinner, the wicked and the scoffer have their hearts set against God, and it spills on to others. The one who delights in the Lord chooses life, and therefore chooses to be fed by the Word of God."

"He paused to look her in the eye. If you choose to delight in God, you can't let your tongue be used for wickedness. Even if spoken for the sake of prayer, if spoken against another in judgment, it is like sitting in the seat of that scoffer."

"So I can't say anything if I see someone sinning?" she asked.

"Speaking out against sin and trying to be the accuser are different. Having good judgment based on the word of God is different than being judgmental. And besides, the sin you spoke of today against Damiria, God has already forgiven and forgotten. Don't you think you should do the same?"

Hedda didn't answer. She looked at the floor and wiggled a bit in her chair.

"I think I need to be alone now."

After her grandfather left she called the beauty shop, and begged them to give her Damiria's phone number. They finally agreed to take her number, and pass it along to Damiria. Hedda waited and hoped she would call. As usual, her grandfather's words impacted her. She wanted to ask Damiria to forgive her, and offer to be that friend who would walk into the church with her.

Maybe, she thought, *Damiria will be that special angel I need in my life.*

To the Warrior Fighting Gossip

Secrets—Inside the Mind of the Gossiper

It is a bit of an unspoken and faulty logic, which reasons that gossip is a woman's sin. Although this battlefield is exemplified here in the lives of Reaneva and Hedda it is not to insinuate that only women gossip. Some recent articles have indicated studies revealing men are right there with women when it comes to gossip, and in some case studies men surpassed the number of women who gossip.

The secrets of the gossiper are often buried deep within, and translate into hurts that have never been resolved, or sin that has never been reconciled. In other words, the one who is prone to a lifestyle of gossip may be one who needs Christ to dig deep to root out a core sin, and apply a healing balm to their wounded soul.

There are a few reasons that are recognized in the psychology of gossip as to why people engage in tittle-tattle about others. One reason is an irresistible need to expose other people's lives. It is an attempt at a means to make us feel better about our own lives, especially if we see another as somehow inferior.

The second reason tags along with the first in that it is a need to be powerful. There are those who gossip because their low self-esteem knows only one way to make them feel like they are somebody. This is accomplished by making another seem to be of lower character, beauty or significance. The reasoning is that if the signs you use to point to others are bigger and uglier than your own, then yours may not look quite so bad.

The third and last reason for gossip is probably the worst of all. Many who engage in gossip, especially against someone who has wronged them, do so for the mere pleasure in their demise. It serves as a means of revenge. It is a way to destroy them legally. Gossip is a social grenade that gets thrown into a circle of people, and points to one in particular with explosive results. This kind of power-seeking gossip can emotionally kill. It can cause the victim to withdraw from social occasions. It can bring on depression, and has been known to lead to suicide. It's no wonder, that the gossiper in Romans 1:28-30 is listed with the murderers and haters of God, and said to be given over to a depraved mind.

Even as I write, I pray, "God forgive me for every idle word." I know there are times I speak out of line against another, and when I do I must confess it. Surely there is a bit of the nit-picker in all of us that needs to be brought to the cross in full repentance every time is rises up, but what needs to be hammered hard is the lifestyle of the rumormonger whose life is marked with a wagging tongue. This is the one that never has a good thing to say about another person. He, who produces negativity, destroys his witness for Christ, and is ruined by his bantering. This is the one whose commentary of others is mostly mockery. Is this you? Is your life marked by a wagging tongue?

To the gossiper: Whether the words you say against someone are true or untrue, it is of equal consequence. To slander another is malicious gossip, and an offense that God takes seriously, but know this—His forgiveness is only a prayer away. Gossip is sin, but not unforgivable. Jesus is always faithful to forgive. He offers the best beginning for freedom from the wagging tongue.

If you are given over to gossip, know that it is not a sin that you want to sweep under the rug, and wish it would go away. It will not go until you cast it out into the light of Christ, and confess your sin before God and others. Gossip continues to find its way out from under the rug, and manages to bring with it more dirt than was initially hidden. Decide today to reject the temptation to speak out against another. Ask for help where it is needed and begin to practice seeing people as God sees them.

To the church: the warrior of God who has become entangled on the battlefield of gossip is hard to rescue, because it is difficult to see that she is wounded. Her wounds are covered completely by the sign she holds in her hand pointing to others. It is also difficult to rescue the gossiper because he carries with him on that battlefield a bomb that has the potential to explode and touch the very one who tries to help, and many simply do not want to be involved in the life of negative people.

Often times, the best way to help these fallen warriors is to hinder them from speaking slander, gently reminding them that their words are damaging. Please know that beneath all the slanderous verbosity is a soul wounded by the arrows of discouragement, pride or bitterness. If they will let you in, look into these areas to begin to minister healing if you can. If their own wounds can be healed, their wagging tongue will likely cease.

To the victim of gossip: Know who you are in Christ. If the tales being spread about you are untrue, righteousness and truth will be your advocate. Cling to Christ and cry out to him as did the Psalmist. Know that He will be your shield.

If the rumors being spread are true concerning sin in your life, know that confession frees you and renders you no longer bound to the condemnation of the wagging tongues.

Finally, to all those who bear the name of Christ, I leave with you the words written by the apostle Paul as he was expressing to the Philippian church how to care for one another. He said this:

"Finally, brothers, whatever is true, whatever is honorable, whatever is just, whatever is pure, whatever is lovely, whatever is commendable, if there is any excellence, if there is anything worthy of praise, think about these things" [13]

If you meditate on these things then such will come from your mouth. Store up good things. Remember to guard your heart and allow only the goodness of God to fill it.

"The good man brings good things out of the good stored up in his heart, and the evil man brings evil things out of the evil stored up in his heart. For out of the overflow of his heart his mouth speaks." [14]

Mariel Anya

BITTERNESS COVERED BY GRACE

Let us then with confidence draw near to the throne of grace, that we may receive mercy and find grace to help us in our time of need. Hebrews 4:16

Sinner's Stain

Softly, quietly the day falls to grace
Silken shadows of my Savior's face
Secret serenade takes my heart to another place

Where loathe of sinner's stain is washed away
Washed away, Washed away
Where trial and pain meet with the cleansing flood
And all is washed away

Clearly, eagerly the night slips away
While sleep and peace lay on a distant shore
Lingering whispers carry me o'er his hiding place

Where loathe of sinner's stain is washed away
Washed away, Washed away
Where trial and pain meet with the cleansing flood
And all is washed away

Calmly, longingly the Lord calls me back
His grace and faith accompany me
Glistening harvest fields plucked white and redeemed

Where loathe of sinner's stain is washed away
Washed away, Washed away
Where trial and pain meet with the cleansing flood
And all is washed away

Mariel's Hammer

A hideous thing hovered in the clouds just above the large cross that stood tall at the entrance to the metropolis area where Mariel worked. The cross was erected in hopes of pointing people toward Christ. Many came to Mississippi to frequent the casino where Mariel worked, and most had to pass by the cross to get there. Those who worked hard to bring this monument of Christ to their city had hearts that cried out to God for a city that would honor the Lord, and enable others to know Christ, and the power of the resurrection. They knew that many would come to visit because of the casino, and the heart of these people was to tell as many as possible about the good news of Jesus Christ. The work to erect the cross had been finished two years prior, and in that short two years had ministered to many passersby through prayer and outreach.

The enemy hated the cross in that city. He was unable to touch it, because God had blessed it, and was using it for His glory. The enemy hated it because people who came to visit often left with a sense of great passion and desire for Jesus. Satan hated the cross for what it represented, and he wanted to destroy it, but he could not.

A plan had been devised in the chambers of hell to kill the people who entered beneath the cross to pray. The death that the enemy had intended was not a physical death. He wanted to kill the spirit in them. He wanted to destroy the joy and the peace. His plot was to take away any form of hope, and throw them into a life of bitter despair. His goal was to bring a death of a spiritual kind, so he posted a demonic stronghold in the sky above the cross. There he sent the demon of discouragement, whose only job was to drive people away. Another demon was placed there to pierce them with shame for not accomplishing the prayer or the time they wanted to offer to God, and if this demon could find a hole in the armor, it would begin to bring in the seed of bitterness.

Jeb drove a bus for the transit system, and his route included a stop at the visitor center where the cross stood. Most days, he managed to get to the cross fifteen minutes before the bus was scheduled to depart, and he always used that time to pray. He prayed for all who would get on his bus, to know the love of Christ. He knew the stronghold was there. God had allowed him to see the demon one day. It was the first time he had ever stopped, and got out.

He had intended that day to go up under the cross and pray, but when he got beneath it a strong wind came in, and clouds formed in the sky. This had initially discouraged him from kneeling down in prayer, and he walked quickly back to the visitor center to buy a cup of coffee.

Before he opened the door, he heard the Spirit of God speaking to him telling him to go back under the cross, and kneel down and worship God. Jeb hesitated at first, but then obeyed, and went back underneath the cross. He knelt down and began to worship. As he prayed he felt several drops fall on his head, and thought it was beginning to rain. But when he touched his forehead the drops felt like oil. He rubbed his fingers together examining the oil that was on his head. Then he looked up to the top of the cross again. When he sniffed his fingers, he detected the scent of myrrh, and as he did he sensed that God was calling him for something great. He cried out to the Lord to be used however He chose. It was a holy moment, and he knew God's anointing had come upon him. He vowed right then to make this place a point of intercession.

He took several photos to mark the moment when God had called him to pray—for this place, and the people who would ride the bus to see the cross. When he got home to look at the pictures, what he saw shocked him. There was something that looked like a demon in the clouds above the cross. At first he wanted to ignore it, but he kept coming back, and looking at it again. This was not a photographic duplicity, but to Jeb it was clearly a picture captured by the hand of God, enabling him to see, and know how to intercede. It was clearly a demonic entity that hovered over the cross with its mouth agape, and its expression fixed with anger. Jeb thought it was a strongman because the breadth of its shoulders was like that of a Goliath. It had dark empty cavities for eyes and it appeared to be raising a fist as if fighting the air.

He had never seen anything like this before. At first he felt maybe he had done something wrong because the superstitions in the family would have taught as much. Jeb had come from a family who had always leaned toward superstitious beliefs, and it was something that he fought against ever since giving his heart to Jesus.

His habits of prayer reflected a Native American heritage, and caused him to approach prayer and the throne of God with the utmost reverence. As he saw this thing in the air, he quickly turned to God for immediate guidance and submission.

Though his mannerisms were a reflection of the Native American, his physical qualities were decidedly of Hispanic nature. His olive complexion darkened at the high spot on his cheeks, and lightened just enough under his eyes to display the thick black brows that formed a nearly straight line above his deep brown eyes, that were accentuated by heavily rimmed glasses. His wavy black hair stuck out under his ball cap, and hung half an inch down his neck.

He adjusted his glasses, and looked again at the photo. In an instant he became afraid of this evil looking apparition, and came close again to embracing the erroneous thinking that had at one time dominated his life concerning the forces of evil having power over him. Though the fear tried to arise in him, what took hold in his mind was the precious word of God. And he rested in the assurance that the Holy Spirit of God lived in him and was greater than anything like this. He determined after that to pray against this stronghold. His wife prayed for him every day at the time he would arrive at the cross, so her prayers would cover him as he interceded for others.

Jeb never saw the demon again when he looked up in the sky, but he knew when it was there, and it drove him deeper into prayer for the city. He entered into warfare on behalf of his community, always with caution, but never again with fear. He knew that the principalities were powerless in his life because of the blood of Christ that covered him. Although he was keenly aware of those powers of darkness hovering over the cross that stood at the entrance to the city, he still knelt beneath it every day, and made that cross a sacred place—a place where he could stand in the gap for others.

Mariel walked past Jeb without turning her head to acknowledge him.

"Have a good day, Ma'am," he said as she went by.

She looked straight past him with her head held high, and her eyes rolling in disgust as she went by. Her bright red dress clung tenaciously to every curve of her body, and the black plaid jacket announced the style and fashion of a woman who had a lot of money. As she stepped off of the bus one of her four inch heels got caught in the grate between the step and the door frame, and the poised and modeled beauty tottered to the right. She reached out to grab hold of something, and a strong hand was there to help her. She grabbed hold, and as she turned to straighten herself out, she twisted her ankle, and fell to the bottom step, hitting the ground. She screamed as the pain struck through her.

"Now look what you have done," she screamed at her helper. "I've twisted my ankle. I can't believe the transit company would hire such an idiot!"

She grimaced at her frustration, and sat there a moment stunned, and feeling embarrassed at having fallen. She wasn't sure how she could pull herself up off the ground, without someone coming to her rescue. She turned to realize that it was not the bus driver's hand she had grabbed. He was standing at the top of the steps behind the person who had helped her.

"Here let me help you up," the stranger said, and lifted her by putting his arm around her waist, and holding on to her shoulder for balance.

Mariel stood up hobbling, giving favor to one foot. She grabbed his hand removing it from her around her waist.

"If you don't mind, I'd like this hand of yours to be gone, please."

The stranger lifted both hands into the air, and let completely go of her.

"Just trying to help," he said.

"Well, dear boy, maybe if you were not so quick to grab hold of my waist, I wouldn't mind your help."

"Well, dear girl," he retorted. "Maybe if you didn't wear to those Pike's Peak heels, you would not have needed my help. Look, can you walk okay?"

"I'm fine," Mariel insisted as she limped away from the bus door. She noticed the bus driver was coming down toward her, and she wanted to get out of his way, but couldn't move fast enough to avoid him. He came right to her with his clipboard in hand.

"Lady, I've called for an ambulance. Can I get your name?"

"You called an ambulance? I am not dying you fool. Why did you do that?"

"Sorry, it's protocol. You looked like weren't getting up, and you were hurt coming off of my bus. It's what I am supposed to do. They should be here any minute. Maybe you should sit down?"

"I will be okay," she said. Just go on your way. I will be fine. I am not sticking around here to go on any ambulance ride, so you might as well call them, and tell them to turn back around. And while you are at it, you can put that clip board up. You don't need my name."

Jeb helped her up and stood to watch as she hobbled into the casino. The man who had tried to help her shook his head as she left.

"Man, I don't think I have ever seen anyone so mean in all my life."

"I know," Jeb said, "But we can't judge. Who knows what sort of things has happened in her life to make her so indignant about everything?"

"You are generous to say so, after she called you an idiot. How can you take that, and go on like it didn't happen?"

Jeb laughed as he climbed back on to the bus.

"She actually called me a fool, and she is right. I am a fool for Christ. Honestly speaking, I can do so many things because He gives me the strength. I try very hard not to be deterred from Him, always remembering I stand only because His grace has made me stand."

Mariel limped inside the casino and sat down at her work station. She *had* to stay because there was no compensation or insurance that came with the job. If she didn't work dealing those cards, then she didn't get paid, and she was in debt so deep she wasn't sure she would ever be able to climb out. It didn't help that she worked for a casino where she would end up losing half her paycheck when it did come in. She needed this money tonight so she could pay her rent tomorrow.

Her boss came by her station just before her shift opened and saw her sitting there rubbing her ankle, and noticed the swelling."

"You okay?"

"Yeah I'm okay, no worries here."

"Let me see you stand up, and put weight on that leg."

Mariel tottered to one side trying not to put too much weight on the leg, thinking she could give the impression of being able to stand. But she shifted her weight just enough that pain shot through her leg. She winced trying to conceal the trauma, but she cried out as she balanced herself on the back of her chair.

"It will be okay, I can work tonight; please don't send me home."

"I think you need to see a doctor. Did that happen here?"

"No, I fell off the stupid bus."

"I don't think you need to be on it tonight. I will get you a ride home."

Mariel slouched down in the chair in defeat.

"Now what am I going to do? Why do I have such a rotten life? Nothing seems to go my way."

Groaning, she tucked her face in her hands, and threw her hands back in exasperation allowing the anger to build, and cause her to speak rashly.

"Fine," she said. "If I can't work today then I won't be back. I'm tired of working in this place anyway. I can get a better job someplace where I am not working in the armpit of the city."

Mariel grabbed her purse, and left limping toward the door.

"And I don't need your help with a ride. I can take the bus."

She hated this place. She hated her boss, and the bus driver who brought her here. She hated life. She didn't know how she was going to pay rent, and hopelessness began to invade once again. Despair had become a common companion, and though she hated feeling this way, it seemed normal to her.

She dreaded seeing that driver again. He was too nice, and she couldn't deal with nice right now. She knew he would look at her with those eyes that pierce right through her. She really didn't want anyone to see her. She especially didn't want *him* to see her.

Just say it! A voice whispered into the stirring of her heart. *Go on, say it*, the voice pressed. *You know you hate men. You know you hate Him. Say it, now. Say it. I hate God.*

Despair pressed in as she sat on that bench waiting.

"I hate him!" she said, "I hate him," she said again throwing her head back. "Ugghh, God, I . . . I can't say it. God, I can't say I hate You."

Despair stayed with her and haunted her as she waited. Its demonic claws tried to burrow into her mind, and force her to renounce God. She was tormented by the barrage but could not bring herself to say words of hate against God. Despair needed to work on her more, and as the bus approached, it called out to the depths of Hell for reinforcements to meet at the cross. She was too soft right now to let this opportunity pass by. These evil combatants knew that the bus would stop at the cross, and could cripple their work in her. Their oppressive muscle could be weakened, and they could lose their grip on her soul. They pushed in.

Screams echoed beyond the natural realm as Despair called out to Sorrow, Bitterness, and Strife. He called out to Fear and Malevolence, and beckoned them to that dark place in the sky for the council to be held against Mariel. Shouts bellowed out a call to battle against one who might turn to God.

The only sound Mariel heard was the sound of the rushing traffic hammering in around her, but there was another sound. It was a covert signal, hidden behind the darkness, which beckoned God's watchmen to arise and stand guard. And the warriors of the Almighty took their place to pray.

Bitterness Takes Sides

Mariel averted her eyes away from Jeb as she boarded the bus once again to head home. She didn't want him being nice to her, and trying to help her. She didn't even want him to say anything. She only wanted to get on the bus and go home, and rest while she still had a place to rest.

As soon as Jeb saw her he got up to help. He was good at ignoring the poor behavior of people. His heart was too tender, and his connection was too close to the Lord to see even the meanest as anything less than a work of the creator.

"Let me help you up," he said.

He got up to stand behind her and gently placed his arm around a shoulder while she still held on to the railing.

Mariel didn't resist. Instead she placed her free arm around his waist until she was able to let go, and she sat down in the front seat. She wanted to thank him, but couldn't bring the words from her mouth.

It is better this way, she reasoned. *At least he'll have no reason to expect any favor from me.* It was usually a long ride back home, so she tried to rest. As she leaned her head against the back seat, she heard the woman behind her talking on the phone. Every word she spoke was negative, and she said nothing good about anyone. Mariel listened, and thought this woman was talking about an ex-husband, condemning him for not being man enough to care for her needs. The woman's voice was a deep, low droning sound that annoyed her. She hadn't paid much attention to who was sitting there when she got on, and she wondered what she looked like. The picture that she had of her wasn't pretty.

Mariel was trying to rest her thoughts and decide what she would do next, and this woman was preventing that. Every negative word began to take invisible stabs at Mariel's stomach that would send pulses of anxiety throughout every inch of her being. She couldn't bear to hear another word, and finally turned around to complain. She was surprised that this woman was beautiful. The woman stood, and turned her back to Mariel pulling her purse up on the seat, looking frantically for something in it.

She was a tall, large-boned woman. Mariel figured she stood about 5'8". The deep voice matched the frame, but the negative words didn't line up with the beauty. Mariel recognized the fashion and accessories that accentuated her beauty. That same beauty did not come out of her mouth. It was obvious that her beauty was only a pretty face that was able to wear the latest beauty treatment and market it well. It made Mariel uncomfortable to think she could be as negative as this woman, but she shrugged the thought.

She wanted the obnoxious language and incessant talking to stop, and continued staring until the woman turned back, and hung up her phone.

"Something wrong," the woman asked?

"Not anymore," Mariel said turning back in her seat.

The woman tapped her on the shoulder.

"Are you okay?"

"Yes," Mariel answered without turning back around. She could tell the woman was leaning in closer. Cupping her hand over her mouth to muffle her words the woman whispered, "Our bus driver is wacky."

Mariel could agree, but did not want to engage in conversation, so she only nodded her head. But the woman came up to the front seat across from Mariel.

"My name is Reaneva," she said extending her hand.

"Mariel hesitated, but took the woman's hand.

"I'm Mariel."

Jeb watched the two women and thought they were a likely pair. Both of them were pretty mean and were, in his opinion, kindred spirits.

These two, he thought, *remind me of two cackling hens.*

As he chuckled at his own wit, the Holy Spirit urged him to correct his thinking about them, and to begin to intercede. He silently entreated God to forgive him for his implicit judgment of these two women, and then asked how he should pray. Once he received his direction his intercession began for the lady in the red dress.

"Lord, he whispered, be her light, and her salvation. When she calls up on you, save her from her enemy. Take her today, and set her feet on a rock. Heal the ankle, and bring strength to her body."

Jeb whispered his prayer so he could not be heard, but all those on the bus saw his mouth moving. Some knew he was praying. Others, such as Reaneva, thought maybe he was a bit strange, and just talking to himself. It didn't matter to Jeb. He wanted his prayers to be spoken, because he believed the words released from his mouth pierced through the darkness in times of spiritual battle. He preferred to pray God's Word, believing it had more effect than his own. As he continued to pray, he could sense the battle that was beginning to ensue. He could tell that something had awakened the enemy, and darkness was beginning to gather. He prayed for all those that were on his bus to be given safe passage away from the enemy. Even as he lifted others, he continued to pray all the more for Mariel, as he listened to Reaneva filling her with contempt for the cross.

"So, you have never ridden the bus home at this time?" Reaneva asked.

"No, I am usually at work now, and by the time I get off, I have a ride to take me home. So, I usually only ride it in the morning."

Reaneva looked behind her.

"And it is usually not this full when I come in."

"You do know why it is full now don't you?"

"No, I guess I don't, but I have a feeling you will enlighten me," Mariel said sarcastically. She was getting tired of this woman's mouth that ran constantly.

"Well, it's something you may want to know. Most of these people are going to visit the cross."

"So, what's that to me?"

"Look at your schedule. The bus stops at the cross, and doesn't leave that spot for twenty minutes."

"Great! Just what I need," Mariel suggested, "a layover with God."

"Well, wait till you see the bus driver. He is a fanatic about the cross. He always gets off, and goes under the cross, kneels down, and prays right there in front of everybody. I just ignore him, and go into the visitor center to get a cup of coffee. You can join me if you want. We can sit in there, and chat till the bus gets ready to leave again. I can tell you some of the crazy things I have seen riding this bus with him," she whispered, nodding her head as if pointing at Jeb.

The more Reaneva spoke, the more she opened the way for Bitterness to join her, and the unseen fiendish influences danced around her conversation with delight, as they began to push at that door for Bitterness to finally take over. She was so close that it really had already entered in, and the only door that remained was the one she had opened for the Lord a long time ago. If they could close that, they could begin to choke out the word that *He* had sown in her.

The oppression that hovered around Reaneva began to work its way into Mariel's mind. Anxiety was arising, and she was feeling that sense of foreboding as she began to remember why she was even on the bus at this time.

"I'll pass," she said to Reaneva, "I think I will sit on the bus and take a nap."

Despair pushed in again, and Mariel sighed leaning her head against the window, and turning away from Reaneva.

Jeb continued to pray as they approached the cross. It was always a welcoming sight for him, and filled him with a great sense of joy, knowing this was an opportunity to be with the Lord. He was always careful to be back to the bus on time, because he didn't want anything to ruin this privilege God had given him. As he drove the bus into the circle driveway, he noticed clouds were forming in the sky. There was still some sun poking through, but the formations were dark. When he parked at the visitor center he got out, and stood at the bottom of the door to offer a hand to help people out, if they needed it. Mariel watched him and realized it wasn't just her that he was so nice to. For a moment, there was a desire to trust him that arose in her. She wanted to believe this guy was different.

She watched Reaneva get off the bus, and she stayed where she was. She didn't plan to go anywhere. She noticed there were a few that stayed. Curiously, she looked around to see who remained. There was a mother with a baby and two small children, and she reasoned when she saw them that she would have not attempted to take all of those kids off of the either. There was an old man at the back of the bus who remained. His head was resting on the back of the seat with his mouth opened as he slept. A couple sat together that seemed to be in close conversation, and did not appear to be going anywhere.

There was a man who was about in his thirties, who looked creepy. He had one side of his head nearly shaved, and on the other side his hair hung down to his shoulder. On the shaved side of his head, he had several piercings. There were silver studs poking out all over that side of his face. He had three in his ear, one in his eyebrow, and one coming off the bottom of his lip. It wasn't so much all the piercings and the tattoos that disturbed her, as much as it was the menacing look on his face. When he saw her looking at him he turned his head directly toward her and glared, shattering right through her instability, causing her to turn away in fear. She looked back to see if the bus driver was still there, and saw he had left, and was walking toward the cross. She suddenly no longer felt comfortable on the bus, and in spite of the difficulty in walking on a sprained ankle, she got off the bus.

She looked toward the visitor's center, and hesitated. Maria really didn't want to see to that overly-talkative woman, so she chose to walk over to the cross. There were benches all around it, where she could sit and wait, until the bus driver went back to the bus again. The best part was that she could at least be alone over there.

Jeb looked up at the clouds. It was visible this time. The same figure he had seen in the picture was now hovering in that place where it had been before. It was like he was looking at the picture again. The same hideous face had surfaced plainly in front of him, hovering above the cross, as if it was waiting for someone. When Jeb turned around to look back at the bus he saw Mariel coming toward the cross, and he waited for her at the bench where he always read from his Bible. Waiting on God to lead the way he prayed.

"Lord, order my steps."

Mariel looked at her watch—fifteen minutes till the bus left. She was determined to not go back to her seat on the bus, until the driver came too. She looked around, and began to feel intimidated at being in the presence of these people whom she perceived as being too perfect for her to be around. There were four couples gathered around the foot of that cross. One single woman was walking around the perimeter, stopping to read each of the devotional stations that had been posted there, and the bus driver remained back away from the cross, looking at the sky. Mariel thought he seemed to be looking beyond the top of the cross, and wondered if he was concerned about rain. She noticed him look toward the clouds, and then at his watch.

The wind picked up, and Jeb hoped that Mariel would not go back to the bus before she could have at least a moment where she encountered God. He bowed his head to pray.

"Lord, move quickly and mightily on behalf of this woman, and bring her to your heart. Let today be the day of her salvation. And Lord, I ask that you would hinder the work of the strongman concerning her life, and let no weapon formed against her prosper. Let her accuser be silenced, that she may hear the voice of the Holy Spirit of God beckoning her to a sweet salvation."

Mariel was taken by this cross. She had always heard about it, but had never desired to see it. She thought that even if she did want to know more about God, He would never want to know her. In fact, why would anybody want anything to do with someone like her?

Suddenly tears were falling, and she couldn't contain her emotions. Mariel was looking back and forth hoping no one was looking. She didn't like for anyone to see her being soft. She surely didn't want anyone coming up coddling her, so she tried to push the tears back, and wipe them away without being too obvious.

Jeb noticed, and he paused a moment asking the Lord what he should do. He noticed there was no time left to talk to her if he was going to leave on time, but if he felt the Lord's leading he would have stayed, and left late. He sensed God saying to just hand her a tissue, and get back on the bus. He walked over to her, handed her a tissue, and turned to walk away. Mariel took it without looking up, but as soon as he walked away she turned her head slightly, and thanked him.

In response, Jeb tipped his hat to her as he was walking away.

"Bus is pulling out, are you going to be okay?"

"Yes, I am coming." she said sniffling, and got up to follow him back to the bus.

The rain began to come down, and those who still remained at the cross came running past her. Her ankle was tender, and the heels didn't help her to move very fast. She took the heels off and walked the rest of the way without them. She still couldn't move very fast, and got pretty wet before getting back on the bus. She still had had an hour ride, and was dreading it.

Jeb helped Mariel get on the bus. He motioned for her to sit in the very front seat right behind him.

"I've turned the heater on. It warms up very nicely in that spot," he said, handing her his coat.

"No, thanks," she said, shaking her head. "I don't need it."

Jeb laid his coat next to her in the seat.

"In case you change your mind."

She sat for only a few minutes before feeling really wet and cold, but wasn't ready to concede to wearing his coat. If she did, he might think she liked him or something. But she kept looking at it. Her thinking was being swayed.

Most people stayed at the cross, and only a few were on the bus as they pulled away. Mariel looked back, and saw that the creepy guy was still there and it made her chill more than ever. She slowly grabbed the coat, trying not to look at Jeb. She pulled it up over her shoulders as the bus stopped. To her relief, that guy got off. She saw the talkative lady coming up near her, and she laid her head back as if she was tired and wanting to rest. She *was* tired, and actually glad for the opportunity to close her eyes a minute, and fell asleep. The day had been too much, and now she was in front of this heater, and it lulled her right to sleep.

The hum of the road made her wake up. It had quit raining, and the wind had died down. Her ankle ached, and she stretched to tend it.

"You probably should get that looked at," Jeb said. "I am really sorry it happened."

Mariel's face looked downcast. She shrugged her shoulders.

"It will be fine. Besides my ankle is the least of my problems."

Jeb kept quiet. He didn't want anything to interrupt. She was talking to him and that was more than he had expected on this trip. They were getting near her stop, and he wanted to interject the love of Christ to her, but he sensed the time was not now. He continued to just listen to her, and prayed she would feel at ease to tell some of her story.

"I lost my job today. My rent is due tomorrow. I paid all but $100 of it, and I was hoping to make that much in tips today. When they told me I had to go home I lost it and ended up quitting. You don't know where I can get a job do you?"

Jeb weighed the moment, and took a chance.

"Can I ask your name?"

"Mariel," she said hesitantly.

"Mariel, I don't know where you can get a job, but I know someone who can provide whatever we need. I will be happy to pray for you, and ask Jesus to help."

"Do you really think that if you ask God to help, that He would care enough to help someone like me? C'mon. I don't think Jesus likes me too much. I have done way too many things that . . ."

"It's not what you do," Jeb interrupted. "It's about what He has done. His love for you doesn't cost anything. When He gives to us, it's not because we deserve it, but because He loves us so much."

"Yeah, I've heard all that before, but it's not for me. I am just going to grow old and bitter. That way when I get nothing from God, then I will at least feel I got what I deserved. No one has ever given me anything free in my life, why should I expect it from God? Besides is He going to drop my rent money from the sky?"

Jeb shrugged his shoulders. "He could."

Mariel sighed "He could but will He?"

"You will never know until you ask. So let's ask Him okay?"

"Are you going to try to lead me in that sinner's prayer? People have done that before, but you see where I am. I am still a sinner, still broke and still bitter.

Jeb would have liked that, but he refrained. "I'll tell you what, I will pray, and you just believe. All you have to do is believe, watch and see what the Lord will do."

"I'll try—to believe, that is."

Mariel expected a long, wordy prayer, but Jeb prayed a short and uncomplicated prayer as he drove nearer to her stop."

"Lord, give Mariel everything she needs for life and godliness. Show her your glory, Jesus, and draw her near to your heart. When she calls on you, please answer. Amen."

"That's it?"

"That's it," Jeb said. "God knows your needs. I don't need to reiterate them. He handed her a small devotional book that he kept in plenty to give away to people. She hesitated, but took it, and put it in her jacket pocket."

The bus stopped, and Mariel got up to leave. She noticed her ankle was feeling better, and she could put weight on it again. She started down the steps, and turned back to Jeb, handing him his coat.

"Thanks. I hope you are right."

After she headed down the sidewalk toward her apartment complex, Jeb continued a silent prayer to God asking Him to rescue this woman, who had probably been beaten by life's trials.

"Nice try." He heard the other woman who sat with Mariel say. He looked into the large mirror to see Reaneva Ashanti. She looked angry. Jeb knew something was different about *her*. She was approachable, but she could turn on a person in a minute. He had always tried to stay away from her. He was sure that Mariel's bitterness was a front to cover up so much pain, but this one was not so. He sensed that there was something deep inside of her that was driven by hatred, and he didn't feel led to engage the conversation, so he let her comment go unaddressed.

"The bad thing," Reaneva persisted, "is that you probably drove her further away from God by promising her He would help. You know in the real world, she won't get anything that she has not earned."

Jeb felt he had to speak up now.

"Well, I guess that is up to God, Ma'am. I don't try to play God. I only share what His word says, and pray it back to Him for others. If he chooses not to give to her, then I guess He knows best. I only do what he asks me to do. I share His love. The rest is up to Him."

Reaneva sank back in her seat grumbling. She hated moments like this. She wanted to be happy that someone took a step of faith, but her own faith walk had been bitter. She couldn't see the enemy pulling her down as she sank deeper into the life of defamation, bantering about the lives of other people to ease her disdain at herself. She was too far away from God to recognize that it was the evil one, who titillated her appetite, using the disparaging fragments of broken lives. She could not see that that this bitterness would turn her further away from eternity with God.

She thought she heard a voice calling her to peace, and she shunned it.

"Well, He has never done me any good. So who cares about love anyway? I choose to shirk love." She slouched in her seat.

"This is my life—my destiny," she said, and at saying it she spoke her own bitter death sentence.

Degradation rushed to her side, and began to give shouts of acclaim to the lower principalities. As this higher principality announced the downfall of Reaneva Ashanti the powers of hell screeched through the hollow voids of the air, reaching other rulers of darkness, and announcing that victory had been attained for Lucifer's empire. She had pronounced her future. By her own mouth she spoke squalor into her life.

"Abundance will not be hers," Degradation shouted. "We have succeeded," he said pointing his evil scepter toward the unseen abyss of Beelzebul. As he spoke a foul cloud of smoke filtered from his nostrils and covered Reaneva's heart. Corruption rushed in to begin its rhythmic mocking chant in her mind that would cause her to open the door further for Hate and Malice to enter in.

Jeb sensed something was going wrong. He prayed for a few minutes, and then stopped the bus at the next stop for her. There was no one waiting to get on. She stood gathering her belongings, and walked toward the front of the bus.

Jeb looked at her, and had compassion. He saw the enemy clearly at work.

"I can pray with you, if you want," he said softly. "There's no one getting on, and it's only you and me. Would you let me pray for you now?"

Reaneva sat down on the front seat behind him.

"I have to ride this bus a lot, and see you more than I would like to see you. So, let's get one thing straight. I do not now, nor will I ever want *you* to pray with me. If you even look like you are going to ask me again, I will have your job."

Reaneva said no more, but got up, and walked off the bus. She turned, and stared at him as he pulled away.

"Lord, be merciful to her," he prayed as he drove away. "Lord, please have mercy on her soul, and free her from the bondage of bitterness."

Mariel went inside and found a note attached to the door. It was from the landlord.

"Stop by and see me before the office closes" is all it said.

"I knew it, I just knew it. Where is that love he was talking about? Where is the redemption? Where is God in all this?"

Mariel decided to go on to the office before going inside, and as she walked to the end of the complex she was amazed at how well her foot was doing. It was good that it did not hurt, but she wondered how she would convince him about what happened today. When she entered the room, she saw Mr. Satler sitting at the computer. He was always kind enough. Maybe he would give her some time.

"Ah, Mariel, he said motioning to the swivel chair. "Come in, and sit down."

Mariel sat in the chair, and had a hard time keeping it still. She sat nervously, fidgeting enough to make the chair move, and cause it to squeak. Still feeling a bit humbled by the bus ride and the prayer, her caustic mannerism had subsided for now. She thought she had better be nice.

"Sorry," she said

Mr. Satler ignored the nervousness.

"Did you come up with the other $100?"

"Not yet," she said looking down at the floor. "I was hoping you would give me more time."

Mr. Satler turned in his chair to pull a folder out of the file cabinet. She thought he might be grabbing her rental file, but he handed her an application for employment.

"What is this?" She asked.

"I need an apartment manager. I know your job is a long bus ride. It's not exactly a career boosting job. It certainly isn't steady, and you owe me $100. If you take the job it pays your rent and utilities and $100 each week. Are you interested?"

"Why me," she asked?

"You go to work every day, keep your place nice, and seem to be pretty responsible. I need someone who lives in the complex, and has time to help me manage this place—mostly paper work and collecting rent for me."

"Do you know Jeb?"

Mr. Satler shook his head. "Do I know who?"

"Jeb, the bus driver."

"No, afraid not. Should I know him?"

Mariel sat still a moment deciding whether to proceed.

Hesitantly she added. "Well, he prayed for me today, and told me Jesus would provide."

Mr. Satler looked up at her. "Jesus? Now I know Him. Do you?"

"No," she said but I think I want to.

Ah an added bonus. Mr. Satler said as he got up from his chair. He went over to pray for this embittered woman, and though he did not see immediate results, he thanked God for the opportunity to be a part of what He was doing in her life.

Mariel took the application, and walked home to her apartment. Shutting the door behind her, she took a deep breath, and leaned against the wall.

What were the odds, she thought, *for something like that to happen to me?*

She thought that maybe she should say yes to Jesus. A wave of conviction flooded through her, and she sensed the scourge of her own tongue which had passed a judgment that she could not pay. For a moment she felt the bereavement of being on the edge of something greater than she had ever known, only to find a chasm lay in between, and she could not cross it. Then she remembered the cross, and the bus driver's prayer that God would answer when she called to Him.

At the cross, unseen forces began to gather in the heavenlies to wage war against this woman who was being quickened by the Spirit. They gathered, and prepared to go out in force against her before she said yes to *Him*. But something else was happening at the cross. The LORD thundered in the heavens, and sent out the sound of His powerful voice. When He spoke, lightening struck across the sky. Those who were at the cross at that moment reported that the lightening looked like torches of fire, shooting like arrows in the sky up above it. The winds blew, and dark clouds formed but the lightening still flashed like a canopy behind them. People rushed in to the visitor center as the hail began to plunder the sidewalk. While they waited inside for the storm to pass, there was a hush that subdued each person inside the center. Jeb sat quietly with them, and thanked God. He knew another sinner was coming to Christ, and the prayer of his heart he quoted from the Psalms.

"He made darkness his covering, his canopy around him, thick clouds dark with water. Out of the brightness before him hailstones and coals of fire broke through his clouds. The LORD also thundered in the heavens, and the Most High uttered his voice, hailstones and coals of fire. And he sent out his arrows and scattered them; he flashed forth lightnings and routed them. He rescued me from my strong enemy and from those who hated me, for they were too mighty for me." [15]

Mariel dropped to her knees, crying out to the Lord, whom she had run from for so long. She began thanking Him for the miracle He worked for her today. In a voice that seemed unfamiliar to her, she began entreating Him for His presence in her life.

"Jesus, it's me, Mariel. I am yours, if you want me. Thank you for showing me great and wonderful things today. They are things too wonderful for someone like me. I am a guilty and bitter woman, but if you will take me, I give my life to you. I ask that you would take the burdens from me that now flood me with guilt. I believe that it is not what I do, and accept that it is what you have already done for me. I believe it, and I receive it."

As Mariel knelt there in her apartment alone with the Mighty God, ministering angels came close, and surrounded her. She felt the ache in her soul, as the Lord began to remove from her the seed sown by the enemy of her heart so long ago. She didn't resist the pain in her heart, as memories of the past seemed to be pulled up to the present with a burning sensation. They came up from deep inside, raw opened wounds that made her cry out with grief. It seemed she knelt there a long time, crying, hurting and mourning. Then she reached into her pocket, and found the devotional the bus driver has given her. She turned to the devotion for the day and read the page taking every word she read to heart.

And you shall be called by a new name that the mouth of the Lord will give. You shall be a crown of beauty in the hand of the Lord, and a royal diadem in the hand of your God. You shall no more be termed Forsaken, and your land shall no more be termed Desolate, but you shall be called My Delight Is in Her, and your land Married; for the Lord delights in you, and your land shall be married. Is 62:3-4

You Have a New Name, was the title of the devotional that followed the Bible verse from Isaiah. It wasn't a lengthy commentary, but it spoke to her like a treasured memoir.

Today is a new day, and you have a new name. All the old stuff that your old name embraced is gone. The wilderness that you have crossed has brought you from exile to the edge of glory, and now is the time to open your eyes, and see the cross before you. It is there as the passage to God's delight. You can't reach Him any other way, only by the cross. No more emptiness, no more desolation, no more being forsaken. You belong to God, and by His mouth you are called, "Devoted to Him." Today is a new day, and you have been given a new name

Mariel sat down on the floor and remained in His presence, allowing the Lord to sing and dance over her. She couldn't articulate what was happening. She only knew He was there, and it seemed something cool and refreshing was being applied to her heart. The word Anya came to mind, and she spoke it, not knowing its meaning. She liked the sound of it and decided it would be part of her name now. Anya was graceful, and it was grace that covered her bitterness and made her delightful. So, to her, it was a good name.

To The Warrior Fighting Bitterness

Bitterness is a powerful opponent. It sneaks up, and strips the warrior of his weapons. Then, when the warrior has nothing left to fight off the enemy, he comes and takes his armor as well leaving the warrior of God defenseless. Bitterness steals hope and douses the flame of the Holy Spirit, with soured relationships and broken dreams. It resents anything that represents faith in God, and we know that without faith it is impossible to please God.

An enemy of contentment, bitterness will make every attempt to squash burgeoning sprouts of joy that come up around it. It kills the attempt to grow good toward others, and is not bothered by stepping on hearts in order to make its way for control.

Bitterness is unreasonable and fights unfairly. It pulls at the core of the person, and strips him of any sense of well being. It is egotistically driven, and focused entirely on self fulfillment, therefore feeding on immature Christians whose lives have been torn apart by relationship failure, moral failure or health failure. It preys on the sick, the hopeless, and the weak in spirit. Without notice, it takes the believer down an unwanted road of despair and destruction.

Look at Israel's decline into failure that kept people from entering the Promised Land. In Exodus 16, they complained of having no food, and began to say things were better back in Egypt because there was food. In their constant complaint, the seed of bitterness was sown, to prevent their faith in God from growing. Even when they had seen numerous miracles, they continued to grumble against the Lord. Little seeds of resentment grew to the point of no return, when finally God gave them over to a bitter end.

As I live, declares the Lord, what you have said in my hearing I will do to you: your dead bodies shall fall in this wilderness, and of all your number, listed in the census from twenty years old and upward, who have grumbled against me, not one shall come into the land where I swore that I would make you dwell, except Caleb the son of Jephunneh and Joshua the son of Nun.[16]

Your weapon against bitterness is forgiveness. When you forgive, you announce pardon for another, and in so doing, you denounce the anger and resentment that tries to steal from your heart. Forgiveness brings healing, where the lack thereof produces death and separation. Forgiveness gives you pardon, and grace brings to you the infilling of the Spirit of God. Unforgiveness births the bondage of bitterness, and kills the life of the Spirit in you.

To the Warrior of God, let kindness and forgiveness rule your heart. Remember that you were forgiven. Therefore, do the same, and in so doing, put away all bitterness.

And do not grieve the Holy Spirit of God, by whom you were sealed for the day of redemption. Let all bitterness and wrath and anger and clamor and slander be put away from you, along with all malice. Be kind to one another, tenderhearted, forgiving one another, as God in Christ forgave you." [17]

PART 3

Sentinels

So many things can keep us from the fullness of God. If we are not watchful, we can find ourselves on arduous battlefields fighting an unscrupulous enemy, who would take us down, and pull us away from Christ. Satan employs many tactics, using covert strategies to fight the Christian. He hides his arsenal in the grey areas of life. Keeping his weapons furtively enclosed, he waits until the opportunity arises to release them like a time bomb onto the unsuspecting soul.

The man or woman of God who is not paying attention to the movement of God can wander away from truth and righteousness, and out from under the covering of the Lord. Like a soldier who has ventured outside the wire he puts himself in danger of standing right in front of the enemy's explosive weapons, with no covering and no help. A chosen path may look easily travelled, but it is filled with spiritual land mines. Unaware of those mines, the soldier walks across that field carelessly, until suddenly one of the mines detonates with the recoil of hellfire, and destroys the very core of his spiritual life.

The mind is like the infamous Little Round Top of Gettysburg. Had that hill been taken, the course of history may have been changed forever. Joshua Chamberlin had to protect it at any cost. Loss of limb or life was of no consequence when compared to the loss of that battle. It was all or nothing, because the opposition, once in, would be unstoppable.

The mind is where the battle rages. This is not new information, but it is still much overlooked information. There is no room for error when it comes to warfare. Not even a fraction can be given to the enemy. Not a nanosecond of time can be afforded in the advancement of God's people. All time and space must belong to God alone.

This is a hard saying. Personally, I squirm in my seat as I write this, because I am all too aware that the battle is difficult. There are so many things that seek to sidetrack my thinking concerning music, movies, social interaction, communication and family. Unguarded and unstable social ideals chant loudly the latest mantra that calls for accepting views that permeate our culture, even those that ride opposition to the word of God.

Sometimes they aren't shouts from the rooftops that scream for attention. Instead, they show up as innocent little nuances that seem to hurt no one. This is when we trust that if we walk in the Spirit, we will not succumb to the lust of the flesh. More commentary will be written on guarding the mind, the heart and the home, but for now let it suffice to say, that if our thoughts are taken captive to Christ, then we will know how to guard our minds, our hearts and our homes.

There are three important areas that must be guarded with diligence, and equally three lies from the mouth of destruction that allays the battle-mind. The mind, the heart and the home must have full time watch guard. Don't let the enemy tell you that the diligence it takes to guard these areas is asking too much. Maintenance is always easier the surgery. If the door is not opened, you make it more difficult for entry. In fact, you should lock the door, and ensure that everything that comes into your mind, your heart or your home will only be allowed entry if it passes through Jesus first. If the strongman tries to enter your life and finds that he has to go through Jesus, he will turn around and run.

The three lies of destruction are (1) it's not a big deal, (2) You should follow your heart and (3) The home is anything other than what God has ordained it to be.

There is no such thing as stepping away from God just a little bit. Jesus said in Matthew 12:30 that you are either for Him or against Him. There can be no opposition in the inner person. If you are not walking with Jesus, you are walking away. Even the tiniest hole in a dam can cause a complete breakdown, and allow unwanted flood waters to break out, and wreak havoc. Likewise our minds cannot open the door a crack without taking a chance at opening the floodgates that will drown our walk with the Lord.

Concerning the heart, we are told in Jeremiah 17:9, that it is deceitfully wicked, and we cannot trust our heart to follow it. Your heart is to be placed in the hands of the Jesus, and bent toward Him. You can trust Him to lead you in righteousness.

The home is first your personhood. 1 Corinthians 3:16 says that as a Christ follower, you are the temple of the Holy Spirit of God. In essence what you allow in *this* house will be replicated in that place you call your family home, and even play itself out eventually in your church home. Your home needs to be swept clean, and made new. After a transformation of your mind, and a rendering of your heart to God, your home will be His home. The man and woman who belong to God are called to guard their mind, their heart and their home, so the strongman cannot come in and bring destruction.

Arion Cadman

Music Warrior
Guarding the Mind

For the weapons of our warfare are not of the flesh but have divine power to destroy strongholds. We destroy arguments and every lofty opinion raised against the knowledge of God, and take every thought captive to obey Christ, being ready to punish every disobedience, when your obedience is complete. 2 Corinthians 10:4-6

Upheaval

Screaming on the inside, Lord hear my cry
Nowhere to run, no place to hide

Escape routes closed, the storm's closing in
Earth shaking battle—don't think I can win

Knowing and thinking, your mercy is great
Indeed this will pass, in you I wait

Chaos around me, the storm whistles its ire
Water is rising, I need to climb higher

Screaming and shouting, Lord, I know you can hear
Upheaval has come, and brought with it fear

Lightning and thunder, the storm heralds its rage
Breakers overtake me, still I engage

Wearied and worn, Lord, I cry out to you
Take this ransacked heart, and create it anew

Playground

It had taken a year of counseling, and a lot of healing grace for Jamee to be able to get to the place where she felt there was a possibility that she could try again at loving someone. It seemed a long year to Simon, but he had no regrets. It gave him time to increase his savings account, and to get to know Jamee's father. In that year he was able to gain her father's respect.

Mr. Adams was very strict with the time he spent with Jamee, even on the phone. He allowed Simon some conversations with her as Jamee felt able to take them, but in the first six months they only spoke twice. After that, it was about once each month, but in the two months before coming to Fisher, it had been more often.

Jamee regained courage and strength to once again get out and do some things in the community. She decided that it would be good to help once again at the conference. It was in its seventh year, and still bringing in a crowd of students. Her father had asked if she thought she could go back, and she decided it was possible, and would be even better if would if Simon would come and volunteer with her.

If nothing else, she thought. *He would be a good support to her.*

Simon drove past Fisher Square Auditorium on his way to meet with Jamee at her father's house. The center was gearing up for the conference. He pulled up in front, and stopped to look around the building. Banners hung outside the building advertising a music group he had only just begun to know. He had heard *Arion Cadman's Music Warriors* only once, but what he had heard, he liked. Their music was alive, and powerfully bold. It wasn't piercing like some of the louder Christian rock bands, it was valiant. It had an audaciously courageous sound that made listening about Christ irresistible, and made singing directly to the Lord easy.

The speakers had both written prolifically about purity and the strength it takes to stay that way. They were known nationally for their writing and speaking prowess, but mostly for the ability to engage the audience in life changing ways. Zachary and Sachiel Angelo were their names, but the banner touted them as Zach and Sach, which was the humorous image that always promoted them.

Simon laughed at the way they had managed to make a word play on their names, use it to draw teens, and then somehow move them from thunderous laughter to intensely deep introspection about their lives before God.

As he walked around the building he noticed all the places that made him think of Jamee. He opened the doors, and went inside far enough to see the volunteer booth that stood clearly facing the center point of the stage. He tried to imagine what it had been like for Jamee that year to be so clearly in view of the stage, when she learned the news about Kambo having been in contact with someone who had AIDS. He wondered how Kambo had faired, if he was around, or if Jamee had seen him since coming home.

Ugh, too many thoughts rolling around in my head, Simon thought.

He bowed his head, and sent up one of those quick prayers to God.

"Lord, I need your help here. There is too much to think about, and I am not smart enough to sort through it all. Help me out here. Tell me what next. Order my steps."

This was a typical prayer for Simon in those times that he felt overwhelmed. He would always surmise that he must not be clear enough on choosing the right path, so he would simply ask God to order his steps, and then try to let go of any stress or anxiety. He decided to head back to the car, and as he came out of the door he looked across the parking lot near the other exit doors. There were two teen aged boys standing in front of a man with long white hair. Simon felt that familiar nudging to walk over that way and strike up a conversation, and did not resist.

Both boys looked like they were about sixteen. One was an average height, and a bit chunky. His hair was light brown, colored with deep black ends. He styled it with the bangs and sides cut toward the front, and swept to the side. It was cut in a way that made it look like he forgot to comb it after getting out of the shower. It made Simon want to chuckle, even though he was used to seeing this style everywhere. This teen's fair complexion made the black ends of his hair stand out even more, and brought a courser look to his face. He was wearing tight jeans, and a thin striped hoodie.

The other boy was taller and thinner. He had strong African features, and long dreadlocks in his hair. He wore torn jeans that hung slightly on his hips revealing just the tip of boxer shorts underneath. Simon thought he was pretty conservative in expressing this style. They seemed an unlikely match for a friendship, but Simon shrugged it off and thought no more about it, knowing that sometimes even the most unlikely find a way to connect.

The old man had his back to Simon, and the two boys faced him. They looked like they were arguing, but Simon determined to address them anyway.

"Hi," Simon said as he drew nearer to them.

No one answered him, but they all turned to look.

Simon quickly assessed everything that he saw in this old man's face. The wrinkled forehead and the deep darkened circles under his eyes were not atypical of an elderly person, but even more than looking aged, this guy's face spoke of evil intent. When he looked at Simon his eyes flattened and lay back, accentuating the sides of his face. The old man's forehead rolled over the top of his eyes, as his hateful stare tried to penetrate the pastor's confidence. But Simon didn't step back.

He wasn't afraid to look back at this man, and endure the silence between them. It was less than thirty seconds, but seemed longer. Simon continued to look, and he saw behind the man's head a negative snapshot of a dragon. He couldn't make out the spirit that was standing with this man, but he saw a glimpse of it, and knew it wasn't of God. He felt repulsed, and he silently prayed for direction as the Holy Spirit bore witness with him that this thing he saw was indeed evil. Simon moved in closer, believing he was doing so in obedience to God. He held out his hand in the middle of them.

"My name is Simon. Are you all part of the set up for this event?"

In another long and awkward silence they all stood there, no one offering his hand back to Simon. Finally the old man looked Simon up and down, and extended his left hand making Simon switch hands in order to shake. His hands—that nail looked like it belonged on the hand of an older man, and it looked sorely out of place.

"What is it you want, Simon," the old man asked?

"I'm sorry, Sir, I didn't catch your name."

"I didn't offer it. You came to me. So, tell me what you need."

Simon shrugged his shoulders. "I was just trying to be friendly."

The tall skinny boy held out his hand. "My name is Lyell," he said, as he poked his head out and looked at the old man with a scowl.

"I work concession here. My brother is Arion."

"Arion Cadman, the lead musician for the Living for One?"

"Yeah, that's right."

"So, *you* don't sing," Simon asked, wishing he hadn't been so outright with his thoughts. Maybe this guy didn't like always being compared to his brother.

"Yeah, I sing," he said. "I just don't sing the same songs."

"What *do* you sing?"

"Well, it's like this," Lyell said as he shifted back and forth, pointing back to the building as if his brother was there."

"Seems all he likes to sing about is Jesus. I like to sing about girls."

The other boy laughed and they grabbed hands interlocking them in a familiar hand shake.

"Yeah, he doesn't like my kind of music. He says his music fights battles in the spiritual places, and mine draws the demons in. Ha! What does he know? He is just a fanatic—a Jesus fanatic. So that's us, Lyell said, He's is the music warrior, and I am the music destroyer."

The boys laughed again smacking hands, and ending in a handshake.

"Enough talk," the old man interrupted. "We have a lot of work to do."

The conversation was cut off quickly as the two boys obeyed the old man's demands, and Simon was left standing in that parking lot, watching them walk away. He stood there until the three had disappeared over the hill toward the end of the trail in the nearby park.

Simon walked back to the car and passed a security guard who was standing there.

"You from around here," the security guard asked.

"No, I'm from Kansas City. I'm here to visit the Adams' family, and help out with the conference here. I just stopped on my way to have a look around,"

"Oh, you're the pastor; I heard about you. Mr. Adams says you are a good man."

The security guard smacked his lips while chewing his gum.

"You should stay away from that one, though."

"I'm sorry?" Simon questioned leaning in a bit to make sure he heard him correctly.

"I mean the old man, Yenene."

"What's his name?"

"His name is Yenene, and he is trouble. Watch yourself around that one. Everyone in town just stays away from him."

Simon turned to look back to the spot he last saw them.

"Well, not everyone, He had two teenagers with him." The security guard was shaking his head. "The short chubby one is related to Yenene somehow. The tall skinny one is the only friend that kid has. Too bad, it has kind of pulled him down."

"Well, thanks for the advice," Simon said as he got into the car. "I will keep my eyes opened."

As he left he prayed, "Lord, show me what to do next with those kids. Order my steps and show me your way." A chill went through him as he prayed, and he wondered what kind of battle was ahead.

Warrior's Call

He tries again
Ol' vile corruption
To steal the soul of man

The Lord calls out
Oh valiant warrior
He's calling you to stand

Stand in the gap
Strong armored soldier
Turn back the soul of man

Treasury vs. Treachery

Lyell met his brother at the entrance to the center two hours before the conference. Their relationship was workable, but the differences they held brought some tension, and sometimes caused the fighting to begin.

"I'm glad you came alone," Arion said putting his arm around his brother. "I don't mind the kid you hang with as much as that old man he is always around. Nobody in town wants to be near him. Isn't he the one that got into trouble a few years back, and had his niece taken from him because of abuse?"

"Yeah, that's him. You just have to ignore him, and he will leave you alone. He's not the best person in the world. You got that one right. But, I won't abandon my friend. That old guy is his grandfather and he is not what I would call a good grandpa. The more I am around Darnell the better he gets treated. So I hang around him a lot."

"It's been a long time since we talked," Arion said. "How is your relationship with the Lord? Are you walking right, and listening to better music?"

It irritated Lyell that his brother could change the subject so easily, but that was his way—always an agenda.

"Nah, it ain't changed. You still claim to have the music treasures, and see me having the music trash?"

"I called it treasure and treachery," Arion said. "I wasn't talking so much about genre. I was talking about whatever we opened our ears to. If I fill my mind with good, I gain treasure, if I fill it with trash, it causes treachery. Your music deceives, and leads you away from God. I like to listen to what speaks truth, and leads me closer to Him. My only treasure is Jesus, Arion said. He is in my life, and I choose to play and listen to music that fills me with good things. It keeps my mind from evil."

"Let's not go there," Lyell said backing away from his brother. "Is that all you ever think about? You constantly talk Jesus, Jesus, and more Jesus? It's all I ever hear from you. Can't we ever just meet up, and say hi, and talk about life?"

"Sorry, little brother, it's just that Jesus *is* my life. I can't help but talk about Him. My hope is built solely on Him. Ever since dad left us, I found I could lean on Jesus."

"Yeah, well, you are no different than dad. You are always leaving us doing your music tours. And what do you get out of it? Nothing, that's what you get—flat out nothing!"

"I get paid enough to get by," Arion said defensively.

"Yeah," Lyell interrupted. "Our mother works hard to get us by. You could be out there making good money to help out. You don't make anything, though, because you are doing all Christian gigs."

"It's called ministry, Lyell. I'm helping people, and Momma is happy with that."

"Well, you're not helping us. So, go on and be Mr. Good Guy. Maybe you and Jesus shouldn't take the time to be concerned about us. No worries, we'll be okay."

Arion changed the direction of the conversation. He didn't want his brother running off again like he did the last time they had this discussion.

"So, mom is still coming tonight, right?"

"I don't know" Lyell said kicking the ground as he calmed down. "She's not feeling too well. I will be here though. I'm working tonight. Where are you heading after the conference?"

"I plan to come home right after, Arion said. "Will you be there?"

"I don't know. I might go with Darnell tonight. He needs a friend right now."

"Hey, I have to go," Arion said. "I know we don't always get along too well, but remember I'm down for you."

"Yeah right," Lyell said tipping his ball cap to one side. "That's what you say. One day you might have to pay up."

"Pay up? Are you sure you are okay?"

"No worries, brother, go on in, and get ready. I will see you tonight. I'm down for you too."

The Thought Surrendered

Simon knocked on the door of the Adams' home. It had been a year since seeing Jamee.

He wondered how she would receive him. He had written to her almost every week during that year so that she could get to know him. He had sent out nearly fifty letters talking about God, how he saw life, and sharing things about himself, including what he saw as his personal downfalls. He didn't send love letters. They were just letters. He didn't want to give her any false impressions of himself.

During that time he had received only five letters from her, but he didn't mind. His intentions were not to woo her, but to try to build a friendship. He was happy with what she did send. There was no mention of the possibilities of courting her when he was invited to come. He had simply been asked to come as support for her, as she ventured out again into ministry.

Jamee opened the door and Simon stood there for a moment speechless. She was beautiful, more than he had remembered. Her hair had grown into long waves that hung gently to each shoulder landing in the front with a smooth perfection. Her eyes looked brighter, and there were no longer the dark circles that had surrounded them before. She was a lovely young woman, carrying a pure kind of beauty.

She blushed, and he realized he was gawking.

"I'm sorry Jamee. I was staring. You have changed over the last year."

"For the better, I hope," she said with a petite giggle.

Simon's heart was pounding. He didn't think he would feel this emotional about seeing her again, but found he was captured by her."

"Simon, are you okay?"

"S . . . Sorry," he said, stuttering.

Man, what is wrong with me. I never lose my bearing," he thought.

This generally unruffled pastor suddenly found himself moved from confidence to uncertainty, and had to make a focused effort to regain his composure, and get his mind under control.

"Well, is your dad home? I'd like to see him."

Jamee smiled. "My parents are waiting in the dining room for you. Dinner is almost ready. Mom thought it would be nice to sit down together, and have a meal."

Simon followed her into the dining room. He grabbed Mr. Adams' hand, and gave it the typical power shake. Then he turned to Jamee's mother, hugging her gently. They sat down at the table while Mrs. Adams went to the kitchen to get some lemonade. Simon was trying to concentrate on what Mr. Adams was saying, but he couldn't take his eyes off of Jamee.

"Jamee, your mom might need some help," her dad said looking at her, and leaning his head toward the kitchen.

Jamee hesitated, but got up, and went to help her mother. As she left the room, Simon's eyes followed her, and he felt again a stirring in his heart. He thanked Mr. Adams for allowing him to come to visit, and then stood suddenly.

"Mr. Adams, do we have time before dinner to talk somewhere?"

"Well, we can make time. Is it urgent?"

Simon pushed his chair in, and tapped his fingers on the back of the chair.

"I am afraid if we don't talk now that I will lose my courage."

Jamee walked into the room with three glasses of lemonade. It was obvious that she wanted to share some time with them before dinner.

"Sorry Dear," her dad said. "I think Simon and I have some man to man discussion, and we will be taking our lemonade in my study. Tell your mom we won't be too long, and ask her to keep dinner warm for us."

Jamee watched as they took their glasses, and left the room. She wished she could go too. She figured it probably had something to do with her, and she wanted to know what was being said. She left it alone though, and returned to the kitchen giving Simon the freedom to talk to her father.

Simon grabbed his briefcase on the way to the study, and when they sat down he opened it up, pulling out his financial statement.

"What's this," Mr. Adams asked?

"I want you to see that I am financially able to take care of Jamee."

"Okay, but what else?"

"Well, I honestly wasn't sure how I felt before coming here. I think for the most part I was acting in what I felt was obedience to God."

"And has that changed since your arrival?"

"I am still acting in obedience to God, but now that I have come here . . . well, I saw such a purity and beauty in Jamee today. I find that I . . . um . . . well, I am very attracted to her. I believe I can love her in a way that will make sense to her, and bring good things to her life."

Simon hesitated a moment, then pressed on. "Is she . . . I mean do you think she is ready for me to court her, and do I have your permission to do so?"

Mr. Adams had gained respect for Simon, and he liked him. He trusted that God was leading him.

"I think she is ready. She has been working at the school as an aide for the disabled students, and has loved the work. She plans to go to university in the spring so she can teach. Her confidence and walk with God is being restored daily. She has definitely come a long way, and I do think she is ready. If she is willing you will both have my blessing. But I want you to remember why you are here. Your coming here was to lend support, not to engage in a courtship. So I would ask you to just do ministry right now, and wait until after that to open the door for dating. Let's go have dinner. There is something that Jamee wants to discuss with you before you both leave to go to the center tonight."

Neither Jamee nor Simon could eat much. There was too much they were both thinking about, and food seemed secondary. Simon kept watching the time so they wouldn't be late, and topics for conversation eluded him. Mrs. Adams broke through the chit chat, and sent the two on their way.

"I know it's early, but you two should go on. Maybe you can have some time to talk before you start your busy night."

"But, the dishes, mom."

"I will help, Jamee's dad said. You go on."

Jamee excused herself from the table, leaving Simon with her parents, and hurried to change into the conference staff tee shirt. She came out holding one of the tees in front of Simon.

"This one is for you," she said. "You can go change down the hall."

"I'll just change at the center," he said. "Let's go."

As they drove toward the auditorium they found everything to talk about, and their conversations carried them to a little pie shop near the building.

"Do we have time," Simon asked?

"There's plenty of time," Jamee said. "This is a pretty nice place to talk. It's relatively quiet, and there are small booths that don't get used too much."

Simon had forgotten that there was something Jamee wanted to talk to him about. It's no wonder her mom sent them off so soon. She must have known that they were not going to get much talking done there.

It was quiet inside. Jamee directed Simon toward the back where the small booths were, and said she would order for them and bring it back. Soon she came carrying one large piece of apple pie and coffee. She sat his coffee down on the table in front of him, and the piece of pie in the middle between them.

"Their pies are big, too big for one person. Do you mind sharing from the same plate? I can get another plate, and cut it in half if it makes you feel better."

"This is fine," he said. "Sit down, and let's enjoy some pie."

As they took up their forks, Simon discovered a playful side to Jamee. Every time he tried to put his fork into the pie to get a bite, she would use hers to push his away.

"I want that bite," she said laughing.

He couldn't get his fork in the pie because of her teasing. Finally he caught her hand as she was stabbing at the pie, and he was taken off guard again by his emotions. He put down his fork, and reached to cup both of her hands in his, and as she responded his mind was reeling. Too many thoughts began to bombard him and he quickly pulled his hand away as the Holy Spirit urged him to take every thought captive to Christ, and place it under submission to the cross.

"I apologize, Jamee," he said. "I got carried away. What was it you wanted to talk to me about?"

I could love this guy, Jamee thought, as she rubbed her hands together still contemplating that special touch.

"I have a favor to ask of you," she said. "Do you remember me telling you about Kambo?"

"I remember."

"He is in town. Actually, he has been here all the time since I returned, but I have not seen him yet, although I want to."

Simon wasn't sure where this was going but he didn't let his mind wander about why this was important to her.

"So what is stopping you?" he answered flatly.

"I want you to go with me."

"Why do you want me to go?"

"Kambo is in hospice. He is dying." She had to fight back the tears, because she didn't want Simon to read any more into it than was there.

"I want to tell him I forgive him, Simon. He has repented, and I am not sure why God won't restore him, but I want Kambo to know before he dies that I have forgiven him. I just don't want to go alone."

"So, I ask again. Why me? Why not ask your parents?"

"I think it will do him good to know that I am okay, and that I have someone good in my life. I don't want him dying, thinking he has destroyed me."

"Am I in your life," Simon asked?

Jamee looked down at the table and spoke timidly.

"If you want to be, then the answer is yes."

Simon wanted to jump up, and hug her, but again contained himself, and simply slipped his hand back on to hers.

"That would be wonderful, Jamee. I do want you in my life, and I will go with you to visit Kambo. It means a lot that you trust me to go with you."

Shiri's Song

Born out of youthful desire
To find my life I leave all behind
Seeking a Kingdom far beyond,
My longing heart climbs higher
Lord, my longing heart climbs higher.

Nothing here can hold me steady,
To find the way, I follow you
To take me home to be with you,
My longing heart sings louder
Lord, my longing heart sings louder.

Listen boys to the song of my soul,
To hear a new way to reach you
To let Jesus come sing over you,
My longing heart sings louder
Lord, my longing heart sings louder.

Shiri's Song

Yenene was preparing the potion of incense that he believed would fill the box with an enchanting aroma. As he did he chanted the calling forth of the demons of lust that would lure the teens of this town. He hated this good reputation that this town had. He determined he would go to his grave, sowing seeds of hell into the lives of these people.

He called his grandson in to help him.

"Darnell," he yelled. "Get down here and help me."

Darnell ran to the basement door where his grandfather often worked, and pleaded with him to let him off tonight. He hated this work. The appeals made to demons, and the rituals his grandfather practiced were repulsive to him. He never wanted to be a part of engaging the support of the underworld, and if he could he would avoid it.

"Get down here. We have to follow the ceremony."

Darnell went to the basement, and stood beside his grandfather. His phone rang as soon as he reached his uncle. Seeing that it was Lyell he let it ring. His uncle enjoyed that ringtone as it rapped about the degradation of women, and he sniggered as it went through its refrain.

The two stood there with their altar built, and began to light, and strategically place candles around the table. As Yenene began his ritual Darnell joined in, and as usual lost himself in the process.

Lyell came to the door, and when no one answered he checked to see if it was opened. When he entered he heard music coming from the basement, and went to see if his friend was down there. He had never been in the basement before. So, he had no clue what was down there.

When he opened the door he shouted Darnell's name. Hearing no reply, he went on down the stairs. Darnell and his grandfather were holding hands encircled around the small table, and it looked like they were praying. That made no sense. He knew they didn't believe in God. When he came to the bottom of the steps the hair on his neck stood up. He felt like he needed to run. Whatever they were praying to, it was not God. He started to turn around and leave, but he heard his brother's name being called out, and it made him stop.

"Hey!" he called out. "Darnell, what are you doing? What is all this, and why are you calling my brother's name?"

The song called *Extinction* was playing in the back ground, and the words were entering his brain and finding a resting place there. It was a song he knew. He and Darnell had played it often. Hearing it now created a familiar spirit that suddenly conjured in the room. What looked like a colorful gas vapor arose in the corner, and began to encircle Darnell's head.

"Darnell," Lyell shouted! "What's going on?"

Neither one turned to look at him. They were so involved in this ritual that they didn't hear him.

I didn't know Darnell did stuff like this, Lyell thought as he was looking around at the basement.

It was all too eerie for him. The song was still playing, and the rhythm of the song was trying to resonate with him, as it usually did when they were together in the park listening to music. But Lyell did not want to link with this music now, because his brother's name was connected somehow to the power of the lyrics. Yenene and Darnell kept cadence with the music, and as they called out Arion's name the lyrics pierced into Lyell's heart with fear and dread.

> Extinction
> Gone, forever removed
> No more life left in you
> Extinction . . . .

Lyell wasn't sure what to do. He yelled again at the two to stop, but they did not hear him. Shadows danced above the candles, creating evil images. A spiritual darkness smothered the room. The stifling despondency crept into Lyell's heart, and he cried out to God. He suddenly remembered his mom. Before he left the house earlier, she had written on a piece of paper a Scripture for the day. It was something she always did, but today was different. She put it in his hand, and held onto his hand for a long time.

"You really need this today," she had told him. "Don't toss it aside. Put it in your pocket. I will be praying for you, so that you will know when to read this."

He stuck his hand in his pocket and pulled out the small notebook paper with flowered border and began to read out loud what was written there.

And I heard a loud voice in heaven, saying, "Now the salvation and the power and the kingdom of our God and the authority of his Christ have come, for the accuser of our brothers has been thrown down, who accuses them day and night before our God. And they have conquered him by the blood of the Lamb and by the word of their testimony, for they loved not their lives even unto death. [18]

Suddenly there was silence. They vapor was gone and the dark atmosphere subdued. Darnell and his grandfather, with glassy, dazed eyes looked up at Lyell. When he saw the look on their faces, his heart pounded, but he continued to read the rest that was written by his mother on that paper. It was the last stanza in the song that she had been working on.

Listen boys to the song of my soul—to hear a new way to reach you. To let Jesus come sing over you—my longing heart sings louder Lord, my longing heart sings louder.

The Lord then led him to read that verse and that stanza again. This time he added his brother's name as he did it. He did not really understand it all, but acted out of sheer desire to protect his family. As soon as Arion's name was connected in that verse with the blood of the Lamb there was a loud shattering noise that sounded like something had broken, but Lyell saw nothing break.

Yenene's face lost all expression as he looked at Lyell, and knew he couldn't touch him. He turned abruptly to Darnell.

"You are useless and worthless, and no better than death itself," he said wrinkling his face and cursing the boy.

"Because of the friends you keep, we are rendered ineffective. We can take no ground tonight. Get out of my sight!"

He then pointed his finger at Lyell. That long fingernail stuck out vividly.

"Leave my house, and don't come back."

Lyell looked over at his friend, watching as Darnell shrugged his shoulders. He had no say over his grandfather, and accepted whatever he said.

Lyell prayed for Darnell as he walked up the stairs. Prayer had never been on his lips, and he marveled at how easily it came. He saw something tonight that began to change his heart and mind about a lot of things. When he got outside he called his mother to thank her for the verse, and tell her what happened here. When she answered he could tell she was having hard time breathing.

"Mom, are you okay?" Mom, are you there?"

He hung up his phone, and ran home as fast as he could. His mind was reeling from all that had happened tonight. He wanted to tell her the good she had done with her verse, and it made him run hard and fast. When he got there he charged into the house and found her on her knees by the bed with the phone on the floor beside her. He was too late. She was gone. It looked like she was praying, and had died right there on her knees. He left his mom in that place, and called the hospital. Not knowing what else to do, he waited there by himself for the ambulance to come.

He started to call Arion, but broke down just thinking of it, and decided that he should wait. As he waited he paced and struggled to sit still long enough to collect himself. He didn't think it would do any good for his brother to come right now, and decided to do this part alone. He knelt down next to his mother's body, laid his head on the bed next to hers and sobbed.

"Mom, I promise I will change," he said crying. "I'm sorry I waited too long for you to see it, but I hope you can see it from Heaven. I *will* change."

The ambulance crew came into the house through the opened door. Finding Lyell kneeling on the floor, they pulled him up trying to calm him. One of the paramedics stayed with him while the other two checked his mother, and pronounced her dead.

After they left to take her to the morgue Lyell stood at the door. His heart was breaking, and he was crying out to God to help him. He was devastated, and didn't want to go anywhere, but he felt he needed to do one thing for his mother tonight.

He drove his mom's car to the stadium even though he didn't have a license. He didn't care. He just needed to get there fast. He was sitting on the edge of his seat all the way, trying to nudge the speed limit to his benefit. He finally arrived, pulled up to the front, and left the car unattended with the door opened and the keys still in it.

The teenager moved through the doors just as the music was about to end. He walked past the concessions where he was supposed to be working, and didn't heed his boss calling out his name. When he entered the auditorium the music was playing softly in the background. He saw his brother close in near the mike, and listened intently as he spoke.

"I know this is a conference about waiting for that right partner in life. Maybe I should be addressing some of those things to you right now, but I sense the Spirit of the Lord saying that there is someone who cannot respond to a call to a life of purity because you are not yet His. So right now, I want to open up the front of the auditorium. Take time to listen to the Holy Spirit of God. If He is drawing you don't resist Him. Come up here, and let us pray for you. Let today be the day of your salvation."

As the musicians continued to play, Arion read from Micah 7:7-8

But as for me, I will look to the Lord; I will wait for the God of my salvation; my God will hear me. Rejoice not over me, O my enemy; when I fall, I shall rise; when I sit in darkness, the Lord will be a light to me.

He paused before sharing the message of this passage about coming out of bondage, and knowing God is faithful to bring us out. Before he could continue he saw someone walking up the center aisle. He was overwhelmed at seeing that it was his brother. He dropped the mike, and ran down to where his brother stood. After they prayed together for his brother to repent, and ask Christ into his heart Arion looked around. No one else came up. He was amazed that the Holy Spirit of God had moved so powerfully that night for him to sense a need for an altar call for one person, and thanked God it was one very special person. Lyell held on to Arion for a long time before finally telling him about their mother. He needed to have that time with his brother before the chaos of her death began to take them into their time of mourning.

To the Sentinel Guarding the Mind

In 2 Corinthians 10:5, we are told to take every thought captive to Christ. We can only do this if we have determined to put that sentinel at the doorpost off our minds.

1 Corinthians 10:12 says: *Therefore let anyone who thinks that he stands take heed lest he fall.*

What Paul was saying to the church at Corinth was to guard your mind. The Corinthian church was proud of their spiritual assessment concerning idols, and Paul took them back to look at the life of the Israelites. He showed them how they fell (or died) in the wilderness because they placed their security in their covenant religiosity, and failed to take captive the thoughts that led them into a spiritual wilderness away from God. The point is to always be on guard against anything that sets itself up against God, not matter how small it may seem.

Simon embodies the concept. You can't always prevent the thoughts, but you can capture every thought, and put it under submission to Christ. Taking authority over all thoughts creates a powerful testimony of God's unfailing grace to enable you to overcome.

While the story of Lyell's life only shows the effects of music on the mind, it is important that the man and woman of God keep in mind the effect of those things seen as well. Remember the path of destruction Amos Marcus Desi took with pornography, and you can easily see that those impure things you look upon are dragnets to death as much as the music. Be careful what you watch or read or hear. Even the seemingly small things can take you away.

The mind is an incredible memory machine, and whatever you see, read, watch on TV will be stored. Be sure too, that whatever you listen to goes into storage and the mind continues to process it. With the visual and audio input your mind tends to develop sensory hearing. A certain song interacts with an emotion. If that song is played again, it causes another stirring of that same emotion each time it is played. The same is true for visual. The brain gets trained to act or react upon seeing certain things. I see a spider, and I react to step on it. My brain is trained to respond this way.

This is important information for the Christian. Romans 12:2, says this about your mind: *Do not be conformed to this world, but be transformed by the renewal of your mind, that by testing you may discern what is the will of God, what is good and acceptable and perfect.*

Transformed means changed. Renewal means more than made new. It indicates a restoration or rejuvenation. So this new way of thinking is supposed to be that which pulls out the old connections, sharpens them, and reconnects them to be conformed to Christ. There is no possibility for such restoration if the old stuff is still being jammed into our minds.

This is where it gets hard, but there is no way to get around it. What you allow into your brain works to train you for action. Then enemy is crafty, and will present subtly those offenses against God that you allow in. They will not look serious, but they will keep your mind from complete renewal in the Lord.

If you watch a show that romanticizes infidelity or *friends with benefits,* you train your mind to find these things acceptable. If that thing you watch stirs an emotion in you, it has potential to lock you in to a corrupted way of thinking.

If the music you listen to is degrading or demeaning, you open the battlefield to an unseen enemy who can rob you of purity of mind. The things that God's people are allowing in their lives are killing a mighty walk with the Lord.

Matthew 6:22 says: *The eye is the lamp of the body. So, if your eye is healthy, your whole body will be full of light.* This verse speaks to the dealings of the inner person. It is, in essence, saying that the body will produce as much light as it has taken in, and is applied to its inner workings. What is induced will be produced.

Don't be fooled. It *does* matter what you watch, and what you listen to. Your choices will determine the strength of your walk. God is faithful now as He was to Israel. He will always provide a way out of bondage, but just as His people walked through the Red Sea, so must you walk through the passages that He provides, to take you away from the enemy.

Be careful if you think you stand. You could be tottering on uneven ground if you are allowing the enemy to pave the way of your mind.

Carolyn Marie Hudler

My son, give attention to my words; Incline your ear to my sayings. Do not let them depart from your sight; Keep them in the midst of your heart, for they are life to those who find them and health to all their body. Watch over your heart with all diligence, for from it flows the springs of life. Proverbs 4:20-23

Lyell Shiri-Kalele

LOYAL FRIEND, SONG OF MY SOUL

Guarding the Heart

"My heart is steadfast, O God; I will sing, I will sing praises, even with my soul. Awake, harp and lyre; I will awaken the dawn! I will give thanks to You, O LORD, among the peoples, and I will sing praises to you among the nations. For Your lovingkindness is great above the heavens, and your truth reaches to the skies. Be exalted, O God, above the heavens, and your glory above all the earth. Psalm 108:1-5

Awaken

Steadfast beating
Sing, my heart, sing
Awaken within me the cymbals of my life
Faithful Lover
Exalt, Oh Lord, exalt
Wash all over me with your glorious love

Heart Surgery

Lyell knew the Lord had entered into his life on the night of the conference. There were so many thoughts and emotions to work through, but one thing he knew for certain—He belonged. It was something that he never thought he could say. He had always known that his mom and his brother cared deeply for him, but he couldn't say he *knew* they loved him. It wasn't anything they did or failed to do really. He lacked a sense of belonging, and that's what outlawed him more than anything.

His mother had always been a Christian. As far back as he could remember, she prayed with her boys, and taught them from the Scriptures. Every day gave them that piece of paper with a Bible verse written on it. She always said she was just packing some meat to feed their souls. He wished now that he had saved them all, and lamented having wadded up so many of them, and tossed them into the trash.

It seemed his anger was always directed anywhere except toward his father. Lyell wondered now if maybe it had landed on Arion more because he was the only other man in the house. It was just six months after their father left that Arion went away to college, and Lyell resented his leaving.

Lyell's dad always said he was a Christian, but the spiritual direction always came from his mom. He never saw his dad go to church, never heard him say a prayer, and had never been taught by him, about the things of God. With that final blow of his dad leaving, Lyell had determined that he wanted no part of a dad who would walk out on his kids, or a God who would let that happen.

Now, having come to the Lord, he thanked God for his mother, and he knew this would become a practice for him every time he sat down to read the Bible. The sweetness of the Word of God reminded him of her.

He had begun using her Bible, and was familiarized with some of the nuances of that particular version. Almost as much as reading the Scriptures, he looked forward to discovering notes she had written along the way as she read.

"Lord, order my steps and light my path as I read your word," he prayed, as he sat quietly in the house, with the Bible opened in front of him. He wasn't sure where he wanted to read, and thumbed through many pages, perusing some of the Old Testament Books, searching for a good place to land. He came across a side note that his mom had written, and it drew attention to a possible resting place for him.

This particular note was written with a fine point pen in purple ink. He almost went past the note and the passage. But the words *heart surgery* brought him back to read the entire note and the highlighted verses. Lyell settled into the chair to read. He wanted time to absorb what she was saying here.

I slept, but my heart was awake. A sound! My beloved is knocking. My beloved put his hand to the latch, and my heart was thrilled within me. Song of Solomon 5:2, 4

He wondered what this verse meant, and what it had to do with heart surgery, so he read more of the purple-inked note.

Heart Surgery, the note began. *Who would have ever thought this beautiful song about the Bride of Christ would relate so closely to heart surgery.*

The margin in his mom's Bible was small, and she wanted to say more about how she had resonated with this verse, so she set an asterisk at the end of her comment, and referred to the notes page in the back. Lyell turned to the back, and as he read her poem it felt as though she was standing right there. His heart melted for the love his mother had for her Savior.

Purple Hearts Explosion

I searched for love in fields of green
When my heart awakened a burgeoning shoot
I postured low in the grasses and waited 'til the gardener came
And he covered me with the loam of his love

Stirred from the silence of nurture
When my senses captured the sweet aromas
I arose in the midst of wonder 'til the scent purposed my eyes
Unfastening all the color of his beauty

I reached for the rose-blushed spectrum of color
When my heart awakened a blossoming fire
I positioned myself in eagerness 'til the great recital
Lacing my toe shoes with botanical knots

Aroused from a sprout I flourished
When my vision ignited by bursting hues
I danced in pirouetting splendor 'til the Gardener came
Marrying me to Purple Hearts Explosion

Lyell meditated on the depth of the poem she had written, and continued reading to understand the connection it had to heart surgery.

I had a dream, last night, he read in her notes.

I dreamed I carried my heart in my hands. It was damaged, broken and losing life-blood. As I carried it, I was looking for someone to help me put it back into my body so I could live.

Lyell sat straight up and sat on the edge of the chair, now anxious to read more.

Everything around me was black and white. There was no color. Even the blood coming from my heart was a dark shade of gray. When I looked up, I saw a green field and walked toward it. It was refreshing, and I needed to rest. So I lay down in the tall blades of grass. The gentle covering of the grass and the soft scent of the air covered me, and I slept.

When I got up, I reached toward the sky, and began pulling colors into the world. It was exciting, as I gathered reds and blues around me, but when I grabbed the purple, Jesus entered in. He looked down at my heart that was lying on the ground. When He picked it up I thought surely He would fix it, but He didn't. He tossed it into the dark areas of the sky—those places that had no color.

He then took His own heart, and held it toward me. When He put his hand to the latch of my heart's door, a holy fire shot out, taking hold of his heart, and pulling it in to my soul. And when His heart became mine it exploded within me with new life. Together we danced as we sang a song I had never sung before, and I saw color everywhere, but the purple burst forth like fireworks in the skies. I awoke and I no longer felt alone and abandoned. Jesus married me to himself. I am His.

"Oh Mama," he said after reading this. "What a testimony of your life. This makes my soul sing. I want that same kind of heart surgery. Do you think that someone like me can have it? I know that I now belong to Jesus, but I want more. I want that fullness that you had."

In the quiet of that room he knelt down, and asked Jesus to take out the old heart, and give him a new one.

"I want that fullness, Lord," he prayed. "I want to walk in the fullness of Your Holy Spirit. Then, I will carry out the things of the Spirit. Oh God of Mercy, Pour out Your Spirit in me."

A hand touched his shoulder in that life-changing moment. It was hot, like fire, but it did not hurt. It felt comforting, but empowering. The presence of God came in, and sang over him with songs of everlasting love. He heard the sound of a heartbeat, and felt a tingling in his chest. It was painful, but the pain was not physical. Then, there was a tender touch on his chest. Suddenly he could hear the sound of a horn blaring, as if it were calling to announce the opening of a ceremony. It was not heard with his ear, but in the silence of his soul. Joyful songs seemed to burst inside of him, and he received the words to songs, hiding the lyrics in his heart.

He danced and sang in the quiet of his home, and when he felt the power of presence of the Holy Spirit of God was fading he cried out for Him to stay.

"I will never leave you or forsake you," he heard Jesus say. Long after the peak of this soulful crescendo, Lyell remained there in the quiet for a while, taking in the lingering splendor of the moment.

He could not explain to others what had happened in that moment; he could only say that he, like his mother, had heart surgery.

Lyell changed his name that day. He added his mother's name, so that he would always remember the legacy of a woman who lived and prayed that one day her son would have a song in his soul. He became Lyell Shiri-Kalele, a loyal friend, who carried in him a love song of his soul.

To the Sentinel Guarding the Heart

You Sing What You Believe

The heart refers to the inner man. It deals with the will and the understanding—the very core of your being. Proverbs, chapter 4 offers an exhortation to protect the inner person. Often times, this teaching from proverbs stops with the 23rd verse, when the best and most pertinent part follows. Proverbs 4:23 tells you what to do, and the remaining verses tell you how to do it. Verse 23 is like a chapter title in the table of contents of an instruction manual for godliness. Proverbs 4:24-5:2 is the step by step directions.

Put away from you crooked speech and put devious talk far from you. Let your eyes look directly forward, and your gaze be straight before you. Ponder the path of your feet; then all your ways will be sure. Do not swerve to the right or to the left; turn your foot away from evil. My son, be attentive to my wisdom; incline your ear to my understanding, that you may keep discretion, and your lips may guard knowledge. Proverbs 4:23-5:2

Protecting Your Heart

1. Watch what you say
2. Keep focused toward the prize, and be careful of what you look on.
3. Think about what you are going to do before you do it to be sure you are heading rightly.
4. Walk with God, and don't even turn an inch toward the devil.
5. Choose God's wisdom, and pay attention to godly discussion that leads to understanding
6. Be discreet.

Of course there is more, but the best of all is to give your heart to God, and then let Him begin to set it toward the direction and purpose for which He has intended. The things that are in your heart are the things that will manifest in your life. If you put ungodliness into your heart by the things you listen to or read or practice you will not be able to gain wisdom. Those things must go first.

The thing about heart surgery is that we all must have it in order to live for Him. He takes out the heart of stone and gives us a heart of flesh. And this heart we need to guard all the more, for it is given by the hand of the Lord. To the sentinel guarding the heart, don't forget your sword, the word of God. God's words can destroy arguments of every kind and tear down anything that sets itself up against God.

Gabriel Alexavier

HERO OF GOD, PROTECTOR OF THE HOME

Be on your guard; stand firm in the faith; be men of courage; be strong. 1 Corinthians 16:13

Heart and Home

The town of Fisher was in mass confusion. The sound of an explosion filled the streets just before the Monday morning classes were to begin. Sirens were bellowing, as they raced to the scene where the town's only high school went under high alert and had begun to evacuate as many students as they could from the building. Flames were beginning to belch out from the eastern corner of the school. Parents were leaving job sites, and rushing from their homes to make their way toward the school, in hopes of finding their child outside in the safety of the schools outer compound.

Fire Rescue evaluated the scene aware that the end of the building that was blazing afire, was the end that held the three automotive bays used by the vocational technical students for training. One explosion had already erupted as the flames hit a car that sat inside one of the bays, and the rescue workers moved in with caution knowing that a reserve of gasoline was not far from it.

Flames surged out of the window, and spilled onto the pavement separating from top to bottom, and momentarily creating a gap in the space between the window and the ground. Firefighters aimed their water hose just below the mushrooming flames that raced rapidly back up to join the larger flames that were spilling from inside the building. Crowds were gathering to watch as they attempted to stop the flames from devouring the school.

Jamee was inside. She heard the fire alarm, and walked with the teacher and the students from their classroom to the door, but turned back at the last minute.

"Where are you going?" The teacher asked. "You need to get outside."

Jamee looked down the long hallway that headed toward the vocational wing.

"I thought I saw someone down there. I just want to make sure there isn't someone stuck, or unable to get out."

"Don't be foolish. That's why we have rescue workers. Come on, Jamee."

She looked for a quick glance at the teacher, but would not go with her.

"I promise I will be right there," she said. "I will just walk down the hall, and take a quick look. If I don't see anyone, I will get out quickly."

As soon as the teacher and the students came out the door, another loud explosive echo resounded from the building. It was gunshot that had a double blast sound effect as it reverberated with rugged recoil. One of the rescue workers knew the sound.

".357," he said. "Someone is still in there, and has a gun."

Jamee thought she heard gunfire, but ignored it and looked in the classrooms down the hallway making sure no one was in any of them. She was sure she saw someone. As she looked straight ahead, she saw smoke beginning to filter through under the shop doors, and hurried to finish her check. She thought she heard crying, but it sounded like a small child, and it didn't make sense that a child would be in here. She kept looking.

Firefighters were working to extinguish the flames, while the police began taking measures to investigate the gunfire situation. Back up was called in and the police chief was notified.

"What's the evacuation status?" The police chief asked.

"We think there may still be three people inside."

Reporters were sending out new data every few minutes, and the news travelled just as fast from one social web site to another. Simon was in his car going to a meeting when he heard the news of the school in Fisher. He pulled over immediately, listened to the news on his phone.

"Firefighters worked to contain the fire which began from an explosion of an unknown source," the reporter announced gravely. "But it appears there are other concerns in this small town high school. Gunshots were reported, and there are three who have not been accounted for. The names of those yet missing have not yet been released, but they believe it is two students and an aide."

"Jamee," Simon gasped. He dialed her number, praying she would answer, but it went straight to voicemail. He called her dad, and got no answer there either. Panic began to set in, and he turned his car around, and headed home.

Jamee called down the hallway.

"Is anyone there?"

The fire seemed to be diminishing in the building, but was still not out. There was a loud crackle of flames burning whatever it touched in the building, and the smell of smoke was thick and pungent. It was beginning to sting her eyes. She knew she had to get out of there soon.

"Please, is anyone here? We need to leave if you are. Please come out."

She thought she heard the child crying again, and she was worried that maybe a little child had somehow come in to the building, and was afraid to come out.

"You can come out. It's okay. I won't hurt you," she said, walking down the hallway towards the last few rooms trying to pinpoint the origin of the whimpering. Jamee opened the door to the classroom near the sound, and jumped back when she looked into the far corner of the room.

There was a teenage boy lying under the table in a fetal position. She walked over to him. When she got came close, he arose suddenly, and the table flew up, and fell backwards against the wall. His face was pointing to the floor, and his dripping wet hair was hanging down in his face. He looked up at her slowly pulling his wet hair away from his eyes to one side. His eyes narrowed and rolled backwards until the pupil disappeared. Then he pulled the gun out of his pocket, causing Jamee to scream.

The special weapons team arrived and was checking the school's rosters waiting to find out who still remained inside, when they heard the scream. While firefighters still worked, the team moved inconspicuously toward the building.

The principal was able to contact Jamee's father through a neighbor to let him know that that his daughter was still in the building. As he ran out the door, he looked at his phone to see if Jamee had called. He saw none from her, but there were several from Simon. He debated about calling him, but decided he already knew something, and was anxious about her safety.

Simon sat in front of the TV in his home so he could be in touch with what was happening, and as he sat he prayed, believing that God didn't give him Jamee just to take her away from him.

"Lord, I feel helpless," he prayed. "I want to protect Jamee, but I can't reach her. So I ask you to encircle her now, and keep her safe. Let no harm come to her. Let no weapon formed against her prosper. Break the arm of the enemy that would take her down. She is yours, and I ask you to send your angels to keep her hidden."

Jamee's heart was pounding, and she was wishing she had left the building earlier. The penetrating smoke was making her lightheaded. She kept her eyes on this teenager, and tried backing away from him toward the door. Without warning, he pointed the gun at her and pulled the trigger. The round clicked on an empty chamber, and he opened it up

"Still one in there," he said. He closed it, and spun it back around again. Tears were coursing down his cheeks. He pulled the trigger back, but before he could let go another teenager burst through the door. She knew this one.

"Lyell?"

He didn't answer, but kept his eyes on that gun.

"Don't do it, Darnell. It's not worth it. Stop and think. C'mon, it's me your buddy Lyell. I'm telling you this is not what you want."

Lyell began walking closer, and Darnell didn't budge. He kept the gun pointed at Jamee, and remained motionless, watching as Lyell came in closer.

"Darnell," Lyell said calmly. "You know you can trust me. Let it go."

Darnell looked back toward the shop area. The smoke was overpowering him, and he began coughing. Jamee was coughing too as she moved closer to the door. She saw Lyell nod his head motioning her to get out. He called out Darnell's name loudly, and caused him to look his way long enough to distract his attention away from Jamee. She bolted out the door, and ran down the hallway as fast as she could. She was looking back to see if he followed, and ran right into one of the special weapons officers. He caught her as she collapsed on the floor in front of him.

The officer stayed with her, and called for the paramedics. The other two moved toward the end of the hallway. It was eerily quiet, but they continued to move forward hoping to hear something that would give direction. Smoke quickly filled the end of the long hallway. As the officers approached one of the class rooms they heard coughing, and moved closer to the door, one of them sneaking under the door's window to get to the room without being seen.

As soon as he placed his hand to the door knob, a shot was fired, and echoed out into the hallway. There was there was a gap that spanned a matter of seconds, where silence permeated the crowd waiting outside. It brought Jamee to consciousness.

"No," she cried out!"

The deputy pushed through the door, and found one student on the floor. The lower part of his arm was dangling from the point where two bones stuck through, and blood was spilling from his arm. He gagged from smoke inhalation, and it made his situation seem more urgent.

The other student was standing over him with the gun in his hand, and the barrel opened up. When Lyell saw them he dropped the gun to the floor.

"It's empty, don't shoot," he said coughing.

The deputy grabbed his arm and hand cuffed him, then he called again for paramedics. Lyell was escorted out and taken to the hospital. The crowd stood by, and watched as they walked Darnell out to a separate ambulance. Jamee broke through and ran over to him.

"He'll be okay, Ma'am. Do you know him? Just looks like he broke his arm. It's an open fracture. He'll be okay."

"The shot?" she asked.

"Looks like it fired into the ceiling, but that's all I know."

Another stretcher was brought out. Whoever it was on that stretcher was covered completely. No one knew immediately who it was. But when Darnell saw it he broke down and cried. Then Lyell remembered the community project for the auto shop was to do free oil changes. He remembered seeing Yenene's car in the shop. Looking at Darnell's reaction now, it wasn't hard to figure out what had just happened, and who was under that sheet on the gurney.

Lyell was released to an officer, who took him to their headquarters office for questioning. Arion met his brother at the police station, and stayed with him while they questioned him about the incident. He was proud of his brother's heroic actions, but hated thinking of the possibilities.

The investigating officer came in, and sat next to Lyell. "I'm Lt. Alexavier—Gabriel Alexavier. I will be doing the follow-up on this incident, so we will get to know each other pretty well in the few weeks ahead. Today is only the beginning."

Lyell nodded his head in agreement.

"I'd like to go over it all again," the officer said. "So, tell me what happened."

"I was leaving the school after the fire broke out and I saw Darnell coming out of the shop with the gun in his hand. I ran after him to try to stop him from hurting anyone. When he saw me, he ran back into the shop area where the fire was blazing, and I went out to the other side of the building to see if I could get in through the back door." He sighed as he recounted his steps.

"But when I got there the fire was already covering the door. So I snuck back into the building, and headed back down the hallway. That's when I heard all the commotion in the classroom."

Lyell shifted a bit in his seat trying to get comfortable.

"Miss Jamee managed to get out. After she was gone, Darnell was going to shoot himself. I wrestled the gun from his hand, and it went off. When it did, he smacked his arm hard against the desk. I knew it was bad when I saw both bones sticking out, but I was glad he didn't die."

"Well," Alexavier said. "He may not feel the same. It's likely he will be charged with arson, and murder. That boy's life is probably over."

"Yeah, I'm sure," Lyell said, "But if he had died then he'd be in Hell. At least now there is hope for him to give his heart to Christ."

"The kid is sick. Why do you concern yourself with him?"

"He was my friend," Lyell said. "Besides, someone once took time to concern themselves with me."

Lyell paused a minute.

"Sir," he said. "If you don't mind my saying, I think more people need to be concerned. You never know what a person has gone through to make them what they are. Maybe the concern of one person can change the course of their life forever—just saying."

As the brothers walked out the door Gabriel overheard Arion question his brother.

"Why did you do it? I know what you said in there, but there is more isn't there? There is another thing that drove you to stand firm in that building."

"I did it because God gave me something great. He gave me life, and now has set up house inside of me. I wanted to guard my home. In a way, I was standing up for what is good and right inside of me, but also God helped me to prevent another evil thing from happening in there. I am called to be a guardian of my house, and that school is part of where I live. It's part of home. So I guess you could say it was for the love God and home."

Gabriel Alexavier's heart sank, and the tough cop looked for a retreat after hearing the testimony of that teenager. He walked downstairs to the little chapel in the station. He went up front by the cross, took off his hat, and confessed to God his lack. Hearing the story of this young man wanting to protect his home pierced his conscience, because he had not taken care of his own home.

"God forgive me," he said. I know my body is the temple of the Holy Spirit, and I have abused it with too much alcohol. No wonder my wife and kids are hurting. I have not done too well on either home front."

He knelt down on the floor, and recommitted his life to Christ. He had seen too much today to take for granted his own family, knowing that stuff like this could hit home.

"Lord, lead me to truth, and show me how to protect my home," he prayed. "I want my kids to grow up being healthy and whole and godly. I want to be their champion before I am anyone else's hero."

Gabriel sat there for the next hour in quiet acquiescence to the direction he felt he should go from here. He believed that what he heard during this time of submission was from God and he knew obedience was required.

Soul and Spirit

Keeping Lamps Ready

"Then the kingdom of heaven will be like ten virgins who took their lamps and went to meet the bridegroom. Five of them were foolish, and five were wise. For when the foolish took their lamps, they took no oil with them, but the wise took flasks of oil with their lamps. As the bridegroom was delayed, they all became drowsy and slept. But at midnight there was a cry, 'Here is the bridegroom! Come out to meet him.' Then all those virgins rose and trimmed their lamps. And the foolish said to the wise, 'Give us some of your oil, for our lamps are going out.' But the wise answered, saying, 'since there will not be enough for us and for you, go rather to the dealers and buy for yourselves.' And while they were going to buy, the bridegroom came, and those who were ready went in with him to the marriage feast, and the door was shut. Afterward the other virgins came also, saying, 'Lord, lord, open to us.' But he answered, 'Truly, I say to you, I do not know you.' Watch therefore, for you know neither the day nor the hour. Matthew 25:1-13

Hidden Love Postlude

That which we love wants to journey our way
Yet we turn love aside to hide, to hide, to hide
Yet never to forget what could have been

Our Bygone Friend, True Self, seems to always elude us
And mock at the reflection in the pond
Where we try to refresh the weariness of travel

That which we love we oft' let go into the night
Today has brought the need for a divergence
As we see our humanness feebly unguarded

Gabriel left the station without speaking to anyone. The day was disturbing, and the call of God on his life was overwhelming. What he knew must take place in the next twenty-four hours was not an easy thing for him, but he had to obey. He stopped by the church on his way home hoping the pastor would still be there. He needed some strong spiritual guidance, and this was the only place he knew to begin.

The church sat up on hill, and could be seen from all directions coming into the downtown area. Monday was a casual day in the building. The senior pastor took Mondays off, and usually it was only the secretary and the children's ministry staff that came in. There was a small men's group that met after work for prayer and fellowship, and Jamee's dad often led the group.

Mr. Adams needed those men today. He praised God for the safety of his daughter, and was eager to gather with the other men. He offered his thanks and praise, knowing it could have been so much worse.

As he settled into the small room in the church to prepare for the study, Gabriel came in asking the secretary to speak with the pastor.

"He's not here," Mr. Adams said, overhearing the conversation. "Can I help in some way?"

"I have some hard things ahead of me that I know I need to take care of, and I was hoping for guidance and some prayers."

"Well, unless you are set on speaking to the pastor, I can help you with that. We can go in the other room and talk if you want."

As Gabriel followed him into the room the Holy Spirit began to stir in this young officer's heart. He didn't know what was ahead, but he sensed that God was in it. Gabriel unveiled before this stranger, his sin against God, and his outbursts of anger towards his family. He asked for prayer that he would have the courage to go home, and seek forgiveness from his wife, and for the strength to put away the alcohol.

As they knelt to pray, again a heavenly host gathered to watch as the Holy Spirit poured out into Gabriel's life, filling him with the gifts of heaven. Before his knees even touched the floor the power of the Holy Spirit began to work in him with a baptism that comes from above. Gabriel sensed that he was being given everything he needed, to walk in obedience before God.

When he left for home, a spirit of derision raced ahead of him to sway his wife from receiving his forgiveness. It gathered from the four

When Warriors Fall

corners of the city the spiritual assassins to come in to destroy this marriage once and for all. Pride, Animosity, Chaos and Fear rushed to join forces against these two people and their family.

They worked in Gabriel's thoughts to derail him.

Just one drink, he thought. *It will ease my nerves.*

He turned to head toward the sports bar that he had stopped at every day after work, and pulled into the parking lot. As he opened the door someone called his name.

"Gabriel!"

No one was there, but he clearly heard his name. Then the Spirit of God interceded for him, and brought to his mind the words from the Scriptures that Mr. Adams had given him, about taking every thought captive to Christ. He could remember the admonition of this godly man clearly.

Remember that every thought needs to be given to God. Don't let your thoughts rule you, but instead let God rule your thinking.

What are you doing, he thought? Get *out of here now, before it is too late,* he said as he fastened his seat belt back up. He sat in the car for a long time. After a struggle with the desire to give in, and go get a drink, he finally took control.

His wife looked at the clock.

"Looks like he is out drinking again," she said in disgust. "I am done! I cannot do this anymore."

The war had begun and she was fighting against forces that were almost too strong for her. All she knew was that she had taken enough, and she wanted no more.

Derision whispered a lie in her ears.

You know he will come home angry again. You don't have to do this. God wants you to be happy. He doesn't expect you to live like this.

Pride spoke, *"You deserve better. Just pack your bags now, and leave him."*

Finally Animosity lashed out against this marriage, spewing vile hatred into the air with more words of hatred.

You can take him for all he is worth, you don't need him.

She ran into the room and grabbed a suitcase.

"Mommy, what are you doing," her daughter asked? Warriors of heaven came rushing in fighting for the heart of this woman of God.

Gabriel turned his car and his heart toward home, and began praying. The more he prayed, the fiercer the battle raged on the home front.

"Go back to your room," Gabriel's wife told her daughter. "Mommy will explain all of this later."

She sat down on the bed after her daughter left, and the battle raged in her mind. She wanted to leave, but the pull of home kept her from doing anything.

"God, this isn't fair," she said. "What do you expect from me?"

She picked up her Bible from the night stand and opened it to her reading plan that took her to Proverbs.

"Trust in the Lord with all your heart," she whispered

The door opened and Gabriel hurried into the house calling for his wife. When he came into the bedroom he saw the suitcase on the, and went over to his wife and knelt down at her feet. She didn't know what to think. He had never acted like *this* before.

"What are you doing, Gabriel," she asked in disgust?.

"I am asking you to forgive me." He leaned backwards on his knees. "I encountered Jesus today."

"Oh, and that's going to make a difference, huh?"

"I don't know," Gabriel said, "All I know is that it will make a difference in me. It already has."

"You're late again," she said. "Did you stop at the bar?"

"Yes, but I didn't go in. I went by the church on the hill, right after work, and I prayed with a man there. I was tempted to have a drink, but I think God gave me the strength to not go in there."

"Oh come on, do you really expect me to believe that?"

"Well, it's true. Here," he said handing her a piece of paper. "This is the man that prayed with me today. He gave me his name and number so I can call him, and plan another time to meet with him."

Fiery blades in the heavenlies kept thrashing as this battle of words continued on between the couple. Neither one was aware that the enemy was using every tactic to prevent them from agreeing. He used fear and doubt, and brought to mind all the hurts of the past. Gabriel stayed on his knees begging his wife not to go. When she turned away from him and began taking clothes out of the closet, Gabriel silently pleaded with God to send an angel to intervene.

"I know I have not been a good husband or father, but I want to make it better. Just say you will forgive me, and agree to stay at least tonight. Then we can talk over a cup of coffee in the morning, and look at our options. Please, forgive me?"

"I forgive you, Daddy," his daughter said.

"Honey, how long have you been standing there? You shouldn't have to hear all this. I am sorry, Baby Girl, but you shouldn't have come."

"The angel told me to come, Daddy."

Gabriel and his wife looked at each other, and then back at their daughter.

"What angel," he asked?

"I was sleeping," she said, "and an angel came, and woke me up. He said that you needed me to come to your room. So I came."

Gabriel looked up at his wife. "Tonight—will you give me tonight?"

She shook her head yes. "But, I give you no guarantees after that." She quietly grabbed her daughter's hand. As they left the room, she turned to look at Gabriel. He was on his knees, praying. She wanted to say more, but kept silent. And in her heart she hoped for tomorrow.

To the Warrior Guarding the Home

As you can see in this short glimpse of Gabriel's life, the home begins in the heart of the father. It may stand true that the mother is the keeper of the home, and the heartbeat of the things that happen in the home, but the father is responsible for the home. It is his direction, given by the Holy Spirit that anoints that home for a purpose. It is his gentle guidance that takes his family on a journey with God. To guard the home means to protect your own heart, to protect your wife's heart and to guard the family through prayer against any entry from the enemy into his home.

It is taken even further into guarding the land. It is not a foreign thought that God cares for the land of His people. A vital part of guarding the heart is to guard the place in which you live. Often this is done through prayer, and at times it is done by taking a stand to just do the right thing for your neighbor, and your community. Godly wisdom will give you direction, and as you seek Him, the courage to do the right thing will become available.

The parable of the ten virgins is often seen as making ready for the return of Christ. This is a true assessment. But there is so much more that is overlooked when confronting the text from a biblical and cultural perspective.

There is much to be said here about guarding the home. To explain this thought in detail, must be reserved for another time and maybe another book; but stay with me as I explain my heart for the home with a few key points and illustrations.

The first and most obvious is that Jesus is the bridegroom, and his church is the bride. What is not commonly known, and should be stressed here, is the context of the first century Jewish wedding. The marriage was sealed with the wedding contract (what we might consider the engagement). The difference being that once *engaged* they were bound to one another. Then the bridegroom would go to his father's house and prepare a place for him and his bride to live. While this place was being built, the bride waited in faithfulness, keeping herself pure, watching for the day her bridegroom would come to take her home.

Proverbs 20:27 makes it clear that our spirit is God's lamp. Our spirit is of the Lord, who searches all the innermost parts of our being. In the language found in Proverbs, the word *lamp* takes on the meaning of the light of Israel, thus the lamp of God's people. It is likened to the inner man.

When considering the word lamp being used metaphorically, we could look at it as the spirit of a man or woman of God who has been sealed in a covenant relationship with Jesus. We know that our greatest hope as Christians is that our Bridegroom would come quickly, and thus we wait for that return.

The oil was very significant for the home. Not only was it used to light the lamps in the home, but even more importantly it was used to light the lamps in the tabernacle. Exodus 27:20 and Leviticus 24:2 tell us that pure oil was presented for use in the tabernacle. Could it be that the oil that is needed to trim the lamp might represent the purity of the bride? I believe so. Thus her purity being maintained the bride is always ready to receive the bridegroom.

We are the sanctuary of the living God, who by His son has married us into His kingdom. Having entered into a covenant relationship with Him, we thus belong to Him. He tells us plainly that He has gone to prepare a place for us, and will return to usher us back to His Father's home (John 14:3). As we wait for Him to return, we keep our lamps (our inner person) trimmed with oil (purity).

Dear Warrior, I leave you with this charge: Be the sentinel who guards the home of your heart, and let this oil of purity spill onto the home of your family as you wait on the Lord. The reward of a heart and home guarded is a mind that is stayed on Christ and a strength that enables you to stand.

Dear Warrior, you *are* called to stand (Ephesians 6:10-20).

Epilogue

A WARRIOR'S VICTORY

Finally, be strong in the Lord and in the strength of his might. Put on the whole armor of God that you may be able to stand against the schemes of the devil. For we do not wrestle against flesh and blood, but against the rulers, against the authorities, against the cosmic powers over this present darkness, against the spiritual forces of evil in the heavenly places. Therefore take up the whole armor of God that you may be able to withstand in the evil day, and having done all, to stand firm. Stand therefore, having fastened on the belt of truth, and having put on the breastplate of righteousness, and, as shoes for your feet, having put on the readiness given by the gospel of peace. In all circumstances take up the shield of faith, with which you can extinguish all the flaming darts of the evil one; and take the helmet of salvation, and the sword of the Spirit, which is the word of God, praying at all times in the Spirit, with all prayer and supplication. To that end keep alert with all perseverance, making supplication for all the saints, and also for me, that words may be given to me in opening my mouth boldly to proclaim the mystery of the gospel, for which I am an ambassador in chains, that I may declare it boldly, as I ought to speak." Ephesians 6:10-20

The picture of the armor has been weaved strategically throughout the lives of those who have been written into this novel. Some used their armor. Some did not. Their names are representative of their lives. Lilith represents change. She had been seared with the brand iron of darkness. God stepped in to bring restoration, and she changed her name back to represent her new stand in Christ. Like Jabez she sought out a mighty God who was able to change not only her name, but her vision for His eternal purpose and plan in her life.

Though the lives here are fictional they represent honest struggles of real people. The heart of this novel is God's restoration. Just as He sought after Israel, He seeks after you. He desires holiness, and calls you to such a standard in life. You *can* live a holy life! Let me say it again. You *can* live a holy life.

A mind that is set on holiness will begin on that path consecrated by the Lord, and will continue to walk in it. Consecration to the Lord means you forsake the lusts of the flesh, and walk in the Spirit (Gal 5:16). Holiness begins with that walk in the Spirit. On your own strength, you cannot forsake the things that are against the heart of God. Walking in holiness means you take every thought captive to Christ (2 Corinthians 10:5), and by this very act demolish strongholds that want to set up dominion in your soul.

Holiness is often mistaken for sinlessness, but a look at the root meaning of the word is not sinlessness but separateness. Hear me out before you think I am giving license to sin—I am not. Holiness is a divine quality that God desires to impart to His people. It is the characteristic of being an alien in this world, a uniquely appointed child of God. According to Leviticus, it is consecrating (or separating) your life unto the Lord, and determining to set your heart, soul and mind on following Him.

Holiness means you are set apart from the ordinary for God's purpose, and indeed set apart from sin. This is not double talk. Considering the Hebrew mindset, sin was an offense to God. To offend God meant loss, punishment and death. Men and women of God who were anointed and set apart for God's purposes were deceived by the enemy, and they sinned. Some died, as did Ananias and Sapphira. Some suffered loss as did David, and as in the case of Moses some were punished, and kept from experiencing the sweetness of God's promises.

Moses disobeyed when he struck the rock in the Wilderness of Zin. David sinned with Bathsheba, and committed murder in order to cover up a lie. Jonah said no to God, and ran from Him. Sarah laughed at God's promise. Rebecca manipulated her husband and her sons. Martha chose to do busy work over sitting at the feet of Jesus. Peter denied Jesus.

Paul's writings are addressed to people in the church dealing with sin. These were holy men and women of God, who were set apart for God's purpose, and failed the Lord in some area of life.

This failure *is* sin. We cannot call it anything else. Here is the point at which I return to the primary message of this book. God is as much at work to restore His people today, as He was with His people Israel. Hell awaits those who choose to walk away from Him, and beloved, it is your choice to walk away or to return with Him. He is waiting and longing for your return. If you will rise up again as did David, Peter and countless others, God will again send you for His purpose. The sin He throws away is gone forever.

As in the life of David, the consequence may always go before you, but God will still use you if you place your life back in His hands, and set your heart and mind back to Him.

As this book closes, I want to finally remind you that you *are* your brother's keeper. If you see your brother or sister sin, you cannot turn a blind eye. To do so is to abandon them on the battlefield of the enemy. Be aware. If someone does not come to carry them off of that horrible field of destruction, they may die there.

Warriors of Christ, we must stand and walk in holiness, and we must enable the weaker to stand again, until they are strong enough to stand on their own. My personal experience tells me that the warrior of God who loves the Lord can fall into sin. The knowledge I have gained from that personal experience tells me that we are over comers. We must have a deeply rooted fellowship with the Holy Spirit who keeps us from sin, and who counsels us in life.

My heart beats for the restoration of God's people, because I am one who has been restored. The one who sins against God hates the sin, hates himself, and feels helpless because he has allowed the enemy to disarm him.

God is merciful. He saw me bleeding to death when I cried out to him confessing my sin, and He rescued me. He sent out battle strong warriors to come and pull me back into the trenches of His safety. He breathed the breath of life back into me and stood me up. He told me that He loves me with an everlasting love. The Lord took me from the pit of destruction, and placed me in a safe haven to heal me, and to retrain me. He made me lie down in the valley of Gilead, and then at the right time he set my feet back on the high places.

If you are in that pit, don't let the enemy lie to you and tell you that you are done. Reach up your hand to Jesus, and cry out for his salvation!

The Bible says to stand. But how do you stand? How do you put on the armor, and what does it mean? I have added a brief commentary to include my thoughts on the armor, and how to pray as you dress yourself in it. I hope it will help you to stand firm and strong in the LORD.

*"Finally, **be strong in the Lord** and in the strength of his might."*

Don't go on your own strength, but allow the LORD to enable you. He is the only one who can make it possible for you to stand against the enemy. In Psalm 18, David said that he cried out to God because his enemy was too mighty for him, and he reported that by His God he could jump the walls, and stand against an army. When you pray, ask the LORD to *be* your strength instead of asking him to give you strength.

Put on the whole armor of God *that you may be able to stand against the schemes of the devil.*

This is your part. Dress yourself in this armor, and always start with the belt of truth. The enemy's arrows penetrate the heart of the soldier of God by loosening the belt of truth so he will lose his sword. The sword, being the Word of God, cannot be found attached to a lie. Let His truth reign in your heart, and on it you can carry the Word of God, your weapon. Put on the entire armor. Nothing can be missing.

For we do not wrestle against flesh and blood, *but against the rulers, against the authorities, against the cosmic powers over this present darkness, against the spiritual forces of evil in the heavenly places.*

Know your enemy. This is warfare knowledge that is found in His word. Don't study the enemy's manual, but prepare yourself in the study of God's Word. If you are well trained in God's word, the truth will be in you, and you will recognize the enemy.

God's word tells us what he looks like and how he acts. It tells us his dominion and instructs us in the wiles he uses. God's word teaches us what we need to know. Know your own battle manual, and you will understand the tactics of the enemy. Beware of any carnal desire to study the enemy's methods by hanging out in his camp. Traps abound in the camp of the enemy. Stay on high ground with the Lord, and you will enter the enemy's camp through prayer and intercession.

*Therefore take up the whole armor of God that you may be able to withstand in the evil day, and having done all, to stand firm. Stand therefore, having fastened on the **belt of truth**.*

Cling to the word of God. Hold fast to good doctrine. Good doctrine here is not intended to mean denominational views. Hold fast to the core tenets of the faith. God came in the flesh in the person of Jesus Christ. He was bruised for our iniquities, and punished for our sin. He died to redeem us. He rose again from the dead and is now seated at the right hand of the Father. He will come again.

*. . . And having put on the **breastplate of righteousness** . . .*

We are hidden now in him and our lives are no more. The breastplate of righteousness is that which covers our heart and enables us to walk in purity before a Holy God. You put this breastplate on by accepting Christ as your Savior, and by making a decision to not grieve the Holy Spirit. The breastplate of righteousness is held on by the enabling power of the Holy Spirit working in your life. Don't leave Him out.

*And, as shoes for your feet, **having put on the readiness given by the gospel of peace**.*

The Roman sandal was a battle-ready shoe because it was equipped with nails that kept the soldier upright when he found himself on a slippery slope. So what will you put on your feet? It can only be the gospel of peace. In other words don't be only a hearer of the word, but a doer of the word. If God's word admonishes you to forgive, then forgive. If the Scriptures pierce your heart to give, then give. James 1:22-25 says that if you only hear then you deceive yourself, and walk away from what you have heard and forget. But if you are a doer, you are blessed of God and able to persevere.

*In all circumstances take up the **shield of faith**, with which you can extinguish all the flaming darts of the evil one; and take **the helmet of salvation**.*

Without *faith* it is impossible to please God. When we take up the shield of faith it pleases God. By faith we are able to resist the fiery darts, and all forms of lust, pride, hatred, and any other evil intentions sent out by the enemy.

Doubt, rationalism, apostasy of any kind cannot enter into the mind that bears the helmet of salvation. This piece of the armor is worn by placing the things of God in your mind, and it bears arms with the shield of faith in protecting the soldier from wrong thinking that leads to destruction.

*And the **sword of the Spirit**, which is the word of God*

The Word of God is alive. It is powerful. It is piercing. It is a sharp sword in the hand of the warrior. It is your number one weapon (Hebrews 4:12). Know the Word of God. Read it. Listen to it. Study it and hide it in your heart. Then use it in your time of prayer. Praying God's Word back to Him is more powerful than any word you could ever use.

My Prayer for

FROM PSALM 46

Oh Lord, God be a refuge for this dear reader, and give him strength. I ask you to be always present—help to her in times of trouble. Lord give her you courage. I pray she will have no fear, even when it seems her life has fallen apart, or when she feels like she is drowning.

I pray you will see that there is a river whose streams make glad the city of God, the holy habitation of the Most High. I ask that the LORD will be in the midst of your world and that you will not be moved;

Lord God, help the reader when morning dawns, or when the nations rage, or when the kingdoms totter; and speak on his behalf. Oh LORD of hosts draw near to him. God of Jacob, be her fortress. I ask that by your enabling of the Holy Spirit that she will be still and know that You are God. Be exalted in his life, indeed in all the earth.

About the Author

Carol Hudler is ordained in the Church of God, Anderson Indiana. She has studied in the areas of Theology, Hermeneutics, Psychology and Humanities with a BS in Pastoral Ministry and an MA in Human Relations. She is prior military, having served in the US Navy and worked in Civil Service with the US Army in the area of Religious Education.

She is currently retired and living with her husband in Missouri, where they serve together with International Student Ministry, Prayer Ministry and Short Term Missions.

Index of Scripture

All Scripture is taken from ESV unless otherwise noted.

1. John 10:10,
2. Proverbs 7:25-27
3. Psalm 103:17
4. John 10:10
5. Psalm 10:9
6. Revelation. 3:21
7. Matthew. 11:28-29
8. 1 John. 1:9
9. James 5:16
10. Matthew. 7:1-5 GWT
11. Matthew. 6:21
12. Proverbs 18:7-8
13. Philippians 4:8
14. Luke 6:45
15. Psalms 18:11-14,17
16. Numbers 14:28-30
17. Ephesians.4:30-32